First published in the United Kingdom in 1991 by
Alan Sutton Publishing Limited · Phoenix Mill · Stroud
Gloucestershire

First published in the United States of America in 1991 by
Alan Sutton Publishing Inc. · Wolfeboro Falls · NH 03896–0848

British Library Cataloguing in Publication Data

Grant, Raymond K.J. (Raymond Kenneth James)
The Royal Forests of England
1. England. Royal forests, history
I. Title
942.00952

ISBN 0-86299-781-X

Library of Congress Cataloging in Publication Data
applied for

Typeset in 11/12pt Garamond.
Typesetting and origination by
Alan Sutton Publishing Limited.
Printed in Great Britain by
The Bath Press, Avon.

The Royal Forests of England

RAYMOND GRANT

ALAN SUTTON

Contents

List of Abbreviations

General

B.M.	British Museum
C.U.P.	Cambridge University Press
Darby, *Dom. Geog.* *Midland Eng.*	H.C. Darby, *Domesday Geography of Midland England.* (C.U.P., 1971)
Darby, *Dom. Geog.* *S.E. Eng.*	H.C. Darby, *Domesday Geography of South-East England* (C.U.P., 1962)
Darby, *Dom. Geog.* *S.W. Eng.*	H.C. Darby, *Domesday Geography of South-West England.* (C.U.P., 1967)
D.N.B.	*Dictionary of National Biography*
E.H.R.	*English Historical Review*
Ekwall, *C.O.D. Placenames*	E. Ekwall, *Concise Oxford Dictionary of English Placenames* (O.U.P. 4th edn. 1980)
Firth and Rait	*Acts and Ordinances of the Interregnum 1642–60* (ed. C.H. Firth and R.S. Rait. London, 1911)
G.E.C.	G.E. Cockayne, *Complete Peerage* (revised edn., Vicary Gibbs)
G.R.O.	Gloucestershire Record Office
H.M.S.O.	Her Majesty's Stationery Office
Jnl. Brit. Arch. Assoc.	*Journal of the British Archaeological Association*
O.S.	Ordnance Survey
P.P.	Parliamentary Papers
P.R.O.	Public Record Office
P.R.S.	Pipe Roll Society
Rolls Ser.	Rolls Series

S.O.D.	Shorter Oxford Dictionary
T.R.H.S.	Transactions of the Royal Historical Society
V.C.H.	Victoria County History of England

Printed Sources

(i) CHRONICLES OF GREAT BRITAIN DURING THE MIDDLE AGES (THE ROLLS SERIES)

Ann. Monast. Burt.	Annales Monastici de Margam,
Ann. Monast. Theok.	Theokesberia et Burton, Vol. I. (ed. H.R.Luard, 1864)
Ann. Monast. Dunst.	Annales Monastici de Dunstaplia et Bermunseia, Vol. III (1866)
Ann. Monast. Wigorn.	Annales Monastici de Oseneia, Chronicon Thomae Wykes, et de Wigornia, Vol. IV (1869)
Chron. Abingdon	Chronicon Monasterii de Abingdon (ed. J. Stevenson, 1858)
Hoveden	Chronicon Rogeri de Hovedene (ed. Stubbs, 1868–71)
Matt. Par. Chron. Maj.	Matthaei Parisiensis Chronica Majora (ed. H.R. Luard, 1872–84)

(ii) PUBLICATIONS OF THE RECORD COMMISSION AND OTHER PRINTED SOURCES

Cal. I.P.M.	Calendarium Inquisitionum Post Mortem (ed. J. Caley & J. Bayley, 1806–28)
Dom. Bk.	Domesday Book (ed. Abraham Farley, 1783)
Dom. Bk. Hants.	Domesday Book Hampshire (ed. J. Munby, Phillimore, 1982)
Dom. Bk. Som.	Domesday Book Somerset (ed. C. & F. Thorn, Phillimore, 1980)
Dom. Bk. Wilts.	Domesday Book Wiltshire (ed. C. & F. Thorn, Phillimore, 1979)
Ex. e Rot. Fin.	Excerpta e Rotulis Finium 1216–72 (ed. C. Roberts, 1835–6)

Rot. Chart.	*Rotuli Chartarum* 1199–1216 (ed. T.D. Hardy, 1837)
Rot. de Lib. regn. Iohann.	*Rotuli de Liberate . . . regnante Iohanne* (ed. T.D. Hardy, 1844)
Rot. Litt. Claus.	*Rotuli Litterarum Clausarum* (ed. T.D. Hardy, 1833–4)
Rot. Litt. Pat.	*Rotuli Litterarum Patentium* (ed. T.D. Hardy, 1835)
Rot. de Ob. et Fin.	*Rotuli de Oblatis et Finibus* (ed. T.D. Hardy, 1835)
Rot. Parl.	*Rotuli Parliamentorum: the Rolls of Parliament* (1783)

(iii) PUBLIC RECORD OFFICE CALENDARS AND TRANSCRIPTS

Cal. Chart. R.	Calendar of the Charter Rolls
Cal. Close R.	Calendar of the Close Rolls
Close R.	Close Rolls
Cal. Fine R.	Calendar of the Fine Rolls
Cal. Inq. Misc.	Calendar of Inquisitions, Miscellaneous
Cal. Lib. R.	Calendar of the Liberate Rolls
Cal. Pat. R.	Calendar of the Patent Rolls
Pat. R.	Patent Rolls
Cal. Treas. Bk.	Calendar of the Treasury Books
Cal. Treas. Pap.	Calendar of the Treasury Papers
Cal. S.P. Dom.	Calendar of the State Papers Domestic
Cal. S.P. Dom. Add.	Calendar of the State Papers Domestic Addenda
Lett. & Pap. Hen. VIII	Letters and Papers, Foreign and Domestic, Henry VIII

(iv) PUBLICATIONS OF LOCAL HISTORY SOCIETIES AND OTHER PRINTED SOURCES

Coll. Hist. Staffs.	*Collections for a History of Staffordshire* (Wm. Salt Archaeological Society)

Memoranda Roll	*Memoranda Roll of the King's Remembrancer*
1230–31	*1230–31* (ed. C. Robinson. P.R.S., N.S., XI. Princeton, 1933)
Sel. Charters, ed.	Wm. Stubbs, *Select Charters* (9th. edn.
Stubbs	H.W.C. Davies. O.U.P., 1929)
Som. Rec. Soc.	Somerset Record Society
Turner, *Sel. Forest*	G.J. Turner, *Select Pleas of the Forest* (Selden
Pleas	Society, XIII. London, 1901)
Yorks. Arch. Assoc.	Yorkshire Archaeological Association

Manuscript Sources

THE PUBLIC RECORD OFFICE

CHANCERY

C47	Chancery Miscellanea
C99	Forest Proceedings
C205	Special Commissions (Petty Bag Office)

EXCHEQUER

Treasury of Receipt

E32	Forest Proceedings
E36	Books

Queen's Remembrancer

E101	Accounts, Various
E111	Bills, Answers and Depositions
E112	Bills and Answers
E137	Estreats
E146	Forest Proceedings
E159	Memoranda Rolls
E168	Notice-of-Trial Books
E317	Parliamentary Surveys. Commonwealth and Augmentation Office
E401	Receipt Rolls, Exchequer of Receipt

RECORDS OF THE DUCHY OF LANCASTER

DL1	Equity Proceedings. Pleadings
DL12	Warrants
DL39	Forest Proceedings
DL42	Miscellaneous Books
KB27	*Coram Rege* Rolls
Sta. Cha.	Proceedings in the Star Chamber
SP16	State Papers Domestic, Charles I
SC8	Special Collections – Ancient Petitions

IN PIAM MEMORIAM

PROFESSOR R.F. TREHARNE, M.A., Ph.D., F.R.Hist.S.

This book has been published with support from the Twenty-Seven Foundation, which is gratefully acknowledged by the author and publishers.

SECTION ONE

CHAPTER 1

Origins and Development to AD 1200

1
Origins and Extent of the Royal Forest

William the Conqueror claimed suzerainty over all the soil of England by right of conquest: accordingly the Norman kings imposed upon their English subjects an iron rule of unprecedented severity. None of William's innovations was more hated and resented than his application of the Norman Forest system to his English kingdom. The *Anglo-Saxon Chronicle* says that the Conqueror 'established a great peace for the deer, and laid down laws therefor, that whoever should slay hart or hind should be blinded. He forbade the harts and also the boars to be killed. As greatly did he love the tall deer as if he were their father. He also ordained concerning the hares, that they should go free. His great men bewailed it, and the poor murmured thereat, but he was so obdurate, that he recked not of the hatred of them all, but they must wholly follow the King's will, if they would live, or have land, or even his peace.'[1]

The Norman kings imposed the Forest system upon suitable districts of England by arbitrary decrees. In the New Forest especially the Conqueror's acts of expropriation created a deep impression upon the minds of contemporaries: the hatred felt for the Forest system caused them to be greatly exaggerated. Florence of Worcester, a monk and chronicler who died in 1118, alleged that William I had depopulated a fruitful and prosperous countryside, and destroyed houses and churches to make way for the deer; so that popular rumour declared that the death of William Rufus while hunting in the New Forest was an act of divine vengeance for the impious act of his father.[2]

So it was with the royal forest of Rutland and Leicestershire, which by 1130 was in the custody of one 'Hasculf the forester':[3] according to a thirteenth-century jury, Henry I had established it by decree, and granted custody to Hasculf, because on a royal progress northward he had observed Riseborough wood, on the eastern border of Leicestershire, to be teeming with game.[4]

By the reign of Henry II the Forest had become such a contentious institution that his Treasurer sought to explain and justify it. In his *Course of the Exchequer* Richard fitzNigel, Bishop of London, explained that the king's forest had been established only in the wooded counties:

> where wild beasts have their lairs, and plentiful feeding grounds. It makes no difference to whom the woods belong, whether to the King or the nobles of the realm: in both alike the beasts wander free and unscathed.

Here the kings of England came to hunt 'as a rest and recreation', putting from them 'the anxious turmoil native to a court'. Consequently:

> the whole organisation of the Forests, the punishment, pecuniary or corporal, of Forest offences, is outside the jurisdiction of other courts, and solely dependent on the decisions of the King, or of some officer specially appointed by him. The Forest has its own laws, based, it is said, not on the common law of the realm, but on the arbitrary decrees of the King; so that what is done in accordance with Forest law is not called 'just' without qualification, but 'just' according to forest laws . . . The greater part of the revenue from forests arises from judicial proceedings and imposts, and it was considered that such unlawful gains might be compounded for by the payment of tithe

4

of the Forest revenues to cathedral churches, as from the forests of Wiltshire and Hampshire to Salisbury cathedral and from the Northamptonshire forests to Lincoln cathedral.[5]

The Norman and Angevin kings imposed the Forest law upon districts where clearing and cultivation had made comparatively slow progress because of the unfavourable terrain. Such for example was the great Upper Jurassic Clay Vale in the south-west, covered in Saxon times by a vast dense oak forest known to its inhabitants as 'Sealwudu', and to the Welsh as *Coit Mawr* ('the Great Wood').[6] By the thirteenth century a belt of royal forests extended over this region of heavy clay soils – Blackmoor and Gillingham in Dorset, Selwood, Chippenham, Melksham and Braydon in Somerset and Wiltshire, and Wychwood in Oxfordshire. The Midland clay plain also was thinly populated in pre-Conquest times, and contained great tracts of woodland. Here too a chain of royal forests later extended on either side of the Severn – Dean in Gloucestershire and Herefordshire, Malvern, Ombersley and Horewell, Feckenham and Kinver in Worcestershire and Staffordshire, and Morfe, Wrekin and Long Forest in Shropshire, with Sherwood in Nottinghamshire as a northern extension. 'The King's forests between Oxford and Stamford bridges' comprised Shotover, Bernwood, Whittlewood, Salcey and Rockingham in the counties of Oxford, Buckingham and Northampton, and the forest of Huntingdonshire. This too was a region of clay soils, densely wooded in Anglo-Saxon times: it included the 'Bruneswald', in which, according to tradition, Hereward the Wake lived as an outlaw at the time of the Norman Conquest.[7]

Another continuous chain of royal forests was established across Hampshire and extended north-eastwards into Berkshire and Surrey. Here early settlements were sparse because the sandy or gravelly soils were sterile and acid.[8] In this vast area, less densely covered with dry oak or birch-wood, were established the New Forest, the forests of Bere Ashley and Bere Porchester, Aliceholt and Woolmer, and Windsor Forest. Other sparsely populated districts decreed to be royal forests were Dartmoor and Exmoor, on the high moorlands of Devon and Somerset, the Forest of the Peak, on the barren limestone uplands of Derbyshire, and Pickering and Scalby, upon the elevated sandstone plateau of the North Yorkshire moors.[9] In the marshes of Lincolnshire the king ordained the Forest law to preserve for himself exclusive rights of hawking and fowling:[10] in the early thirteenth century the local inhabitants had to pay handsomely for exemption from its restrictions. In 1204, for example, the vills of Surfleet, Gosberton, Quadring and Donington had to purchase from King John a charter disafforesting their marshes,[11] and in 1230 the forest of Kesteven itself was disafforested.[12]

Comparatively densely populated counties, however, such as Norfolk, Suffolk, Kent, Hertfordshire and Middlesex, where the rich loamy soils favoured intensive settlements, seem never to have been burdened by the Forest law. Moreover, inhabitants of many parts of royal forests where the soil favoured tillage and settlement was closer, purchased their freedom from the Forest law by large fines paid to the Crown at an early date. Such was Essex north of the 'Stanestreet' – a fertile boulder clay region – which was disafforested by King John in 1204 for a fine of 500 marks and five palfreys.[13] Similarly the more fertile and populous northern vales of Berkshire were disafforested in 1227, whereas the poorer and more sparsely populated land in the south-east of the county remained within the royal forest of Windsor.[14]

Within the bounds of the royal forests a comprehensive body of laws was developed to protect the hunting rights of the Crown. The four beasts of the English forest were the red deer, the fallow deer, the roe and the wild boar, together called 'the venison'; lesser beasts such as hares and rabbits, wildfowl and birds used in falconry, and fish in the 'forbidden rivers', were also protected. The forest inhabitants were forbidden to possess bows and arrows or any other means of taking the game, and their dogs must be 'lawed' (i.e., their claws cut) so that they were unable to run in pursuit of the wild beasts. The 'vert' – that is, the trees and other forms of vegetation which afforded food and shelter for the game – was also preserved by numerous and oppressive regulations, which forbade the people to clear and cultivate waste land, restricted their rights of cutting wood for building and fuel, and of pasturing their animals on the wastes, and even made it an offence to enclose their crops against the deer.

The Forest laws were administered by a complex hierarchy of

Forest officials – Chief Justices of the Forests, Wardens, foresters of fee and a host of subordinate foresters who performed the duties of gamekeepers. These professional Forest officers were assisted by the verderers, regarders and agisters, who were elected in the county court from among the knights of the locality. There was also an elaborate system of Forest assemblies and courts – swanimotes, attachment courts, Forest inquests and the triennial inquiry known as the regard, leading up to the Forest Eyre, which in the twelfth and thirteenth centuries was a ponderous judicial and fiscal engine comparable to the General Eyre.

The essential feature of the English royal forest was therefore the existence within its boundaries, side by side with the common law, of a distinct legal system enforced by its own courts and officers, and designed to preserve the vert and venison for the king's pleasure and profit, not only in the royal demesne, but also in extensive areas beyond it. This system was created and maintained by the arbitrary will of the king in face of the hostility of his subjects, who considered that its interference with their liberties was contrary to natural law.

2

The Hunting Rights of the English Kings Before the Norman Conquest

The pre-Conquest kings of England shared the passion for the chase of their Norman successors. Asser tells us that King Alfred excelled in the art of hunting,[15] and it was said of the pious Edward the Confessor that every day after his devotions he indulged in the sports of hunting and hawking.[16] Within their demesnes these kings had extensive woods, such as the Confessor's woods of Chippenham in Wiltshire, which were four leagues long and four wide.[17] In these woods, according to the *Dialogues of Aelfric*, a treatise of the early eleventh century, the king's huntsmen took 'harts, boars, roe deer and sometimes hares', with hounds, with nets and with boar-spears; the king also fed and clothed his huntsmen and gave them occasional gifts of a horse or a bracelet.[18]

But there is no evidence that kings of England before the Conquest claimed exclusive hunting-rights in the woods of their subjects as William I and his successors did. Canute by his legislation claimed hunting rights in his own woods which were much the same as those of any other landowner – 'I will that every man be entitled to his hunting in wood and in field, on his own estate. And let every man abstain from my hunting: take notice where I will have it untrespassed upon, under penalty of the full amercement.'[19] So offences against the game in the king's woods were to be punished by a fine, according to the ordinary law of the land, and not by a special Forest court according to a separate Forest law.

By the time of Edward the Confessor, however, there existed the nucleus of a Forest administration. In the Forest of Dean Edward granted to three of his thegns land in Dean in Longbridge hundred 'quit of geld for keeping the forest'.[20] His huntsmen held land of him in what later became the royal forests of Chippenham, Savernake and Clarendon,[21] and his 'foresters' in what later became the forests of Mendip and Windsor.[22] These last-named royal servants were called in Anglo-Saxon 'woodwards' – a term translated by the Norman clerks who compiled the Domesday Book as 'foresters'. We do not know whether the two terms describe very different officers, or whether the 'foresters' were an innovation introduced into England by the Confessor from Normandy, where he had spent the best years of his life.[23] There is in fact some evidence of continuity between the administration of the king's forests before and after the Conquest. In the time of the Confessor Alvric the huntsman held of him lands in North Newnton, Burbage and Harding; by 1086 these holdings had been granted to Richard Sturmy, first of a long line of hereditary wardens of Savernake Forest.[24]

3
Frankish and Norman Origins of the English Royal Forest

Whereas in pre-Conquest England the hunting rights of the king did not differ materially from those of any other landowner, in the

Carolingian Empire the Forest was essentially a royal institution. Forests could be established by the king alone; within their bounds no one might hunt the game or fish in the rivers without his authority, and the cutting of wood was severely restricted. Foresters protected the game against poachers, and amercements for Forest offences formed one of the regular sources of income provided by the royal demesne.

After the collapse of the Carolingian Empire, the dukes of Normandy in the tenth and eleventh centuries took over in their duchy many of the former attributes of the royal power. There were extensive woods within their demesnes, and in them they exercised exclusive rights of chase, restricted the rights of their subjects to cut down the natural cover of the game, and took the profits of the Forest pleas. Grants of demesne land to subjects reserved ducal rights over 'vert and venison': when for example the Conqueror, as Duke of Normandy, granted to the abbey of Caen the woods of Mauperthuis, Torteval, Foulogne and Quesnay-Guesnon, he reserved 'in his lordship' the stags, roes and wild boars in those woods, and stipulated that the monks should not at any time cut down those woods in order to cultivate or build upon the land.[25]

By the beginning of the thirteenth century, 'the Forest administration in many of its aspects is the same in Normandy and in England. The greater number of the terms employed in England are Norman.'[26] At the head of each of the two Forest administrations was a Chief Forester, or Chief Justice of the Forest, and under him were wardens, foresters or bailiffs, who were often constables of neighbouring castles, and who kept each forest or group of forests. Foresters of fee and sergeants of fee held their hereditary offices by service of helping to administer the Forest law, attaching offenders to appear at the Forest courts, and gathering in the Forest revenues. The 'pannage' assembly in Normandy, like the English 'swanimote', made arrangements for the agistment of the ducal woods – i.e., for feeding the local people's swine on the acorns and beechmast during the autumn months, and collecting the 'pannage' dues paid for this privilege. In Normandy, however, the verderers, regarders and 'pannagers' had certain emoluments attached to their offices, which were often hereditary; in England the corresponding Forest officials were elected in the county court from among the knights of the locality, and served unpaid. There is no evidence moreover that before the Conquest the dukes of Normandy enforced the Forest law beyond the bounds of their ducal demesnes.

It may well be that after the Conquest the development of the Forest administration in England in its turn influenced that of the parallel system in Normandy. But nevertheless it seems clear that the Forest system was a Norman institution, and that the English writers who condemned it as one of unprecedented tyranny were substantially justified.

4
The English Forest Under the Norman Kings: 1066–1135

The Norman kings established forests in well-wooded and sparsely populated districts where there were extensive royal demesnes. In Wiltshire, for example, the royal manors of Lydiard Millicent, Chippenham, Melksham, Calne, Bromham, Warminster, Westbury and East Knoyle formed the nuclei of the royal forests of Braydon, Chippenham and Melksham, and Selwood in the west. In the east of the county Savernake, Chute, Clarendon and Groveley Forests were created around the king's manors of Bedwyn, Wootton Rivers, Collingbourne Ducis and Amesbury.[27]

William I's most notorious creation was of course the New Forest in the south-western corner of Hampshire, unique in that holdings in it and around it formed a separate section of Domesday Book.[28] The nucleus of the New Forest was an infertile and almost deserted district; this central hunting reserve appears not to have been organized into townships and hundreds like the rest of the country.[29] It was extended by inducing landowners to exchange their holdings for others on the forest outskirts. Thus in 1086 one Aelfric held Milford of the king 'in exchange for forest' (de excambio forestae).[30] The Conqueror furthermore took the unprecedented step of evicting some hundreds of families from thinly populated areas in south-west Hampshire.[31] Domesday records that in Eling '16 villeins' and three bordars' dwellings were expropriated in the

Forest';[32] by 1086 seven-eighths of Lyndhurst were in the Forest and 'now there is nothing except two bordars there'.[33]

Other royal forests, though not mentioned by name in Domesday, had clearly been established by the time of the Survey. Twenty-one places in Worcestershire, recorded therein as having been afforested, lie mainly within the boundaries of Feckenham Forest as defined in thirteenth-century perambulations.[34] In William I's manor of Bromsgrove, for example, he had put into his forest 'four leagues of woodland' in Willingwick and Chadwick, and four leagues in Kidderminster.[35] Half the extensive woodland of his demesne of Cookham in Berkshire was in Windsor Forest,[36] and land in Buckholt returned in 1086 as being in the forest gave its name to another Hampshire forest.[37]

The valuation of such royal demesnes put into the forest was substantially reduced. In the New Forest Ringwood had in the time of the Confessor been valued at £24, but in 1086 at only £8.10s. Christchurch was reduced from £19 to £10, and Holdenhurst from £44 to £24.[38] This devaluation was due in some instances at least to depopulation, but in others to the restrictions enforced by the Forest officers, and by the transfer of certain revenues from the bailiffs of the royal manors to the foresters themselves. In Nether Wallop, Over Wallop and Broughton the reeve had 'formerly had honey and pasture to make up his farm, and wood for building houses', but by the time of Domesday these manors were in the royal Forest of Buckholt, and 'the foresters had these things and the reeve nothing.'[39]

These revenues were substantial. The king's manor of Brill in Buckinghamshire rendered £12 annually 'for the issues of the forest' (of Bernwood),[40] and in Oxfordshire Rainald, almost certainly a royal forester, paid the king £10 a year for the profits of the 'demesne forests' of Shotover, Stowood, Woodstock and Wychwood, and the lands appurtenant thereto.[41] William fitzNorman, lord of Kilpeck, paid a farm of £15 for the Herefordshire forests he kept, probably Archenfield and Treville.[42]

By 1086 the Conqueror was enforcing the Forest law far beyond the limits of his own demesnes, which caused the Forest system to be bitterly hated and opposed. In south-west Hampshire, for example; the holdings of great lay and ecclesiastical tenants-in-chief such as the Earls of Shrewsbury and Chester, and the Bishop of Winchester, had been put into the New Forest.[43] Here too there is evidence of depopulation and devaluation. The manor of Hordle was held by one Odilard from Ralph of Mortimer: Domesday records that 'the king holds the woodland in the forest, where six men used to live' and eight-and-a-half hides in Through am, assessed as land for seventeen ploughs, and held by five different tenants-in-chief, were declared to be worth 'nothing, because it is all in the forest'.[44]

Depopulation extended into Wiltshire: in the Bishop of Winchester's manor of Downton, in what later became Clarendon Forest, the Geld Rolls record that there were 'two hides from which the inhabitants have fled because of the king's forest'.[45] Into the Berkshire part of Windsor Forest William I put four hides of Winkfield manor, belonging to the abbey of Abingdon. The monks bitterly recorded that these four hides had been 'put beyond the pale' (*exterminatae*).[46] Many other holdings, such as Ashwood in Staffordshire, held by the canons of Wolverhampton, were declared to be 'waste on account of the king's forest (of Kinver)'[47] – that is, that they had lapsed out of cultivation.

Subjects retained some rights in their afforested woods. In his wood of Ripple in Worcestershire the Bishop of Worcester had formerly had 'the honey and the hunting and all profits, and 10s. over and above'. After the king had put the bishop's wood into his Forest of Malvern, the bishop still retained 'its pannage and (wood for) firing and the repair of houses'.[48] But nevertheless the valuation of such lands was substantially reduced. Hordle, held by Ralph of Mortimer, was reduced from £8 to 100s.; four hides in Sopley, held by William son of Stur, fell in value from £10 to 50s, because all the woodland in that manor had been put into the New Forest.[49] Wyegate, held by William of Eu, had before the Conquest been assessed at six hides, but by the time of Domesday it had been put into the Forest of Dean 'by the king's command', and there remained for taxation purposes 'only a fishery worth 10s.'[50]

At the Conqueror's death in 1087 the succession to the throne was disputed, and Rufus was compelled to enlist the aid of the English. He promised to surrender Crown rights over vert and venison in the woods of subjects. But when the danger to his crown was past he forgot his promises.[51] According to William of Malmesbury, he put to death those who took his deer in his forests, rich and poor alike.[52] Other chroniclers assert that his foresters exercised supervision over the woods of subjects, to protect the deer and prevent felling and clearing, and amerced those whom they found guilty of Forest offences.[53] In some cases at least forest offenders were committed to trial by ordeal, a procedure by which it was notoriously difficult to get convictions. Eamer, a monk of Christchurch, Canterbury, relates how fifty Englishmen were arrested and accused of having taken and eaten the king's deer. They denied the charge, and were immediately subjected to the ordeal of the hot iron. On the third day, when their hands were examined, they were found to be unburned, so that their innocence was considered proved. The king is said to have exclaimed angrily, 'What is this? Is God a just judge? Let him perish who will believe this henceforth! Answer shall be made from now on to my judgment and not to God's, which is swayed this way and that at anyone's petition.'[54]

At his coronation Henry I issued a Charter of Liberties promising to abolish or modify oppressive exactions. But he too was determined to maintain the Forest system founded by the Conqueror – 'I have kept the forests in my hands as my father had them, by the common consent of my barons.'[55] He also created new forests – in Rutland and Leicestershire,[56], in Bedfordshire[57] and in Yorkshire;[58] by the end of his reign the whole of the county of Essex seems to have been subject to the Forest law.[59] The impression made upon the minds of his subjects is indicated by the exaggerated statement of Odericus Vitalis, monk and chronicler, that Henry I:

> claimed for himself the hunting of the beasts of the forest throughout all England – and granted to a small number of nobles and friends only the privilege of hunting in their own woods.[60]

Breaches of the Forest laws were punished with severity. A

chronicler says that Henry 'wished to see little or no distinction between the public punishment of those who slew men, and those who slew the deer', i.e., by hanging.[61] Onerous restrictions were imposed upon Forest landowners and inhabitants. Waste land in the forest which had been cleared and brought into cultivation without authority ('assarts') was seized, together with other property of the offenders, and substantial fines exacted for their recovery.[62] Henry I's charters show that Forest landowners who took wood in their own woods without royal licence were guilty of the Forest trespass of 'waste'; their dogs had to be 'lawed'.[63] The unauthorized erection of buildings and enclosures within the forest constituted the offence of 'purpresture', and bows, arrows and other weapons were forbidden to be carried there.[64]

Henry I sent out from time to time experienced professional administrators like Geoffrey de Clinton and Ralph Basset[65] to hear pleas of the forest at special Forest Eyres. Accounts rendered at the Exchequer at Michaelmas 1130 for fines and amercements levied by them in fourteen counties show that the Forest had become an important source of royal revenue.[66] The Earl of Warwick, for example, owed the king £72.6s.8d. and two chargers for taking a stag, Walter Espec had been amerced in 200 marks on a similar count, and Baldwin de Redvers in 500 marks for a 'Forest offence'.[67] Foresters were called to account for oppressive and dishonest conduct. Walter Croc, the forester of Warwickshire, had been convicted of seizing two hundred pigs in the forest which did not belong to him, and of unlawfully taking 30 shillings for which he had not accounted. His bailiwick was forfeited and he had to pay a fine of 3 marks of gold for its recovery.[68] The clergy too were subject to the jurisdiction of the Forest judges. The Abbot of Westminster was amerced in 20 marks, one of his canons in 10 marks, and a Wiltshire priest 7 marks, for various Forest offences.[69]

These developments increased the efficiency of the Forest system, which became more and more important to the Crown as an instrument of financial exaction. The system therefore became increasingly burdensome and unpopular in the eyes of the English people.

5
Temporary Collapse of the Forest System Under Stephen: 1135–1154

Stephen's right to the throne was dubious, and he was compelled to purchase support by promising concessions. By his second charter, issued in March or April 1136, he promised to give up all forests created by Henry I, reserving to the Crown only those which had existed under William I and William II.[70] But his success in putting down the rebellion of Hugh Bigod and his party during the summer led him to break his promises. When he came to hunt at Brompton near Huntingdon, he held a Forest court and imposed many punishments for Forest offences. A chronicler declared this to have been a violation of his oath,[71] implying that the forest of Huntingdonshire was one of those he had promised to disafforest. Subsequent grants of disafforestment – for example, of the lands and woods of the nuns of Barking[72] and of Tendring hundred[73] suggest that Stephen exacted substantial fines for the freedom from the Forest law which he had previously conceded freely as a general measure.

On the outbreak of civil war in 1139 between Stephen and Matilda, however, the power of the Crown to enforce the Forest laws, like the other laws of the land, was reduced to nothing. The chronicler says, with exaggeration, that 'the herds of thousands of deer, which previously had flooded the whole land in large numbers, were quickly wiped out'.[74] When Matilda arrived in England she purchased the support of powerful nobles like Geoffrey de Mandeville, Earl of Essex, and Aubrey de Vere, Earl of Oxford, with charters acquitting them of Forest offences committed up to the time they came over to her. They were not to be answerable at the Forest law for timber cut in their woods, and were given licence to plough up assarts or forest clearings and bring them into cultivation without penalty.[75] To a powerful supporter in the West Country, Miles of Gloucester, the Constable, who became Earl of Hereford in 1141, she granted the Forest of Dean and the castle of St Briavels in fee: on his death in 1143 they were duly inherited by his son Roger of Hereford.[76] Stephen probably made similar concessions, and in any case was powerless to revoke those made by Matilda. Thus by the death of Stephen in 1154 the tremendous administrative system built up by the Conqueror and his sons for the protection of vert and venison had been in abeyance for more than a decade.

6

Restoration and Development of the Forest System Under Henry II and Richard I: 1154–1198

On his accession in 1154, Henry II repudiated the concessions extorted from Stephen. The whole of the county of Essex, for example, was treated as royal forest, and during the years 1155 and 1156 had to pay a total of over £235 for assarts or unauthorized Forest clearings.[77] The Forest of Dean and the castle of St Briavels, granted away by Matilda, were reserved to the Crown when in 1155 the king confirmed the various possessions inherited by Roger, Earl of Hereford.[78] Alan de Neville, who was his Chief Justice of the Forest from 1165 until 1177, enforced the Forest law with vigour and determination at Forest Eyres in twenty-eight counties.[79] Forty years later a Huntingdonshire jury swore that he 'first appointed . . . verderers . . . regarders and other evil customs'.[80] He did not hesitate to lay hands upon clergy who took the king's deer, and in 1168 he was excommunicated by Thomas Becket, Archbishop of Canterbury, because he had kept the archbishop's chaplain in chains.[81]

Monks and clergy were the chroniclers of the times; the violation of clerical privilege by Forest officers naturally earned their severest strictures against the Forest system. John of Salisbury was Becket's confidential adviser, and dedicated his *Policraticus* to him in 1159. He says in that work that kings of England:

> have not feared to execute men, whom God redeemed by His blood, for offences against the game. In their audacity they have dared to claim for themselves animals which are wild by nature and are made by right for those who can take them . . . What is more astounding, decrees have made it a crime to prepare snares for birds . . . or to catch them by any kind of trap, punishable by confiscation of goods or by mutilation.[82]

St Hugh, Bishop of Lincoln, denounced the oppression of the poor by the royal foresters to Henry II's face; and in 1187 he aroused the furious anger of the king by excommunicating Geoffrey fitzPeter, then Chief Justice of the Forest, for enforcing the Forest law against clerical offenders.[83]

In the first article of the so-called Assize of Woodstock Henry II threatened to revive the brutal penalties for Forest offences inflicted by Henry I.[84] But in fact, as William of Newburgh says, Henry II 'loved the joys of the chase as much as his grandfather, but was more . . . merciful in punishing trespassers against the law established for the protection of the deer.' He 'committed trespassers of this kind to prison, or to exile for a time.'[85]

By this time the object of the Forest Eyres was profit rather than punishment. Remission of traditional methods of trial could be bought by money payments. At the Wiltshire Forest Eyre of 1166 Ailric of Studley was accused by Matthew Croc, warden of Chippenham Forest, of cutting oaks at night time in the forest. He was adjudged to trial by battle against Matthew, but bought himself off by a fine of 40 marks.[86] In the reign of Rufus, as we have seen, Forest offenders were put to trial by the ordeal, but by the reign of John they were paying fines to be excused from this procedure.[87]

At times of crisis the king was forced to promise concessions regarding this burdensome and detested institution. In 1173 and 1174 the Angevin empire was theatened by enemies at home and abroad. Henry II, in a desperate attempt to deprive his rebellious English barons of popular support, promised to abolish the entire Forest system.[88] But as soon as the rebellion was suppressed, the king enforced the Forest law with vigour and severity. He was in great need of money to pay his mercenary troops and to meet the expenses of the war of 1173–4: the great Forest Visitation which he carried out in person in 1175 was a means to this end. On 1 June he held court at Reading, by 1 August he was at Nottingham, and on 11 August he heard pleas of the forest at York.[89] By Michaelmas 1176 long lists of 'the king's amercements for (offences concerning) his forest' in twenty-seven counties were presented at the Exchequer.[90] All classes of his subjects felt the weight of the Forest law. The heaviest penalties naturally fell upon the territorial magnates.

In Hampshire Herbert fitzHerbert and William de Cahaignes were adjudged to pay 500 marks each, and Adam de Port, a leading baron, £200.[91] Loyalty to the king during the rebellion of 1173–4 did not save barons who had taken the king's deer: Everard de Ros and Adam and Robert de Brus, northern magnates who had been among Henry II's most notable supporters, were heavily amerced – Ros in 100 marks and the others in £100 each.[92] The lands of some Forest offenders were seized by the king, and the sheriff subsequently accounted at the Exchequer for their issues.[93] In other cases such lands were handed over to the feudal overlord, who was responsible for payment of part of the amercement.[94]

The Forest officers were summoned to give an account of their stewardship. Fulk de Lisours, warden of Sherwood Forest, and William his clerk, were fined £100 each 'for waste of the forest in his bailiwick'; Hugh of Kilpeck, forester of fee in Herefordshire, had to pay 100 marks, and Peter of Allexton, forester of fee of Rutland Forest, 40 marks.[95] The towns did not escape the prosecutions: the burgesses of Worcester had to pay 20 marks, and the township of Cambridge 40 marks.[96] Humble men by the hundred were condemned to pay sums which must have seemed to them enormous: William the smith of 'Aissour' (Ashford) in Oxfordshire[97] was fined 20 marks, Ralph the smith of Shenfield in Essex half a mark, and William son of Emma of the same county, who owed half a mark 'for a cart he had in the forest'.[98] Many of these poor men abandoned their homes and fled. William the potter of Worcestershire, for example, had been amerced in half a mark, 'but he was nowhere to be found'.[99] The sheriffs subsequently paid into the Exchequer the proceeds of the sale of the chattels of these outlawed 'fugitives from the forest law'.[100] Some of them sought sanctuary in a church:[101] one who did so was Henry Maloisel, who afterwards bought acquittance with a fine of forty shillings at the Gloucester Forest Eyre in 1185;[102] another, Robert of Melcombe, offered five marks at Somerset Forest Eyre in 1199 for leave to 'abjure the forest'.[103] Over eleven hundred Forest amercements were separately enrolled on the 1176 Pipe Roll, ranging from five shillings to 500 marks, besides small amounts for which the sheriffs accounted in lump sums. They totalled nearly £13,000, of which £4,650 was paid into the

18

Exchequer in 1176 and £5,234 in 1177.[104] This was a very substantial addition to the royal revenue, which, it has been calculated, did not amount to more than £21,000 annually before 1173.[105] Many of the sums due were ordered to be paid directly to the Jews,[106] a fact in itself indicative of the king's financial plight.

In 1184 Henry II initiated a great plan of forest re-organization. The so-called Assize of Woodstock, promulgated partly at least in that year,[107] provides a comprehensive statement of the Forest law and administration as it existed at that time. Articles which appear to be new required owners of woods in the royal forest to appoint woodwards to keep the vert and venison in them, and to find sureties for the faithful discharge of their duties. In every forest county four knights (the 'agisters') were to be appointed to make the arrangements for feeding swine in the king's demesne woods between 15 September and 13 October, and to receive and account for the 'pannage' dues. No one was permitted to 'agist' his woods in the forest before the king. Twelve other knights were to be appointed to have general responsibility for the safe keeping of vert and venison.[108] These unpaid officers were to be an important and characteristic feature of the English royal forest.

After the promulgation of this important Forest assize, the king took the unprecedented course of sending out four commissions of Forest judges to hold concurrent Forest Eyres.[109] He was clearly determined that the Forest law should be enforced upon his unwilling subjects. Under his strong rule it was in truth a heavy burden upon all classes, and a cause of misery and hardship for his humbler subjects. Ralph Niger, his enemy, says bitterly of him:

> He granted to no one dwelling within the forest metes liberty to gather twigs in his own woods without supervision by the foresters, or to bring even impenetrable thickets into cultivation . . . He conferred immunity upon the birds of the air, the fish in the rivers, and the wild beasts of the earth, and made poor men's plots their feeding-grounds.

Referring to the perpetual rents exacted for crops grown on forest 'assarts', Niger says, 'He also made an unprecedented forest law, by which innocent people will be for ever made to pay for the trespass of another.'[110]

After the death of Henry II in 1189 there was a respite. The ministers who ruled England during the absence of Richard I on Crusade seem for a decade to have pursued a conciliatory policy. But in 1198 the king's need for money for his war in Normandy was so great that resort was made once again to the Forests. The General Eyre of 1198 in the northern counties – which, according to Hoveden, 'reduced the whole country from coast to coast to beggary' – was followed by a Forest Eyre, which he describes as 'another kind of torment for the confusion of the men of the realm'.[111] In each Forest county the judges read out at the Forest Eyre an ordinance which repeated the provisions of the Assize of Woodstock with certain modifications and additions. The pasturing of pigs in the forest, and the passage of carts along the forest roads were prohibited during the 'fence month', the time of fawning – i.e., from 10 June until 8 July. The different offences against the vert, such as the cutting of branches and underwood, the digging of turves, and the construction of hedges, ditches, sheepfolds or houses within the forest were enumerated and declared to be punishable by very heavy amercements. The forest judges also gave very detailed instructions for the viewing and assessment of assarts by means of the triennial regard.[112]

By the end of the twelfth century, therefore, the main features of the English Forest system had been established.

NOTES

1. *Anglo-Saxon Chronicle* (Rolls Ser.) I 355: II 190.
2. *Chronicle* (ed. B. Thorpe, Eng. Hist. Soc., London 1848) II 44–5.
3. Pipe R. 1130, 87.
4. E 32/140/3, printed G.J. Turner, *Select Pleas of the Forest*, 45.
5. *Course of the Exchequer*, (ed. Johnson) 59–60, 103–4.
6. Darby, *Historical Geography of England* (1936) 10, 96, and map p. 95; Stenton, *Anglo-Saxon England*, 43, 64–5; Crawford, *Map of Britain in the Dark Ages* (O.S., South Sheet).
7. Darby, op. cit., 97; Stenton, op. cit., 281–2, and end map; Crawford, *Map*.
8. Darby, op. cit., 90, 95, 131.
9. ibid., 98.
10. See E32/249 m. 2; Pipe R. 1209, 76.
11. *Rot. Chart.*, 128.
12. Cal. Chart. R. 1226–57, 122.
13. *Rot. Chart.*, 132. The 'Stane Street' (A120) runs west from Colchester to the county boundary.
14. Cal. Chart. R. 1226–57, 39; Darby, op. cit., 213.
15. *De rebus gestis Aelfredi*, cap. 22, 76 (ed. W.H. Stevenson, pp. 20, 59.)
16. Wm. of Malmesbury, *De gestis regum Anglorum* (Rolls. Ser.) I 271.
17. Domesday Book (ed. Abraham Farley. 1783) I 64b.; 'The Domesday league may have comprised 12 furlongs or 1½ miles.' (Darby, op. cit., 201.)
18. *An Anglo-Saxon Reader*, ed A.J. Wyatt (C.U.P., 1925) 40.
19. Secular Dooms, cap. 81 (*Sel. Charters*, ed. Stubbs, 88.)
20. *Dom. Bk.* I 167b.
21. *V.C.H. Wilts.*, IV 392.
22. *Dom. Bk.* I 30, 98b.; III (Exon. Domesday) 443.
23. F. Liebermann, *Über Pseudo-Cnuts Constitutiones de Foresta* (Halle, 1894), 14–16.
24. *V.C.H. Wilts.*, IV 420–21, 438–40.
25. Ch. Petit-Dutaillis, 'Les Origines Franco-Normandes de la "Forêt" Anglaise', in *Mélanges d'Histoire offerts à M. Charles Bémont* (Paris, 1913) 62–66, 68–70.
26. ibid., 72.
27. *V.C.H. Wilts.* IV 392.
28. *Dom. Bk.* I ff. 51–52.
29. See Map No. 2 in *Dom. Bk. Hants.*
30. *Dom. Bk.* I f. 51b.
31. Petit-Dutaillis, 'Studies' II 169–70; Baring, 'New Forest' (E.H.R. 1901, 427ff.; 1912, 513ff); Darby, *Dom. Geog. S.E. Eng.*, 324; 'New Forest Docs.' ed. Stagg, xi–xii.

32. *Dom. Bk.* I 38b.
33. ibid., 39.
34. C47/12/10; Pat. R. Suppl. 6a.; Bazeley, 'Extent of the Forest' (*T.R.H.S.*, Fourth Series, IV 1921) 171: Darby, *Dom. Geog. Midland Eng.* Fig. 83, p. 246.
35. *Dom. Bk.* I fo. 172.
36. ibid., fo. 56b.
37. ibid., fo. 51b.
38. ibid., fo. 39.
39. ibid., fo. 38b.
40. ibid., 143b.
41. ibid., 154, 154b.
42. ibid., 181: Darby, *Dom. Geog. Midland Eng.*, 88.
43. *Dom. Bk.* I 41b., 44b., 51.
44. ibid., 51–51b.
45. *Liber Exoniensis*, fo. 2B.; Darby, *Dom. Geog. S.E. Eng.*, 337; *Dom. Geog. S.W. Eng.*, 39.
46. *Dom. Bk.* I 59; *Chron. Abingdon* (Rolls Ser.) II 7; *V.C.H. Berks.* I 309.
47. *Dom. Bk.* I 247b.; *V.C.H. Staffs.* IV 21, 45.
48. *Dom. Bk.* I 173; Darby, *Dom. Geog. Midland Eng.* 245.
49. *Dom. Bk.* I 48b., 51.
50. ibid., 166b.
51. *Anglo-Saxon Chronicle.* (Rolls Ser.) II 192; *Symeon of Durham* (Rolls Ser.) II 215.
52. *De gestis regum Anglorum* (Rolls Ser.) II 372.
53. *Chron. Ramsey Abbey* (Rolls Ser.) 210; *Reg. Malmesbury Abbey* (Rolls Ser.) I 330, 332.
54. *History of England* (Rolls. Ser.) 102.
55. *Sel. Charters*, ed. Stubbs, 116, 119.
56. See above, p. 4.
57. Pipe R. 1191, 109.
58. *Regesta regum Anglo-Normann*, (ed. Johnson, C. & Cronne, H.A. O.U.P. 1956) II 103.
59. Round, 'Forest of Essex' (*Jnl. Brit. Arch. Assoc.*, N.S. III, 1897) 39.
60. *Ecclesiasticae Historiae* (ed. A. le Prévost. Paris, 1838) IV 238.
61. *Chron. Stephen* etc. (Rolls Ser.) I 280.
62. See e.g. Pipe R. 1130, 51, for a fine of 20 marks made by a Surrey landowner 'that he may have his house and assart and be quit of his trespass'.
63. See e.g. charters granted to the monks of Chertsey in Windsor Forest, and to Colchester Abbey in the forest of Essex (Dugdale, *Mon. Angl.*, 1817) I 431; Cartulary Colchester Abbey, ed. S.A. Moore (Roxburghe Club) I 20–21, cited Cronne, 'The royal forest in the reign of Henry I' in *Essays in British and Irish History*, p. 10.
64. 'Laws of Henry I', art. 17, in *Die Gesetze der Angelsachsen*, ed. F. Liebermann (Halle, 1903) I 559.

65.   A.L. Poole, *Domesday Book to Magna Carta*, 388.
66.   Pipe R. 1130, 7–159.
67.   ibid., 32, 106, 153.
68.   ibid., 106.
69.   ibid., 20, 56.
70.   *Sel. Charters*, ed. Stubbs, 143–4.
71.   Henry of Huntingdon, *Historia Anglorum* (Rolls Ser.) 259–60.
72.   *Inspeximus*, Pat. R. 2 Hen. VI m. 18, cited Round, 'Geoffrey de Mandeville', 378.
73.   Round, 'Forest of Essex', 37–9.
74.   *Chron. Stephen* etc. (Rolls Ser.) III 4.
75.   Charters of Matilda 1141–2, printed Round, 'Geoffrey de Mandeville', 92, 168, 182.
76.   B.M. Lansdowne MSS. 229, fo. 123, cited Hart, 'Royal Forest', 12.
77.   Round, 'Forest of Essex', 39–40.
78.   Flaxley Cartulary, ed. A.W. Crawley-Boevey (1887) p. 8.
79.   Pipe R. 1166–68, 1170–71, 1173–75.
80.   E32/38 m. 2.
81.   Ralph de Diceto, *Opera Historica* (Rolls Ser.) I 332.
82.   *Policraticus*, ed. C. Webb (O.U.P., 1909) I 30.
83.   Map, *'De nugis curialium'*, 5; *'Magna vita S. Hugonis'* (Rolls Ser.) 125, 176.
84.   *Sel. Charters*, ed. Stubbs, 186; and see Petit-Dutaillis, 'Studies' II 192–93.
85.   *Chron. Stephen* etc. (Rolls Ser.) I 280.
86.   Pipe R. 1169, 158.
87.   ibid., 1199, 88, 225.
88.   Benedict of Peterborough, 'Chronicle' (Rolls Ser.) I 94.
89.   ibid., 92–94; *Hoveden.* (Rolls Ser.) II 79: Ralph de Diceto, *'Opera historica'* (Rolls Ser.) I 402.
90.   Pipe R. 1176.
91.   ibid., 193, 194; Pipe R. 1177, 142.
92.   ibid., 112, 115, 116: J.H. Round, Introduction to Pipe R. 1177, xxi–xxii.
93.   Pipe R. 1176, 135, 185, 187.
94.   ibid., 215.
95.   Pipe R. 1177, 53, 95, 104.
96.   ibid., 1176, 37, 74.
97.   Ashford Bridge and Ashford Mill are in North Leigh parish in Wootton hundred ('Place-names of Oxfordshire' II 274.)
98.   Pipe R. 1176, 8, 32, 75.
99.   ibid., 39.
100. ibid., 1170, 102: 1179, 83–84: 1185, 207.
101. ibid., 1185, 167.
102. ibid., 147.
103. ibid., 1199, 237.
104. Pipe R. 1176, 1177.

105. Ramsay, *Angevin Empire*, 186, 194.
106. Pipe R. 1177, 14, 15, 21, 22 etc.
107. Petit-Dutaillis, 'Studies' II 1192–93.
108. arts. 4, 7. (*Sel. Charters*, ed. Stubbs, 187.)
109. *Hoveden*. II 289–90; Pipe R. 1185, 1186.
110. *Chronica*, ed. Anstruther, 167–69; Stubbs, 'Constitutional History' I 530 n. 2.
111. *Hoveden*. (Rolls Ser.) IV 63–65. For the accounts at the Exchequer for the issues of these Forest Eyres, see Pipe R. 1198–1202, passim.
112. *Hoveden*., loc. cit.

The Forest System at its Height During the Thirteenth and Early Fourteenth Centuries

CHAPTER 2

Parks, Hays, Chases and Warrens

1
Parks

There were within the royal forests, or on their outskirts, a number of royal parks in which the deer were preserved with special care. Domesday records a wood at Oakley in Buckinghamshire which would have yielded two hundred pigs had it not been in the king's park in the royal forest of Bernwood.[1]

These parks were usually enclosed by a ditch and earth bank, topped by a wooden palisade, though by the reign of Henry III the royal parks of Devizes and Woodstock were enclosed by stone walls.[2] The expense of maintaining these enclosures was usually borne by the Crown,[3] but in the case of Northampton park the tenants of lands nearby owed the labour service of maintaining specified lengths of the park enclosure.[4] From time to time instructions were given for feeding the deer with hay, and occasionally with oats, when other food was scarce.[5]

The custody of parks and woods in royal manors within the forest was for long a matter of contention. It was finally decided by King and Council in 1237 that custody should belong to the bailiffs of the manors, provided that they swore to answer faithfully to the Chief Justice of the Forest for the safe keeping of vert and venison, and did not pasture any animals in 'enclosures, hays or forest pastures belonging to the said manors' without the consent of the Chief Forest Justice 'according to what shall be most to the King's profit'.[6]

Many of the king's parks were kept by 'parkers', who often had sub-parkers under them. The hereditary parker of Windsor park held of the king twelve acres of land, and in return 'found one or two men daily for keeping the said park'.[7] The parker of Guildford, however, held his office during the king's pleasure, and received two pence a day,[8] while William, son of Matthew of Odiham, appointed in 1292 for life to be parker of the king's park there, received an annual stipend of 16s. 8d.[9]

Royal parks, such as Guildford park, on the outskirts of Windsor Forest,[10] King's Cliffe, Brigstock and Northampton parks in Rockingham Forest,[11] and Woodstock park on the outskirts of Wychwood Forest[12] were subject to the full measure of the Forest law. The beasts of the forest were of course protected, and the smaller game also, such as hares and rabbits.[13] Some isolated royal parks which were not within the forest nor adjacent to it, like Kenilworth park in Warwickshire, were under the jurisdiction of the Chief Justice of the Forest, but others, like Eltham park in Kent, were not.[14]

There were also many parks belonging to subjects, both within the forest and outside. Any landowner might make a park in his lands, provided that they were outside the forest. If they were within it, he had to obtain the king's licence to inclose and impark them: as early as 1130 Roger de Raimes had been fined 40 marks for breaking this law.[15] Such licence to impark transferred the owner-ship of the deer in the woods from the king to the lord of the manor: the Forest law and the Forest officers no longer operated in them.[16] The owner of a private park within the forest was bound to maintain the park enclosure, so that the king's deer should not stray into them through any breaches therein – otherwise the parks were seized by the Forest officers.[17] 'Deer-leaps', constructed so that the deer could get into private parks but could not get out again, were ordered to be removed by the Forest judges.[18]

Pleas of trespasses in private parks were heard, as a general rule, at the General Eyre, according to the common law.[19] By the Statutes of Westminster 1275 a person convicted of such trespass was to pay substantial amends to the plaintiff, and an amercement to the king, and find sureties against repeating the offence. If he could not pay, he was to be imprisoned for three years, and if he could not then find sureties he was to be banished from the realm. Fugitives were to be 'exacted' in the county court and outlawed. 'By these statutes the punishment for trespassing in [private] parks was more severe than for similar offences in the forests.'[20] Exceptionally, such pleas might be heard by the Forest justices. Thus at the Essex Forest Eyre in 1292 Walter le Hunte was sentenced to three years' imprisonment in Colchester gaol 'for his trespass in taking bucks and does in the park of Hugh son of John de Neville, a manor in the King's wardship, at Langham.'[21]

During the latter half of the thirteenth century, commissions of oyer et terminer were frequently issued for pleas of trespasses in private parks. In 1250 Geoffrey de Langley, Chief Justice of the Forest, was instructed to:

> hear and determine in all counties through which he passes, by inquisition or otherwise, pleas of trespasses done in parks, warrens and fishponds, whether in the Forest or without, whosesoever the parks, warrens and fishponds be, and touching trespasses of the king's forbidden rivers, so that he answer to the king for the fines and amercements arising therefrom.[22]

Langley went about this task with characteristic zeal. In February 1251 the king, who 'had heard that many are being kept in the king's prisons for trespasses in parks and fishponds, of which they are accused', ordered him 'to cause them to be delivered in sufficient bail, according to the ancient customs and laws of the Forest'.[23]

2
Hays and Chases

Within the bounds of the royal forests there were many royal hays. 'Hay' means a hedge or enclosure; many of the demesne hays were enclosed woods which formed the nuclei of royal forests. In 1300 a jury declared that Henry II 'had afforested all the woods and groves of the county of Huntingdon . . . except his hays of Weybridge, Sapley and Harthay, which were his demesne woods before.'[24] Most of the Forest offences presented at the Hungtingdon Forest Eyre of

1255 were committed within these hays, or in the districts lying around them, and royal gifts of deer, timber and firewood from the Huntingdon Forest were made chiefly from them.[25]

The king's foresters had a special duty to protect the deer within the hays, but sometimes abused their authority in this respect. At the Parliament of York in 1334 the 'community of the realm' complained to Edward III that:

> if any [domestic] animals enter by a breach into the King's enclosed hays in his forest, the foresters . . . take them and detain them until they receive a heavy ransom, and they cause animals found outside these hays to be chased into the hays and then detain them, so that they may take such redemptions from them for their own use, not permitting them to be replevined by the sheriff or to be delivered.[26]

But some royal hays were extensive forest areas which could not possibly have been entirely enclosed. The Hay of Lythwood in the Long Forest in Shropshire, for example, included a number of woods and townships, and 'the Hay of Hereford was a forest district some six miles in length, including part of the county town'.[27] The seven 'hays' of Cannock Forest were likewise bailiwicks or major sub-divisions of that forest.[28]

A 'chase' was usually a district where the right of hunting the deer belonged to a subject. The chase of Cranbourne, in Dorset and Wiltshire, was held in the twelfth and thirteenth centuries by the Earls of Gloucester and Hertford. The Hundred Rolls of 1275 show that the earl's foresters made attachments of vert and venison, took tolls from carts passing through the chase, made 'scotales'[29] and other illegal exactions.[30] Some of these chases had formerly been royal forests. The royal forest of Dartmoor was in 1239 granted by Henry III to his brother, Richard Earl of Cornwall, and his heirs, 'to hold as the King held it'.[31] Such private forests sometimes maintained the machinery of the royal forest administration almost unchanged, as in Pickering Forest in Yorkshire, and the forests of Lancaster, granted in 1267 by Henry III to his son Edmund, Earl of Lancaster, and his heirs.[32]

But medieval nomenclature was not always consistent. In the thirteenth century the royal forest of Exmoor was sometimes referred to as 'the chase of Exmoor',[33] and royal letters patent in 1295 referred to 'the free chase of William de Braose, which is called the forest of St Leonard'.[34]

3
Warrens

In royal warrens the king reserved to himself the exclusive right of hunting certain beasts other than the four beasts of the forest. The hare was the principal beast of the warren. The Somerset Forest Eyre roll of 1257 shows that it was protected in the warren of Somerton in the same way as the four beasts of the forest: when a hare was found dead there an inquest was held by the four neighbouring townships, and those who had taken hares were attached to appear at the eyre, committed to prison on conviction, and usually released on payment of a fine.[35] The fox and wild cat were also considered to be beasts of the warren;[36] in certain warrens the rabbit was preserved,[37] as were game birds such as the pheasant and partridge.[38] It was furthermore decided in 1339 by the Court of King's Bench that the roe was a beast of the warren and not a beast of the forest, on the ground that it chased away the red and fallow deer, and that therefore land-owners who had the right of free warren in their lands within the royal forest might hunt the roe on those lands.[39]

The king had the right to create warrens in all his demesne lands,[40] and one warren at least, that of Cambridge, also included within its bounds lands held by subjects.[41] If a royal warren were within the bounds of the royal forest, it was of course subject to the Forest law, and the deer were preserved in it:[42] but there were also many royal warrens outside the forest. Two at least of these, the warren of Staines in Middlesex, and the warren of Cambridge, were under the jurisdiction of the Forest officers. At the Huntingdon Forest Eyre of 1209 Jacob of Chinnock, a Jew, was amerced in 10 marks 'for a hare which he killed in the warren of Cambridge',[43] and in 1232 Brian de l'Isle, Chief Justice of the northern and eastern forests, was commanded to sit with the sheriff of Cambridge to hear pleas of this warren.[44] But entries on the 1286 Huntingdon Forest

Eyre roll suggest that the king's rights there had been long disregarded.[45] The royal warren of Staines was, before its diswarrenment in 1227, likewise subject to the authority of the king's officers of Windsor Forest, who held pleas of the warren there.[46]

There were also of course many warrens belonging to subjects, which had been granted by royal charter. In 1232 Henry III granted to Peter des Roches, Bishop of Winchester,

> that he and his successors may for ever have free warren in all his demesne lands in England throughout each one of his manors; so that no one may enter the said warren to take the fox, hare, partridge or pheasant without the bishop's licence, on pain of amercement of ten pounds.[47]

If the proposed warren were within the bounds of the royal forest, a preliminary inquiry by a local jury was held to determine the effect on the rights of the Crown.[48] When suits were brought in the king's courts by landowners against trespassers in their warrens, the amercement went to the king, but when the case was heard in a franchise court, the amercement went to the holder of the franchise.[49]

Substantial fines were paid for charters of warren: in 1255 the abbey of Worcester paid a mark of gold to the king, a mark of silver to the queen, and 2 marks 9s. to the Chancellor and his clerks.[50] Henry III exploited this source of revenue by selling the right of warren to any landowner who desired it.[51] The barons at the Parliament of Oxford in 1258 complained and sought a remedy:

> because, although forests have been disafforested by the king's charter, . . . so that anyone may freely hunt in those districts, the lord king has granted at his pleasure to many men warrens in his aforesaid liberties, which are granted to the detriment of the concessions aforesaid.[52]

NOTES

1. *Dom. Bk.* I 30b.
2. Close R. 1227–31, 164; 1231–34, 63.
3. Cal. Lib. R. 1226–40, 23, 83, 229, etc.
4. Close R. 1227–31, 19; 1247–51, 58 etc.
5. Rot. Litt. Claus. 1204–24, 29, 79 etc.
6. Cal. Pat. R. 1232–47, 186–87.
7. E32/194/3d, 4, printed Turner, *Sel. Forest Pleas*, 55, 57; Cal. I.P.M. II 298.
8. Close R. 1247–51, 503.
9. Cal. Close R. 1272–79, 389.
10. E32/194/3d., 4, printed Turner, op. cit., 54–58.
11. E32/62; 68/3; 72/7d., printed ibid., 4, 29, 40.
12. Bazeley, 'Extent of the English Forest', (*T.R.H.S.*, 4th Series, IV, 1921) p. 143 n. 6.
13. E32/68/3; 194/3d., 4, printed Turner, op. cit., 54, 58.
14. Pat. R. 1216–25, 361; Close R. 1242–47, 151; Bazeley, 'Extent', 144.
15. Pipe R. 1130, 58.
16. See e.g. a licence granted in 1232 to impark Kelvedon wood in Essex (Close R. 1231–34, 50.)
17. Cal. Close R. 1288–96, 97, 163.
18. E32/5/37d.; 258; 309/13; Turner, op. cit., cxvii–cxviii.
19. Articles of the General Eyre, *temp. Hen. III* (Statutes of the Realm I 234.)
20. Turner, op. cit., cxx–cxxi.
21. Cal. Pat. R. 1292–1301, 82.
22. Cal. Pat. R. 1247–58, 76; and ibid., 204.
23. Close R. 1247–51, 412.
24. Wright, *Common Law in the English Royal Forest, Appendix, p. 13.*
25. ibid., p. 22.
26. Cal. Close R. 1333–37, 307.
27. Bazeley, 'Extent', 143.
28. Cantor, *Mediaeval Forests of Staffs.*, 40, and Map on p. 45.
29. See below, p. 118.
30. *V.C.H.* IV 458–60.
31. Cal. Chart. R. 1226–57, 247.
32. ibid., 1257–1300, 78.
33. Petit-Dutaillis, 'Studies' II 151 n. 2.
34. in Sussex (Turner, *Sel. Forest Pleas*, cix n. 1.)
35. E32/152/5d.
36. Close R. 1231–34, 212; *Placita de Quo Warranto* (Rec. Com.) 804.
37. Turner, *Sel. Forest Pleas*, cxxix.

38. Rot. Chart., 185.
39. KB27/315/106; Cal. Pat. R. 1338–40, 246–47.
40. Statutes of the Realm (Rec. Com.) I 144.
41. E32/44/3.
42. E32/152/5d.; printed Turner, *Sel. Forest Pleas*, 41, 130–31.
43. E32/37/Id.
44. Close R. 1231–34, 134.
45. E32/44/3; printed Turner, *Sel. Forest Pleas*, 129–31.
46. *Rot. Litt. Claus.* 1224–27, 195, 197.
47. Close R. 1231–34, 109: cf. ibid., 16, 212 etc.
48. Cal. Pat. R. 1258–66, 123.
49. Turner, op. cit., cxxv–cxxvii.
50. *Ann. Monast. IV Wigorn.* (Rolls Ser.) 443; cf. *Rot. de Ob. et Fin.* (Rec. Com.) 68, 88 etc.
51. Matthew Paris, *Chron. Maj.* (Rolls Ser.) V 356.
52. Petition of the Barons, art. 9 (*Sel. Charters*, ed. Stubbs, 374).

CHAPTER 3

The Local Forest Courts

1
The Swanimote

In medieval times swine were 'agisted' or driven into the woods in autumn to feed on the acorns and beech-mast; 'pannage' dues were paid by the owners of the pigs to the lord of the wood. The Assize of Woodstock, as we have seen, made provision in 1184 for the agistment of the king's demesne woods in the forest.[1] The four 'agisters' responsible for this were usually elected in the county court,[2] though on one occasion at least Henry III himself appointed two agisters in Wychwood Forest.[3] They took an oath that they would faithfully discharge the duties of their office:[4] in 1362 William of Hutton held certain lands in Cumberland 'by service of coming with a book to Gatesgill in Inglewood Forest at Michaelmas, in order to hear the oaths of the keepers of the swine-herds of the forest in time of pannage.'[5]

The foresters, verderers and agisters met at a forest assembly to make arrangements for the agistment of the king's demesne woods. This assembly was called the 'swanimote' or 'swainmote', from an Old English word meaning 'a meeting of swineherds'. The Charter of the Forest conceded in 1217 that henceforth swanimotes were to be held in the forest three times a year only – on 15 September, at the beginning of the pannage season, when the agisters counted the

35

pigs as they entered the forest, and again on about 11 November, at the end of it, when they collected the pannage dues from the owners of the pigs as they came out. It was later enacted that 'At that Time the Forest should again be cleared, and no Animal (except Deer) admitted from 11th November until 23rd Day of April (Old Stile) which Period is called the Winter Haining.'[6] The foresters and verderers were to meet on 10 June for the third session of the swanimote, to see that all animals were removed from the forest: they were not allowed to be pastured there during the 'fence month', which lasted from 10 June until 8 July, because the deer were supposed to be fawning during that time. No persons other than the foresters, verderers and agisters were to be compelled by distraint to attend the swanimotes,[7] which were to be not Forest courts, but merely assemblies of the local Forest officers for certain administrative purposes.

Those who agisted their pigs in the forest after the season of mast without authority were liable to have them seized by the Forest officers, and compelled to find sureties for appearance at a Forest court.[8] Article 9 of the Forest Charter had conceded that 'every free man may agist his wood in the forest at his pleasure, and may have his pannage',[9] but Henry II's edict, that the king's demesne woods must be agisted first, continued to be enforced during the thirteenth century by the seizure of pigs agisted in other woods.[10] In 1279 the inhabitants of Mendip Forest in Somerset complained that the warden summoned to the swanimote all free tenants within the forest, and four men and the tithing from each township, 'and if they do not come they incur fines, to the great grievance of the country, although the king has no demesne and . . . no profit from those fines.'[11] In 1349 the jurors of the several wapentakes of Yorkshire presented that William of Kirkby, late bailiff of Pickering, every time he held a swanimote of Pickering Forest, 'extortionately attempted to amerce at his pleasure the townships within the forest' which failed to send five men to attend the swanimote, 'even though there were not five tenants within them', and compelled them to pay by seizing their ploughs. Kirkby replied that what he had done was in accordance with the custom of the forest from time immemorial.[12]

2

The Attachment Courts: Proceedings Relating to Trespasses of the Vert

The Charter of the Forest provided in 1217 that the verderers and foresters should meet every forty days throughout the year.[13] The foresters were to present the Forest trespasses they had discovered, and the verderers were to record them on their rolls, with the names of the offenders and their sureties or other means of compelling their appearance at a Forest court. Since the principal business of these courts was the 'attachment' of offenders to answer for their trespasses, they were usually called 'attachment courts', but sometimes they were confusingly referred to as 'swanimotes', and, on one occasion at least, as 'the forest hundred'.[14]

It appears from the records of the forests of Galtres in Yorkshire, Sherwood and Dean that in practice the Forest courts were usually held there every six weeks.[15] In the forest of Inglewood in Cumberland Thomas of Milton was hereditary warden from 1222 until 1268, and he held 'the King's pleas of attachment within the forest, and petty pleas concerning himself, always the day after the Lancaster county court'[16], which sat every six weeks.[17] By 1295, however, attachment courts were being held there every twenty-eight days.[18]

In 1287 the judges sitting at the Nottingham Forest Eyre distinguished 'small pleas of the vert', which could be heard and determined at the next attachment court, and major pleas, which had to be remitted to the next Forest Eyre. Anyone discovered cutting wood in the forest without authority was to be compelled to find two trustworthy sureties for his appearance at the next attachment court. If the wood were valued at four pence or less, the offender was to be amerced at the attachment court before the warden of the forest, or his deputy, and the verderers. The amercement was to be paid at the next attachment court, and belonged to the Crown.[19]

The rolls of the attachment courts of Galtres Forest, held at Huby and Easingwold between 1289 and 1293, record many amercements for such small pleas of the vert. On 27 December 1293 a jury convicted 'Thomas the fisherman and Walter Sager' of carrying away by night to Newton-on-Ouse wood belonging to the Treasurer of York Minster. They were amerced in six pence each. John Rimer was fined a like sum 'on account of his sisters who carried wood upon their backs'.[20] William Surale of Tollerton was amerced in twelve pence 'because he came at night with his cart into the forest to commit a trespass'. Thomas Cockerel, vicar of Sutton-on-the-Forest, had to pay eleven pence for having taken 'dry wood in the King's demesne', and William Woodhead of Castleton six pence 'for having carried away windfallen wood belonging to the King'.[21]

Other minor offences for which amercements were imposed at the Galtres attachment courts included cutting grass without licence, allowing cattle and pigs to escape into the king's demesne woods, and evading payment of the agistment dues, taking honey and wax in the forest, fishing without permission, and taking birds with limed twigs.[22] The prior of St Andrew (a small Gilbertine house in Fishergate, York) refused to warrant Thomas son of William of Warthill for having dug turves upon the moor of Stockton-on-the-Forest: Thomas was amerced in twelve pence for purpresture. Other offenders were fined for breaches of the laws for the protection of the venison. Such were 'John the hayward of the assarts' of Sutton-on-the-Forest, who had 'led a certain dog in the forest, in the lord King's chase, contrary to the prohibition'; William of 'Jugeland' and William the miller of Towthorpe, who had to pay twelve pence 'because they came with bows and arrows to Strensall at night time to some women, for the purpose of fornication' – or so they said; and Walter of Aldwark, fined six pence 'because he was found at night within the covert in York, in the fence month'.[23]

The foresters levied contributions of food and other things upon the forest inhabitants for their maintenance. Payment of these contributions, known as 'puture', was enforced at the attachment courts by amercement, distraint and imprisonment.[24] The conduct of the woodwards, who kept the woods of subjects within the forest, was reviewed by the foresters and verderers at the attachment courts. The woodwards were from time to time amerced for failing to take from Forest offenders sufficient security for their appearance at the next attachment court, or for making illegal exactions from the Forest inhabitants.[25]

Major pleas of the vert had to be remitted to the next Forest Eyre. The Nottingham proclamation of 1287 laid down that if the tree or sapling which the offender had cut down were valued at more than four pence, he was to be compelled at the attachment court to find further sureties for his appearance at the Forest Eyre. The value of the wood cut was to be estimated by the foresters and verderers, and the trespasser was to pay it to the verderers in full attachment court. In the case of a third such offence, the malefactor was to be imprisoned in the king's prison at Nottingham, from which he could be delivered only by special order of the king or of the Chief Justice of the Forest – and he usually had to find twelve sureties for his appearance at the next Forest Eyre.[26]

Trespassers who dwelt outside the forest limits, and who possessed no land or chattels within them, could not be attached by the Forest officers.[27] Therefore, if they committed any such trespass against the vert, they were to be sent to gaol at once. For a third offence, the offender was:

> to lose his horses with his cart, or his oxen with his wagon, or their price; and that price is to be paid in the next and full attachment court to the verderers, or to the four neighbouring townships, for the use of the lord King . . . to answer therefor . . . before the justices in eyre (for Forest pleas).[28]

Disputes about clerical privilege occurred in the attachment courts. At Easingwold in Galtres Forest 'Master William of Pontop, parson of Huntington', was attached in 1293 for having cut down a 'green oak' in the lord of the manor's wood. He was summoned three times, but he refused to come, and his sureties were therefore amerced. The verderers ordered his oxen to be seized by way of distraint, and finally that he himself should be arrested for contempt. Master William was compelled to appear, to acknowledge the jurisdiction of the king's court, and to agree to pay a fine.[29]

There were frequent complaints of extortionate practices. In 1279 the people of Mendip Forest in Somerset complained that 'every forty days throughout the year the summons is made of the free men and townships outside the King's demesnes, to the great grievance of the country . . .'. The Forest warden said that he did this so that inquiries should be made regarding Forest offences, but the people objected to it when there was 'no beast dead or maimed, nor any lawful indictment by a forester or any other certain man according to the assize of the forest.'[30]

Edward I's 'Ordinance of the Forest' admitted in 1306 that:

> the People of our Realm are, by the Officers of our Forests, miserably oppressed, impoverished and troubled with many wrongs, being everywhere molested. For sometimes the Accusations of the Forest, and Indictments, commonly so called, are not made by lawful Inquests of true and law-worthy men of the Country, preceding them, as justice doth require, but on the command of one or perhaps two of the Foresters, or on the command of one or two of the Verderers, who from hatred or otherwise maliciously, that they may extort money from someone, do indict or accuse whom they will; and thereupon do follow grievous Attachments, and the innocent Man is punished, who hath incurred no Fault or Offence at all.

The Ordinance therefore enacted that henceforward all presentments of trespasses of vert and venison should be made by foresters in full attachment court, that the truth of the matter should be ascertained by a sworn jury, and that subsequent presentments should be confirmed and sealed by all the Forest officers, including the foresters, verderers, regarders and agisters.[31]

NOTES

1. See above, p. 19.
2. Cal. Close R. 1279–88, 34, 338.
3. Close R. 1234–37, 145.
4. ibid., 1251–53, 56.
5. Cal. Fine R. 1356–68, 239.
6. 20 Car. II c. 3.
7. art. 8, Charter of the Forest (*Sel. Charters*, ed. Stubbs, 346.)
8. *Rot. Litt. Claus.* 1204–24, 473.
9. *Sel. Charters*, ed. Stubbs, 346.
10. E32/239/3; Bazeley, *Forest of Dean*, 255.
11. C99/101; Turner, *Sel. Forest Pleas*, 127.
12. KB27/355/67; N. Riding Record Series IV N.S. 171–77.
13. art. 8 (*Sel. Charters*, ed. Stubbs, 346.)
14. E32/140/3; B.M. Add. Roll 28404; Turner, *Sel. Forest Pleas*, xxxvi–xxvii, 70.
15. E32/33, 237, 239–41; E101/134/16; Turner, op. cit., xxx: Hart, 'Royal Forest', 55–56.
16. Cal. Inq. Misc. I 156.
17. Holdsworth, *Hist. English Law* (7th. ed.) I p. II.
18. E32/7.
19. E32/127/10d.; cf. a similar proclamation at the 1282 Glos. Forest Eyre (E32/30/33); Turner, op. cit., xxxvii n.I., 62–64.
20. E32/239/3.
21. E32/237; 240/2.
22. E32/237; 239/1–2; 241/1.
23. E32/237d.; 239/1; 240/1.
24. E32/240/1.
25. E32/237; 239/1.
26. See e.g. *Rot. Litt. Claus.* 1204–24, 417; Close R. 1234–37, 276 etc.
27. E32/63; B.M. Add. Roll 28405; Turner, *Sel. Forest Pleas*, xxxiii–xxxiv, 73, 90.
28. E32/127/10d.; Turner, op. cit., 63.
29. E32/240/1–3; see also E32/237; 239/3.
30. C. 99/101; Turner, op. cit., 127.
31. Statutes of the Realm (Rec. Com.) I 147–48.

CHAPTER 4

Proceedings Preliminary to the Forest Eyre

1
The Regard

The regard was a triennial inquiry into the state of the vert in the forest, and trespasses against it. Its primary object was to prevent the destruction of the trees, bushes and other forms of vegetation which afforded food and shelter for the king's deer, but it was soon used to furnish the central administration with a detailed record of sources of royal revenue in the forest, arising for the most part from breaches of the law relating to the vert.

The earliest version of the articles of the regard dates from the Assize of Woodstock in the reign of Henry II,[1] though there is evidence that the regard itself was initiated by a Forest Assize promulgated by Henry I.[2] These articles were elaborated by Richard I's Forest Assize in 1198, which was also decreed that the regard was to be held every three years.[3] Every regard was made by twelve regarders, who, like the verderers and agisters, were unpaid and elected in the county court from among the knights of the locality. Where there were several forests in the same county, there was a separate regard for each; in Staffordshire, for example, twelve regarders made the regard in Kinver Forest, and twelve others in

Cannock.[4] The larger forests were subdivided for this purpose. In 1285 there were twelve regarders for each of the three bailiwicks into which Inglewood Forest in Cumberland was divided,[5] while in the forest of Essex about the same time twelve regarders made the regard of Colchester, twelve the regard of Ongar, and twelve the regard of Chelmsford.[6]

By the reign of Henry III a regard was held just before the Forest Eyre and in preparation for it. The sheriff was instructed to call the foresters and verderers together; the places of regarders who were dead or infirm were to be filled by the election of others in the county court. Foresters and regarders were to swear scrupulously to make the inquiries set forth in the articles of the regard. If the foresters were ignorant of any relevant matter, or wished to conceal it, the regarders were nevertheless bound to investigate and record it. Their returns were to be enrolled and sealed and kept until the coming of the Forest justices.[7]

By 1229 the Articles of the Regard had assumed almost their final form: the twelve articles issued in that year[8] were re-issued subsequently with occasional variations of minor importance. The first articles dealt with 'Assarts', which are defined by the 'Course of the Exchequer', written between 1176 and 1179, as 'Clearings . . . that is, when any woods or thickets in the forest which are suitable for meadows and homesteads are cut down . . . the roots are torn up, and the land is ploughed up and brought into cultivation.'[9] The Charter of the Forest in 1217 had granted acquittance of all assarts, waste and purprestures made before 28 October in that year:[10] the regard required all assarts made since then to be measured and recorded in detail. New assarts made since the last regard were to be enrolled separated from old assarts, with information as to all crops grown on them. Most of the assarts recorded were small: the smallest were clearly the work of individual peasants who had encroached upon the forest covert and wastes in order to grow food for themselves and their families. Encroachments were naturally most extensive in the more fertile valleys and coastal plains. The Crown turned these activities into a source of revenue: after an inquisition *ad quod damnum* licenses to assart were granted in return for payment of a fine and an annual rent thereafter.

43

The second and third articles of the regard directed a similar inquiry to be made regarding 'purprestures' – that is to say, any unauthorized buildings, enclosures, excavations or other man-made features in the forest which interfered with the freedom of movement of the deer, or was likely to frighten them away. The Charter of the Forest in 1217 expressly exempted mills, fishponds, marlpits and ditches made by free tenants in their lands and woods outside the covert of the forest.[11]

The right of owners of woods within the forest to cut wood or underwood in them was strictly limited. The Assize of Woodstock conceded that such owners might take what was necessary for them 'by view of the King's foresters'[12] – i.e., for repairing their houses (housebote), for fuel (firebote), and for fencing (haybote). The fourth and fifth articles dealt with the cutting of wood beyond this limited right, an offence called 'waste'. The regarders were to inspect the king's demesne woods with special care: all stumps of oak and beech trees cut down since 1218 were to be counted and recorded, and damage to underwood and outer branches was to be noted.

The remaining articles dealt with various other rights and revenues of the Crown within the Forest. A return was to be made 'of the sea ports in which ships or boats ply for the export of timber or underwood from the forests': all forges and mines operating in the forest were to be set down, whether they were in the royal demesne or not, and who received the dues and rents paid for them. Inquiry was to be made whether anyone had unlawfully pastured animals in 'the lord King's hays and chases where no one had common': as to honey and the eyries of goshawks, sparrow-hawks and falcons in the forest, and who had the right to them according to law and custom: and whether anyone was in unlawful possession of bows, arrows, crossbows, hounds, 'or any other means of doing evil to the lord King's beasts'.

The Charter of the Forest laid down that:

> the inquest or view of the lawing of dogs kept in the forest shall henceforth be made when the regard ought to be made, to wit, every three years, and then it shall be done by the view and testimony of law-worthy men . . . He whose dog shall then be found unlawed shall pay three shillings as an amercement: henceforth no ox shall be taken for lawing. Lawing shall

44

commonly be by the assize, such that three claws shall be cut off the forefoot without the ball of the foot: dogs shall not henceforth be lawed except in places where they were accustomed to be lawed in the time of the first coronation'

of Henry II (i.e. in 1154)[13] The purpose of 'lawing' was of course to prevent dogs from running after the deer in the forest, but it soon became yet another means of financial exaction. In the fourteenth century, for example, the tenants of lands in the soke of Scalby in Pickering Forest made a return every three years of their dogs which were not lawed, and paid a collective fine therefor: 'the bailiff of the castle . . . levied the fine in its entirety and received it from the Soke.'[14]

The returns to the articles of the regard were enrolled upon the regarders' rolls, and formed the basis of part of the proceedings at the Forest Eyre. But in the meantime it was the duty of the Forest officers to seize for the king any woods within the forest in which waste had been committed,[15] and sometimes the owner's chattels and livestock also.[16] Any assarts made without warrant, and any crop grown on them, were likewise seized,[17] and houses, sheepfolds or other constructions and enclosures erected without licence were to be thrown down. The offenders were attached to appear at the next Forest Eyre,[18] and the owners of property seized had to obtain a royal writ directing the Chief Justice of the Forest to replevin them until then.[19]

The unpaid office of regarder was a very unpopular one among the knights of the forest districts, involving as it did the enforcement of a system which the forest inhabitants considered thoroughly hateful and oppressive. Moreover, the regarders were liable to amercement at the Forest Eyre for any failure to perform their duties − for example, for failing to appear to take the regarder's oath and to make the regard after election;[20] for failing to appear before the Forest justices with their returns on the first day of the Forest Eyre;[21] for loss of their rolls;[22] for incompleteness in their returns;[23] or for making a presentment which was proved at the Forest Eyre to have been false.[24] No wonder then that many men bought from the Crown exemption from election as regarders.[25]

For the forest landowners and inhabitants generally the regard was therefore a grievous burden. In 1187 the men of the royal forest of Lancashire gave the king a fine of 100 marks to postpone it for three years.[26] Many landowners paid large sums for a grant of acquittance of the regard: in 1307 the Abbot of Eynsham paid 100 marks for such a grant in respect of his woods of Eynsham and Charlbury in Wychwood Forest, and Eton, in Shotover Forest. The abbot was to appoint sworn woodwards to keep these woods; the covert of Eton wood was not to be destroyed and the king's Forest officers were still to have authority to deal with venison trespasses.[27]

Ordinary folk in the forest who could not purchase freedom from the regard sometimes reacted with violence. At the Pickering Forest Eyre in 1334 fourteen men were presented because they had 'with force and arms prevented the regarders from making their regard in the said forest in Raincliff'.[28]

As the Forest Eyre fell into desuetude, so did the regard. From the middle of the fourteenth century the number of counties in which it was held declined, and it disappeared almost completely south of the Trent after 1387. It continued to be held in the north, however, in the forests of Inglewood, Sherwood, Galtres and Pickering, using the same articles of the regard as before.[29]

2

The Attachment of Trespassers Against the Venison

The decrees of the Norman and Angevin kings reserving to themselves hunting rights over the lands of subjects were bitterly resented; rich and poor, clergy and laity alike incurred the penalties of the Forest law. To enforce it the warden of each royal forest had under him a staff of foresters; they were assisted by the verderers – unpaid knights of the locality, elected in the county court. A typical example of procedure occurs on a Rockingham Forest presentment roll. On 11 June 1248 James of Thurlbear, a forester:

came into the park of Brigstock about the first hour [i.e., just after sunrise], and found . . . John the son of Stephen Cut of Slipton, carrying a doe's fawn. And the said James arrested him, and caused Richard of Aldwinkle, the verderer, to be summoned.

He came the next day 'and questioned the said John . . . and he said that he had no accomplices'. The poacher:

was sent to Northampton to be imprisoned. And the sheriff was then Alan of Maidwell. And the skin of the aforesaid fawn was delivered to John Lovet, verderer, to have before the justices of the forest.[30]

The Forest officers were bound to secure the appearance of offenders at the next Forest Eyre. This was usually done in the first instance by committing the accused persons to prison. The wardens of many royal forests were also constables of neighbouring royal castles, and so had a gaol at their disposal. Trespassers in Windsor Forest, for example, were frequently committed to the gaol in Windsor castle.[31] Galtres Forest had its own gaol in York: in 1369 John of Thornton held in chief a messuage in York by service of keeping the Forest gaol 'which is in the said messuage', and was paid 5d. a day by the bailiffs of the city of York.[32] Where the Forest warden had no gaol, he handed his prisoners over to the keeper of a neighbouring royal gaol. So Richard de Munfichet, hereditary warden of the royal forest of Essex, was at various times between 1234 and 1259 ordered to hand over Forest trespassers whom he had arrested to the sheriff of Hertfordshire, the constable of Colchester castle, or to the keepers of the London gaols of the Fleet and Newgate.[33]

Long intervals elapsed between successive Forest Eyres, so that poachers often lay for long periods in gaol, awaiting trial.[34] Imprisonment at this time entailed very great hardship: prisoners depended on their families or friends to bring them food, so that poor and friendless men fared ill.[35] Prisoners frequently died of cold and hunger;[36] it is not surprising that many forest offenders preferred flight and outlawry. Some Forest wardens treated their prisoners with great severity. On the other hand, the warden of Rockingham Forest was indicted in 1293 for having allowed

47

William son of Mary of Gretton, an imprisoned poacher, to go home every night, in return for a payment of half a mark.[37]

Prisoners who could pay the necessary fines, usually half a mark or twenty shillings, according to their means, obtained from the king or the Chief Justice of the Forest a writ releasing them on bail until the next Forest Eyre.[38] They had to find sufficient sureties for their appearance there, and take an oath not to break the Forest law in future.[39] The king sometimes took pity on poor prisoners who could not find sureties, and ordered their release on taking the oath only.[40]

Property within the forest belonging to trespassers against the venison was seized as a further means of ensuring their appearance at the next Forest Eyre. The warden was usually responsible for the safe keeping of such property, whether lands, woods, horses, oxen, or dogs, and for replevying them until the next eyre upon receipt of the appropriate royal writ.[41]

The sheriff was often called upon to arrest and attach Forest offenders, when the Forest officers had failed to do so. The Assize of Clarendon in 1166 provided that he should arrest men who fled into his county after a Forest offence in another county.[42] Offenders arrested by the foresters were in many cases handed over to the sheriff to be kept in custody until the Forest Eyre;[43] if they escaped from prison, or were released without proper warrant, the sheriff was liable to amercement. He was bound to appear before the justices on the first day of the Forest Eyre, and produce his prisoners, or the appropriate writs for their delivery on bail.[44] Some trespassers lived outside the forest bounds, and had no property within it, so that the foresters could not attach them: in such cases it fell to the sheriff to seize their lands.[45] The sheriff also had to account for the proceeds of the sale of chattels of 'fugitives of the forest'.[46]

All presentments of major Forest offences made by the foresters had to be enrolled and sealed by the verderers.[47] These rolls recorded all deer taken in the forest with or without authority, details of all trespasses, the names of offenders and suspects, and of sureties or gaolers responsible for producing them. These 'rolls of presentments' had to be produced at the Forest Eyre, and formed the basis of many of the proceedings there before the Forest justices.[48]

3
Special Inquests of the Venison

If a beast of the forest were found wounded or dead, the foresters and verderers called together the men of the neighbouring townships to make inquiry as to the cause of death or injury, and the identity of anyone suspected of having killed or wounded it. Similar inquests were held as to the identity of those who had committed venison trespasses discovered by or reported to the foresters, the guilt of persons indicted of such offences,[49] and, in one case at least, as to the ownership of greyhounds found running in the forest and suspected to have been brought there to hunt the king's deer.[50] These Forest inquests began to be held at least as early as the reign of King John,[51] and they resembled the coroner's inquest very closely.[52] The inquiry was usually made by four townships, but sometimes five, six or even seven townships were summoned for this purpose.[53] It was held soon after the trespass had been discovered, usually at the scene of the trespass or a place nearby.[54] The Forest officers, sometimes presided over by the deputy warden of the Forest, called the townships before them one by one, and examined them on oath. Sworn evidence was also given by the foresters, verderers, woodwards, and others such as eye-witnesses: suspects also were examined on oath.[55] Those indicted or suspected of venison offences were in most cases compelled to find sureties of appearing at the next Forest Eyre[56], but in serious cases they were committed to gaol.[57] Their chattels were seized and valued by the foresters and verderers and then handed over to men of substance in the neighbourhood, who were bound to answer for their value at the next Forest Eyre.[58] Evidence such as arrows, and snares set for the deer and discovered by the Forest officers, and the heads and skins of deer found dead, was handed over to the verderers, or to law-worthy men of the neighbourhood, for production at the Forest Eyre.[59] The flesh of deer found dead or recovered from poachers was given to the lepers, the poor or the sick of the locality.[60] Greyhounds belonging to poachers, or found running after the deer in the forest, were seized for the king, and sent to the Forest warden or to the Chief Justice of the Forest.[61]

If a township did not appear at the Forest inquest when first summoned, it was required at a subsequent inquest to find sureties for appearance at the Forest Eyre.[62] Sureties had also to be found by townships whose evidence at the inquest was considered unsatisfactory, by the four nearest neighbours, by the finder of a dead deer and the owner of the field in which it was found, and by any individual whose absence from the inquest had brought him under suspicion.[63]

4

General Inquests of the Forest

The 'special Inquests of the Forest' were concerned with a single specific Forest offence, and were intended to gather evidence for the Forest Eyre. But by the reign of Edward I the intervals between successive Forest Eyres became ever longer, so that new and less cumbrous procedures were devised, using the familiar machinery of the local jury of inquiry.[64] The scope of these 'general inquests of the Forest' was extended to include all manner of Forest trespasses committed in the locality. For example, on 2 June 1301 a stag was found 'wounded and dead' in Wakefield bailiwick in Whittlewood Forest. There followed an inquest held before John Tingewick, deputy warden of the forest, and the foresters and verderers, by the four neighbouring townships and a jury of twelve, 'regarding this trespass, and all other trespasses committed since the last inquest'.[65] These 'general inquests' were frequently held in full attachment court;[66] sometimes, when a 'special inquest' held on the spot soon after a venison trespass had failed to elicit any useful information, the whole proceedings were adjourned until a 'general inquest' could be held at the next attachment court, so that further inquiries could be made in the mean time.[67]

During the reign of Henry III special commissions, often headed by the Chief Justice of the Forest, were sent out whenever there seemed need, to inquire into breaches of the Forest law.[68] When during the next reign the Justice of the Forest came into the forests of Whittlewood, Rockingham, King's Cliffe and Salcey to hold a general inquest, the foresters, often headed by the warden and his deputy, appeared before him and, in some cases, handed to him their rolls of presentments. The woodwards were generally present, and sometimes the regarders and the agisters also. Often a jury of twelve 'knights and law-worthy men of the neighbouring parts of the forest' was summoned to give evidence on oath 'as well regarding malefactors of the lord King's venison as regarding the vert, and other matters touching the said forest'.[69] The neighbouring townships were summoned – four, five and sometimes more.[70] In one instance at least each township sent four men and the reeve.[71] They made presentments of venison offences, and offences against the vert such as cutting down trees and branchwood, and sometimes of assarts and purprestures also.[72] From time to time they indicted the officers of the forest – the wardens and their deputies, the foresters, the woodwards and the agisters:[73] the central administration clearly used these general inquests as a check upon them. The Justices' clerks recorded the proceedings upon their rolls, and accused persons had subsequently to stand trial at the next Forest Eyre,[74] or, in certain cases, before the king in Parliament.[75]

But as the intervals between successive Forest Eyres lengthened in the second half of the thirteenth century, commissions were issued during these intervals to the Justices of the Forest and others, not only to inquire into Forest offences, but also to hear and determine them (*oyer et terminer*).[76] Between 1293 and 1297 the Justice of the Forest, or his deputy, exercised jurisdiction at general inquests in the northern forests of Sherwood, Inglewood and Galtres, as he would have done at the Forest Eyre. For example, at Blidworth in Sherwood Forest in 1294 it was discovered that three foresters of the bailiwick of Nottingham had not levied the amercements of the attachment court pleas as the Justice of the Forest had ordered them to do. They were committed to gaol, but were subsequently delivered after finding sureties for the proper discharge of their duties, under a penalty of twenty shillings. Twelve men presented by the foresters and verderers at the same inquest for trespasses against the vert were also committed to gaol, and later amerced in two or three shillings each.[77] By the middle of the fourteenth century the Forest Eyre had virtually been superseded by commissions of *oyer et terminer*, and by general commissions of inquiry into the state of the forests.[78]

These developments present a close parallel with what was happening in the common law, where the General Eyre, with its comprehensive Articles, had by the middle of the fourteenth century been replaced by courts having more limited commissions.[79]

NOTES

1. art. 10 (*Sel. Charters*, ed. Stubbs, 188)
2. Petit-Dutaillis, 'Studies' II 173–76.
3. *Hoveden*. IV 65.
4. E32/184/3d., 7; 187/2.
5. E32/5; Turner, *Sel. Forest Pleas*, xx n. 3.
6. E32/12/8, 9d., IId; 13/25d., 28d., 31.
7. See e.g. Close R. 1231–34, 31.
8. Pat. R. 1225–32, 286–87.
9. ed. Johnson, 60–61.
10. art. 4 (*Sel. Charters*, ed. Stubbs, 345.)
11. art. 12 (ibid., 347.)
12. art. 3 (ibid., 187).
13. arts. 5, 6 (ibid., 345–46); Cal. I.P.M. II No. 638.
14. Cal. Pat. R. 1345–48, 37–38.
15. Close R. 1242–47, 268, 434 etc.
16. *Rot. Litt. Claus.* 1204–24, 56.
17. ibid., 93.
18. ibid., 407; Close R. 1234–37, 88 etc.
19. *Rot. de Ob. et Fin.*, 325; Close R. 1242–47, 468 etc.
20. E32/188/14; *Coll. Hist. Staffs.* V i 169.
21. E32/41/5; 185/7d.
22. Pipe R. 1199, 33.
23. E32/12/8, 9d., 11d.
24. E32/5/36d.; Turner, *Sel. Forest Pleas*, lxxxi n, 3.
25. Cal. Pat. R. 1247–58, 47, 101, 198 etc.
26. Pipe R. 1187, 17.
27. Cal. Pat. R. 1301–7, 493; cf. Cal. Chart. R. 1226–57, 113, 116, 182 etc.
28. DL42/I/262a.; N. Riding Records, N.S., III 16–17.
29. E32/215; Young, 'Royal forests', 157–58.
30. E32/63; Turner, *Sel. Forest Pleas*, 81–82.
31. Close R. 1231–34, 89–90; 1234–37, 432 etc.
32. Cal. Fine R. 1369–77, 20.
33. Close R. 1231–34, 383: 1234–37, 295; 1254–56, 337: 1259–61, 17.
34. Cal. Close R. 1288–96, 406, 432.
35. ibid., 1272–79, 391.
36. E32/62; Turner, *Sel. Forest Pleas*, 3, 4; cf. Gross, *Sel. Coroners' Rolls 1265–1413*, 79, 80 etc.
37. E32/82/3.
38. *Ex. e Rot. Fin.* II 24, 113, 203 etc.; Close R. 1237–42, 102, 470 etc.
39. *Ex. e Rot. Fin.* I 293: E36/76/19r. (Sherwood Forest Book, 55–56.)

40. Close R. 1231–34, 36.
41. Close R. 1231–34, 521: 1237–42, 64, 471; 1247–51, 124, 515; Cal. Close R. 1279–88, 222.
42. art. 17 (*Sel. Charters*, ed. Stubbs, 172.)
43. Close R. 1231–34, 36, 422 etc.
44. E32/41/5, 6, 6d.; 249/11.; Turner, *Sel. Forest Pleas*, lxiii, 7, 14, 17, 22.
45. E32/68/3d.; 72/6d.; Turner, op. cit., 23, 32, 39, 42, 58; Fisher, *Forest of Essex*, 98.
46. Pipe R. 1170, 102; 1179, 83–84 etc.
47. Charter of the Forest 1217, art. 16. (*Sel. Charters*, ed. Stubbs, 347–48.)
48. See e.g. rolls for Salcey, Kingscliffe, Rockingham, Whittlewood and Sherwood Forests *temp. Edward* I (E32/78, 79, 82, 83, 128; Turner, *Sel. Forest Pleas*, 69–116.)
49. Turner, *Sel. Forest Pleas*, 22, 27, 71–72, 106–108 etc.
50. ibid., 78–79.
51. E32/62; Turner, op. cit., 4.
52. See Gross, *Sel. Coroners' Rolls*, xxiv–xxxi.
53. Turner, op. cit., 97–100.
54. ibid., 75, 76, 82, 87 etc.
55. ibid., 70–71, 75, 77, 80, 97–98, 99 etc.
56. ibid., 76–77, 83–84.
57. ibid., 87–88, 90–91.
58. ibid., 70, 94.
59. ibid., 78, 81, 83, 87, 91, 95.
60. ibid., 82, 84, 87, 89.
61. ibid., 13–14, 81.
62. ibid., 87, III.
63. ibid., 70–72, 87.
64. Holdsworth, *Hist. of English Law*, I 312–17.
65. E32/83/6.
66. E32/78/5; 79/3–7.
67. E32/79/4; 83/4.
68. Cal. Pat. R. 1232–47, 123; 1247–58, 116 etc.
69. E32/78/5; 82/1, 2, 4, 7; 83/8.
70. E32/68/4d.; 83/3.; Turner, *Sel. Forest Pleas*, 37, 108–111.
71. E32/79/4.
72. E32/78/3–5.; 83/8.
73. E32/78/2, 4.; 82/2, 3, 5.; Turner, op. cit., 37.
74. E32/65; 68/4d.; Turner, op. cit., 36, 37, 108–112.
75. Cal. Pat. R. 1281–92, 281, 286, 332–333 etc.
76. ibid., 1266–72, 96; 1281–92, 522; 1292–1301, 47 etc.
77. E32/130. See also E32/6, 131, 242.
78. See below, p. 167.
79. Holdsworth, *Hist. of English Law*, I 264–74.

CHAPTER 5

The Forest Eyre

1
Suitors and Articles

Between six weeks and two months before a Forest Eyre was held in any county, a writ was issued from the Chancery ordering the sheriff to see that a regard was made.[1] Then their commissions were issued to the Forest justices by royal letters patent,[2] and a writ sent to the sheriff ordering him to summon all those who owed suit at the Forest Eyre to appear before them in the day and place appointed. Those summoned to attend were the archbishop, bishops, abbots, priors, earls, barons, knights and all of lesser degree who held land in free tenure within the bounds of the king's forest in that county, together with four men and the reeve from every forest township. The foresters and verderers with their rolls of attachments, the regarders with their rolls – all sealed with their seals – and the agisters with their accounts of the agistment of the king's demesne woods in the forest were also bound to attend.[3]

Until 1215 men dwelling on the outskirts of the forest were also summoned: at the Rutland Forest Eyre in 1209 the verdict of the knights of the county was that all men of the county of Leicester ought to come who dwelt outside the forest of Sauvey 'as far as two leagues'.[4] But Magna Carta conceded that 'men who dwell outside the forest shall not come henceforth before our Justices of the Forest by the common summons, unless they be impleaded, or be pledges of anyone who had been attached for a forest trespass.'[5] This concession was confirmed by the Charter of the Forest in 1217,[6] and seems to have been honoured by the central administration.[7]

In one category of offences, however, the jurisdiction of the Forest justices extended outside the forest bounds. The deer within them were the property of the king: none might kill them even if they strayed outside. At the Somerset Forest Eyre held at Ilchester in 1270 it was presented that a fawn had come out of Exmoor Forest and had been taken by Henry Boniface, Richard Absalom and Thomas son of Henry of Bossington.

> They appeared, and because it is proved that they took that fawn outside the forest bounds, and carried it to their houses in the township of Bossington, which is within the forest, going through the forest with the same fawn, therefore they are committed to prison. They were brought out and made fine by ten shillings.[8]

The obligation of doing suit at the Forest Eyre was an onerous one, especially for tenants in chief who held land in many counties. The barons at the Oxford Parliament in 1258 complained that they were on occasion summoned to attend the General Eyre in one county and the Forest Eyre in another on the same day, and were amerced at the Eyre they did not attend, unless they had a royal writ of acquittance.[9] Consequently many subjects found it expedient to purchase from the king such a grant of acquittance of the common summons to the Forest Eyre.[10]

Barons, prelates and heads of religious houses who held land in free tenure within the forest bounds were allowed to appear at later Forest Eyres by 'attorneys'. At the Hampshire Forest Eyre in 1280 the Abbots of Waverley, Titchfield and Netley sent six 'brothers', and the Abbot of Beaulieu sent 'Matthew his monk'.[11] The Archbishop of York headed the list of those who appeared by proxy at the Nottingham Forest Eyre of 1287.[12]

By the second half of the thirteenth century the justices for Forest pleas were armed with a set of Articles resembling those of the General Eyre,[13] – designed, like them, to enforce the law, bring local officials to a sense of their duties, and fill the king's coffers by exacting amercements from everyone in default.[14] At the Cumberland Forest Eyre of 1285 these Articles were twenty-nine in number[15] and fell roughly into three categories. First, inquiry was made into the conduct of the local Forest officers: whether the foresters had made any unlawful exactions; which foresters of fee had taken money from their subordinate foresters for their appointment; which foresters had without authority pastured their beasts in the forest; whether any of them, or any of the verderers or other Forest officers, had concealed any offence; and whether attachments had been made by the boys who assisted the foresters (which was illegal because the boys had not taken the foresters' oath). A list of wardens and deputy wardens of the forest since the last eye was required: inquiry was made as to whether the regarders and agisters had performed their duties faithfully and well. At many Forest Eyres these questions brought to light long lists of illegal exactions, usurpations of Crown rights, and acts of waste and destruction in the forest by the warden and his subordinates.

The second group of Articles was concerned with offences committed and liberties unlawfully usurped by the forest land-owners and inhabitants. Some of these matters had already been dealt with by the regard, such as waste, assarts and purprestures, forges, honey and eyries, and sea-ports exporting forest timber: the returns to these Articles merely referred to the regarders' rolls. But there were also new Articles, inquiring whether the forest pastures were over-burdened by the unlawful pasturing of horses; whether any of the forest dwellers refused to pay the lawful dues for the agistment of their pigs in the forest; who claimed any right in the forest which was to the king's detriment and to the damage of the forest, such as the right to have hounds to hunt the hare and fox, to have dogs unlawed, and to take timber in their demesne woods without supervision by the foresters.

The remaining Articles were concerned with sources of Crown revenue within the forest – as to the value of windfallen wood and who received it; what iron, lead and tin mines there were in the forest, and their value; sea-coal; and the herbage dues from the king's demesne pastures.

The returns to these Articles were made at the Forest Eyre by the foresters and verderers and by a jury of 'twelve knights and free men', and sometimes also of sworn representatives of the forest townships.[16] The Forest judges used them as the basis of part of their proceedings, and imposed amercements in respect of offences disclosed therein.

2
Procedure at the Forest Eyre: the First Day

On the first day of the Forest Eyre all those who owed suit had to appear. Defaulters were amerced according to their means. At the Huntingdon Forest Eyre of 1286, for example, over a hundred persons were amerced in sums ranging from 12d. to £5 'for default on the first day'.[17] Important and wealthy men had to pay more: at the Yorkshire Forest Eyre in 1262 Simon de Roche-Chouard, a canon of York and a kinsman of the king, was fined £20 'for common summons', and the Chancellor of York had to pay twenty marks.[18] The foresters and verderers, regarders and agisters had also to appear on the first day and produce their rolls, on pain of amercement.[19] If they had died, their heirs were bound to produce their rolls in their places.[20] The owners of woods were bound to present their woodwards before the justices, to take an oath to perform their duties faithfully,[21] and it is likely that this was done on the first day.

Trespassers attached to appear at the Forest Eyre also had to be produced by their sureties on the first day, when the justices' clerks entered their names on the Court record.[22] Failure to do so entailed amercement for the sureties, even though the accused persons appeared later on during the eyre.[23] 'Essoins', or valid excuses for non-appearance, were also made on the first day.[24] Death was the usual reason given: long intervals elapsed between Forest Eyres, and the Court files began with long lists of names headed, 'Those essoined of death on the first day.'[25] Men engaged elsewhere on the king's business obtained a royal warrant for their non-appearance, directed to the Forest justices,[26] and the Barons of the Exchequer issued similar writs of warranty to men engaged in business at the Exchequer.[27]

If an accused person failed to appear at the Forest Eyre, and was not 'essoined', the sheriff of the county in which he had lands and chattels was ordered to distrain him to appear later on during the sitting,[28] or at a subsequent Forest Eyre in a neighbouring county.[29] Failure to do this entailed a penalty for the sheriff himself. At the Nottingham Forest Eyre in 1334 five sheriffs were fined a total of £7 for not carrying out orders to seize the lands of offenders in their counties.[30] In other cases distraint was levied upon those legally responsible for the offenders, to compel their production. For example, on the Master of the Knights Templar for offending Knights,[31] since they had no property of their own by which they might be distrained. The Mayor of London was bound to produce citizens of London,[32] and in other boroughs the bailiffs were ordered to levy distraint upon defaulting burgesses.[33]

If, however, the trespasser had no lands or chattels by which he might be distrained, and no one was willing to act as his surety, the sheriff was ordered to cause him to be 'exacted', or called in the county court on five days in succession. If he did not then appear, he could be adjudged an outlaw; he was thereby deprived of civil rights and his property was forfeited to the Crown.[34] A very large proportion of those presented for venison trespasses at the Northampton Forest Eyre in 1209 preferred flight and outlawry to standing to right at the eyre.[35]

Just as all franchise holders were bound to appear at the General Eyre to make good their claims to liberties, so subjects who claimed privileges in the forest had to substantiate them before the Forest judges. A royal charter was usually produced: by the latter part of the thirteenth century it had become the practice for it to be transcribed upon the Forest Eyre rolls.[36] At the Huntingdon Forest Eyre of 1286 the Bishop of Ely claimed to have the right to hunt and take deer 'found between Somersham and the high road from Huntingdon to Ramsey'. A monk of Ely Priory appeared at the eyre on his behalf, and produced a number of royal charters in support of his claim. The judges examined the foresters, verderers, regarders and other jurors upon oath; they declared that the bishop had secured the exercise of that liberty by bribing a forester, and that he had no legal right to it. The bishop also claimed that a great part of the marsh of King's Delph was within his liberty. This claim was rejected too after the judges had examined the rolls of the Huntingdon Forest Eyre of 1245, which showed that the marsh was in Huntingdonshire and within the royal forest, and did not belong to the Isle of Ely. Other claimants at this Forest Eyre could produce no royal charter, and claimed to exercise their liberties by prescriptive right: some of them sought the verdict of a jury on their claims.[37] Doubtless the two Statutes of Gloucester, which allowed that uninterrupted exercise of a liberty from the beginning of Richard I's reign should confer a good legal title,[38] applied to the Forest law also.

Frivolous claims received severe treatment from the Forest justices. At the Huntingdon Forest Eyre of 1255,

> Master Robert le Baud of the Hospital of Huntingdon came before the Justices and alleged that the lord King ought not to have attachments either of vert or of venison, and that neither the foresters nor the verderers ought to make any attachment thereof in the town of Huntingdon. And this he wished to establish in every kind of way, so that by his chatter the Court was disturbed and the business of the lord King hindered: therefore he is committed to gaol. Afterwards he found (two) pledges . . . Subsequently he is taxed at half a mark.[39]

3
Pleas of the Venison

The most important category of pleas, which yielded the greatest revenue to the Crown, was that of the 'Pleas of the Venison'. Presentments were usually made by the foresters and verderers jointly,[40] but also in some cases by a jury of presentment of twelve or twenty-four,[41] and by neighbouring townships, numbering from four to ten.[42] Each township was probably represented by the reeve and four men. The employment of a jury together with the neighbouring townships in making indictments corresponded with the practice at the General Eyre.[43]

In most cases the foresters and verderers substantiated by their oral evidence before the Forest justices the details of Forest offences entered on their presentment rolls; in such cases the justices regarded the offences as having been sufficiently proved. Many of the entries on the Huntingdon Forest Eyre roll of 1255,[44] for example, are mere paraphrases of corresponding entries on the Huntingdon presentment roll for the period 1248–53.[45] But this did not always happen. At the Northampton Forest Eyre of 1255 William of Forest

Hill, a forester, was presented by the verderers as a suspected poacher. But when the justices called upon the verderers to substantiate their indictment, they declared that William was 'not guilty nor suspected of any trespass'. Thereupon the judges pronounced William acquitted, and amerced the verderers for contradicting their rolls.[46]

In some cases the judges closely examined the verderers. At Northampton in 1255 it was presented that:

> Philip of Staines, a man of lord Hugh fitzRalph, was found in Kingscliffe Park with a bow and four barbed arrows, and with a dog and two boys . . . And Roger of Fotheringay and John Caperun, the verderers, being questioned as to the boys, who they were and whence they came, say that they fled, and that it cannot be discovered who they were. Questioned as to the dogs, as to what breed they were, Roger of Fotheringay says that they were braches,[47] and John Caperun says that they were mastiffs. And because they are verderers, and ought to agree and tell the truth in all things, and now they differ in their stories before the Justices, therefore they are committed to gaol'.[48]

And of course they would have to pay the king a fine for deliverance.

Accused persons might pay for the privilege of having the question of their guilt or innocence decided by a petty jury. At the Huntingdon Forest Eyre in 1209 John Joede and nine others were declared to be in mercy for complicity in a venison trespass committed by Richard of Bradenham. John paid a fine of forty shillings for a sworn inquest regarding the indictment, which resulted in his acquittal.[49] In three cases at the Huntingdon Forest Eyre in 1255 the accused sought to clear themselves by calling upon the foresters, verderers and four neighbouring townships to give evidence upon oath; the jurors declared them not guilty, and they were acquitted.[50] This was similar to procedure at the General Eyre: when persons were presented by the hundred jury as suspected of crime, the four neighbouring townships were often asked for their testimony, which decided their guilt or innocence.[51]

Persons accused at the Forest Eyre did not always get off by obtaining a jury verdict. At the Nottingham Forest Eyre of 1287, Nicholas the riding hayward of Bestwood Hay in Sherwood Forest and his men were presented for various offences against vert and venison. In his defence Nicholas alleged that the accusations had been made at the original inquest by enemies he had made by seizing their beasts in the Hay. He asked for another inquest to be made by Forest officers and jurors, from which his enemies were excluded. But the second inquest confirmed the indictment made by the first. Nicholas was committed to prison, and later paid a fine of forty shillings before the Barons of the Exchequer.[52]

As a special privilege the accused was allowed to defend himself by compurgation. A charter of Henry III granted to the burgesses of Scarborough in 1256 that the borough and manor of Falsgrave should be disafforested: no Forest officer was to attach, summon or distrain anyone within the bounds of the borough or manor for a Forest offence. If any of the burgesses or men of the manor were indicted for such an offence they might 'defend themselves . . . by the oaths of 36 men before any of the King's Justices of the Forest, unless they be taken by the verderers or foresters of fee with the mainour' (i.e., red-handed).[53] At the Forest Eyre held at Scarborough in 1286 several burgesses secured their acquittal in this manner; others paid a fine of half a mark or a mark to be excused from taking the oath and finding the 'oath-helpers'.[54]

The Charter of the Forest conceded in 1217, on behalf of the young Henry III, that:

> No one shall henceforth lose life or limb for our venison, but . . . he shall pay a heavy ransom, if he has wherewith to be ransomed; and if he has not, let him lie in our prison for a year and a day, and, if after a year and a day he can find sureties, let him be released from prison; if not, let him abjure the realm of England.[55]

In practice, no record was usually made upon the Forest Eyre rolls of any presentment if it did not result in an amercement, or a fine made by the accused, for example, for delivery from gaol[56], or for having the case decided by a jury. There is no mention on the eyre rolls of imprisonment for a fixed term: the penalties varied according to the wealth of the offender rather than the gravity of the offence. At the Northamptonshire Forest Eyre of 1255, for example, the usual amercement was half a mark or a mark, but Simon of Overton the parson of Old was amerced in five pounds for taking a roe, and

Walter de Grey, a knight, made fine by £20 because he and his men had led greyhounds in the forest, but without taking anything.[57] As the intervals between successive Forest Eyres grew longer, the number of amercements at a single eyre increased – penalties of between 12d. and 40d. were imposed upon the humbler tres-passers,[58] and crippling amercements ranging from one to 500 marks upon laymen and clerks of substance.[59] Offenders usually had to find sureties for payment of the fine, and sometimes also for their future good conduct in the forest.[60] Poor men, however, from whom the Crown could hope to extract no money penalty, were frequently pardoned 'for the King's soul'.[61]

The sheriff was responsible for collecting a large proportion of the fines and amercements paid for breaches of the Forest law, and for delivering them into the Exchequer. At the end of a Forest Eyre the judges gave into the Exchequer the 'estreats' of the eyre – that is, a list of the fines and amercements made in each county. The sheriff received a copy of the estreats which concerned his county, and collected most of the smaller items at least. These he paid into the Exchequer at Easter or at Michaelmas, and the Exchequer clerks marked them off on their copy of the estreat roll.[62]

Payments of fines and amercements was compelled by distraint levied by the sheriff and his men. In Inglewood Forest the warden did not 'permit the sheriff or any bailiff to enter the forest with bows and arrows, except to distrain money for the king, and that only by view of the foresters'.[63]

By this time punishments of offenders against the venison were less severe than those inflicted upon criminals condemned in the common law courts. At the Northampton Forest Eyre of 1255 it was presented that two poachers had been arrested red-handed in 1252, and committed to gaol in the custody of the sheriff. They had subsequently been arraigned for common law theft at an assize of gaol delivery. The sheriff failed to point out the mistake in the indictment, with the result that the two poachers were hanged. Had they been tried at the Forest Eyre, they would have escaped with a fine.[64]

The Forest officers were called upon at the eyre to account for all deer taken with proper authority. At the Huntingdon Forest Eyre of

1286, for example, the deputy warden of the forest produced royal writs for 115 bucks and 48 does given as royal gifts since 1276, and the verderers reported that 134 deer had been taken for the king's use.[65]

4
Pleas of the Vert

Offences of cutting wood in the forest of more than a certain value were, as we have seen,[66] remitted to the Forest Eyre. If the offender failed to appear, his sureties were amerced. The usual penalty for the vert offence itself was twelve pence, but important offenders had to pay much more. The Abbot of Ramsey, for example, was in 1255 amerced in twenty marks for his tenants' trespasses in his woods and for the failure of his woodwards to restrain them.[67]

In Edward I's reign clerical privilege was sometimes claimed, but unsuccessfully. At Huntingdon Forest Eyre in 1286 it was presented that 'John le Gray, the carter', two carpenters and two others:

> all servants and members of the household of John of Raveningham, the parson of Ellington, entered the wood of the abbot of Sawtry at Grafham, at night, with horses and carts belonging to the said parson, and with bows and arrows. They cut down fourteen saplings, and carried eleven of them to the said parson's court. But while they were in the said wood the said abbot's woodward came and wished to attach them, and they shot arrows at him, and by the use of force returned to the aforesaid John's house. He received them with the aforesaid trespass and mainour [i.e., the saplings] . . . and caused them to be used for his own profit. And therefore the bishop of Lincoln is commanded to cause the aforesaid Master John to come [to the Forest Eyre] to have his aforesaid servants to right. Afterwards Master John came and made fine for himself and his aforesaid servants for the said trespass by five marks.[68]

The Forest warden or his deputy, or in some cases the recipients, had to produce at the Forest Eyre royal writs authorizing gifts of timber and wood from the forest, and the judges' clerk made a record of them upon the eyre rolls.[69] Failure to produce such a warrant meant that the person who had taken the wood would be charged with its price, and an amercement besides.[70]

5
The Regard: Other Business at the Forest Eyre

Another important part of the proceedings at the Forest Eyre was based upon the regarders' rolls, which reported 'New Assarts', 'New Purprestures' and 'New Wastes of Woods' made since the last eyre.[71] Lands and woods concerned were ordered to be seized for the king, but could usually be recovered on payment of a fine. In addition to an amercement for the offence, a further sum had to be paid for any crops grown on the assarted land: twelve pence for every acre sown with winter corn or rye, and six pence an acre for spring corn, oats or beans.[72] The tenants of the land were bound to account at every subsequent eyre for payments on the same scale, which were enrolled as 'Old Assarts', or 'Old Purprestures'. 'Wasted woods' had to be enclosed so that animals could not eat the young shoots and so prevent regrowth. The owners paid half a mark at every subsequent eyre until the woods had grown back into their former state; these payments were enrolled as 'Old Wastes of Woods'.[73]

The agisters accounted for revenues received since the last eyre – for the pannage dues for the feeding of pigs upon the mast in the autumn, and for the herbage dues for the pasturing of horses and cattle on Crown pastures, especially in the king's parks and demesne hays.[74]

By the fourteenth century the Forest judges had acquired jurisdiction in cases of non-repair of bridges in the forest. At the Pickering Forest Eyre of 1334 the Abbot of Rievaulx and the Prior of the Hospital of St John were amerced for failing in their duty to keep bridges in the forest in repair, 'so that men were unable to pass over and made a detour in the forest, to the injury of the deer, and treading down their pasture'.[75]

6
The Itinerant Justices for Pleas of the Forest

Many of those appointed to go on circuit to hear and determine forest pleas were common law judges. Such were William de l'Isle and John of Birkin, who went on circuit between 1221 and 1223,[76] and John de Lovetot, Richard de Crepping and Thomas de Normanville, who did so during the reign of Edward I.[77] These examples could be multiplied indefinitely, and they help to explain the parallel developments in the common and the Forest law.

Forest wardens sometimes sat at the Forest Eyre. Thomas of Milton, hereditary warden of Inglewood Forest, who was a judge of the Court of Common Pleas, heard pleas of the Yorkshire forests in 1232.[78] But it was obviously inexpedient that local Forest officers should hear Forest pleas in the counties in which their own bailiwicks lay. In June 1232 John son of Philip, hereditary warden of Kinver Forest in Staffordshire and Worcestershire, was one of four judges commissioned to take pleas of the Forests of Staffordshire and Shropshire – but there is a subsequent entry on the Close Roll that 'John son of Philip has been removed from that justiceship, because he is a forester of fee in those counties'.[79]

Some Forest judges were secular clergy, such as Walter Mauclerc, later Bishop of Carlisle, who went on circuit in 1221 with Brian de l'Isle.[80] Master William Powicke, who went on the Forest circuit in 1262, was a clerk and a common law judge.[81] Regular clergy were rarely included in the Forest commission, but in 1245 the Abbot of Abingdon was one of five judges who went on circuit in the counties of Northampton, Buckingham and Huntingdon.[82]

Such appointments were anathema to spiritually minded English clergy. Robert Grosseteste, the saintly Bishop of Lincoln, in a letter to Henry III refused to admit Robert Passelewe to the living of St Peter's Northampton because he was a Forest judge. To have handed over to him the cure of souls, declared Grosseteste, would have been a flagrant breach of canon law.[83] In several other letters the bishop inveighed vehemently against Henry III's appointment of abbots and other religious as judges of the General Eyre:[84] his arguments must have applied *a fortiori* to similar appointments to the Forest bench.

The appointment of such royal servants to church benefices of course eased for the Crown the financial burden of providing for them. In the fourteenth century, however, there are references to money payments to Forest judges and their clerks. In 1355 they sat at Salisbury to hear pleas of the forests of Clarendon, Groveley, Buckholt and Melchet.[85] The sheriff of Wiltshire was subsequently ordered to make payments out of the amercements and fines levied at the Forest Eyre: five shillings a day for thirty-five days to Henry Sturmy, one of the judges, and one hundred shillings for twenty days for Peter atte Wood, 'clerk and keeper of the rolls before . . . the justices in eyre for pleas of the forest'.[86]

7
Venue, Territorial Jurisdiction and Periodicity of the Forest Eyre

The itinerant Forest justices usually sat at the county town, and heard pleas of all the royal forests within the county. For example William le Breton and his colleagues began their eyre on 6 June 1255. They sat at Huntingdon to hear pleas of the forest, which was then coterminous with the county.[87] Where, however, the greater part of a forest lay within one county, the Forest judges usually heard pleas there relating to a small part of it which extended into another county. Pleas relating, for example, to the Buckinghamshire part of Salcey Forest were heard at Northampton,[88] those concerning the Worcestershire part of Kinver Forest were determined at the Staffordshire Forest Eyre at Lichfield,[89] and those for the Herefordshire part of the Forest of Dean at Gloucester.[90] But where extensive areas of a forest lay in two or more counties, then pleas relating to it were heard partly in one county, and partly in another. The Forest judges sat for example at Reading for the Berkshire part of Windsor Forest, and at Guildford for the Surrey part.[91]

From the twelfth to the fourteenth centuries, the intervals between successive Forest Eyres grew longer. Between 1165 and 1212 there were ten eyres.[92] During the troublous times at the end of King John's reign and the beginning of the next there were of course no Forest Eyres, but between 1221 and October 1236 there were four more.[93] In November 1236 the forest was divided between two Chief Justices.[94] From then until 1272 there were six eyres south of the Trent,[95] and four north of it.[96] There were similar developments in the common law. Between 1227 and 1263 'there was a strong tendency towards an average interval of seven years between successive visits of the general eyre', and this interval was recognized in 1261 by the king and his judges as the minimum.[97]

During the reign of Edward I General Eyres became fewer, and in the next reign almost ceased.[98] So with the Forest Eyres: during Edward I's reign of thirty-five years there were only two Forest Eyres south of the Trent, and one north of it.[99] A Forest Eyre was opened at Nottingham on 14 January 1287 by William de Vescy,[100] and none held there until Ralph de Neville sat on 25 April 1334[101] – an interval of forty-seven years. Likewise at the Hampshire Forest Eyre opened at Southampton on 9 July 1330, presentment was made of a venison trespass committed in the New Forest on 9 November 1283. Most of the accused were dead, but Richard Payn was fined twenty pence for an offence committed nearly forty-seven years previously.[102]

The decline of the Forest Eyre, like that of the General Eyre, was due partly to the 'lack of governance' in Edward II's reign, but partly also to the development of new forms of revenue-raising, and of new and less cumbrous machinery for the enforcement of Crown rights and the supervision of local officials.

NOTES

1. See e.g. E32/67/6; 68; 74/1 etc.
2. Cal. Pat R. 1247–58, 412; Turner, *Sel. Forest Pleas*, 1–1i.
3. Close R. 1227–31, 238; ibid., 1254–56, 193.
4. E32/249/11; Turner, *Sel. Forest Pleas*, 6.
5. art. 44 (*Sel. Charters*, ed. Stubbs, 298.)
6. art. 2 (ibid., 345.)
7. See e.g. Close R. 1227–31, 274–75.
8. E32/153; Rawle, 'Exmoor Forest', 63.
9. Petition of the Barons, art. 13 (*Sel. Charters*, ed. Stubbs, 375.)
10. Close R. 1254–56, 207; Cal. Chart. R. 1226–57, 218 etc.
11. E32/161/2; *New Forest Documents*, ed. Stagg, 95.
12. E32/127/17; E36/76 f. 70r.; 'Sherwood Forest Book', 141.
13. Turner, *Sel. Forest Pleas*, lviii–lxix.
14. Holdsworth, *Hist. of English Law*, I 268–71.
15. E32/5/38, 38d.
16. E32/140/2, 3; 185/9; Turner, *Sel. Forest Pleas*, 44; *Coll. Hist. Staffs.* V i 150–51.
17. E32/45/1d.
18. Close R. 1261–64, 378.
19. E32/41/5, 6; Turner, *Sel. Forest Pleas*, II, 25.
20. E32/41/4d; Turner, op. cit., 26.
21. ibid., lvii–lviii.
22. E32/30/1; 45/1; 145/1 etc.
23. E32/41/6; 68/4; Turner, op. cit., 14–15, 35.
24. E32/41/6d; 68/4; Turner, op. cit., 20, 35.
25. E32/45/1; 145/1. etc.
26. Close R. 1247–51, 286.
27. E159/5 Hen. III/8d.; E168/6 Hen. III/1.
28. E32/41/5; 68/3d; 153/8d; Turner, *Sel. Forest Pleas*, 22, 23, 32, 42.
29. E32/41/6d; 72/7d; 194/4; Turner, op. cit., 21, 40, 58.
30. E36/76/49–51; 'Sherwood Forest Book', 105.
31. E32/45/4d, 7.
32. ibid., m. I.
33. E32/72/7d; Turner, op. cit., 41.
34. Pollock & Maitland, *Hist. of English Law*, I 539, 554; II 449–50, 580–81.
35. E32/62; Turner, op. cit., 1–6.
36. E32/13/2d–7; E32/188/1d; *Coll. Hist. Staffs.* V i 155–56, 157; Turner, op. cit., lxvii.
37. E32/44/4d, 5.

38. Holdsworth, *Hist. of English Law*, I 88.
39. E32/41/5d; Turner, op. cit., 25.
40. E32/41/5, 5d, 6, 6d; 68/3–4d; Turner, op. cit., 11–37, 42.
41. E32/72/7d; 194/3d; Turner, op. cit., 40–41, 44, 54.
42. E32/185/9; 187/5, 7d.
43. Holdsworth, *Hist. of English Law*, I 268–70; Gross, *Coroners' Rolls*, xxxiii–xxxiv.
44. E32/41/5; Turner, op. cit., 21, 23.
45. E32/39(a); ibid., 74–79.
46. E32/68/3; ibid., 28.
47. 'a kind of hound which hunted by scent' (*O.E.D.*)
48. E32/68/1; Turner, op. cit., lxii n.I.
49. E32/37/1.
50. E32/41/6; Turner, op. cit., II, 14–16.
51. Gross, *Coroners' Rolls*, xxxii–xxxiii.
52. E32/127/6r; E36/76/ff. 67r.–68v; 'Sherwood Forest Book', 137–39.
53. Cal. Chart. R. 1300–26, 190–91.
54. DL 42/1/318a; N. Riding Records, N.S., III 178–79, 181–83.
55. art. 10 (Stubbs, *Sel. Charters*, 346–47.)
56. See e.g. E32/41/5, 6d; Turner, op. cit., 20, 24, 29.
57. E32/68; Turner, op. cit., 29–38.
58. Cal. Close R. 1288–96, 165; 1296–1302, 338.
59. ibid., 1272–81, 251, 367; 1281–92, 55, 237, 349.
60. E32/161/3d; *New Forest Documents*, ed. Stagg, 100, 167–76.
61. E32/44/2d; 45/4d., 5; Turner, op. cit., 29, 30.
62. Pipe R. 1176, 6–8; 1230, 61; 1242, 40; *Coll. Hist. Staffs.* II 138–39; Cal. Close R. 1327–30, 344.
63. Memoranda Roll 1231, 48–49; Close R. 1254–56, 275; Cal. Inq. Misc. I 156.
64. E32/68/4; Turner, op. cit., 33–34.
65. E32/44/5d.
66. See above, pp. 37–64.
67. E32/41/2; Turner, *Sel. Forest Pleas*, lix–lx; Rawle, 'Forest of Exmoor', 53.
68. E32/44/4.
69. E32/41/2d; 44/5d.
70. ibid., m. 4.
71. See above, pp. 42–45.
72. See e.g. E32/2/6, 10; 152; 184–186; Rawle, 'Forest of Exmoor', 55 ff.
73. E32/231/7–9; Turner, *Sel. Forest Pleas*, lxxviii–lxxix.
74. E32/41/4d; 44/7d; Turner, op. cit., 59–60.
75. DL42/1/258, 259a; N. Riding Records, N.S. III 2–3, 4–6.
76. *Rot. Litt. Claus.* 1204–24, 516.
77. E32/5, 30, 125, 161; Foss, Judges, sub nom.; P.R.O. Lists & Indexes IV 164, 195.

78. Cal. Inq. Misc. I No. 471; Close R. 1231–34, 137–38.
79. ibid., 145–46.
80. *Rot. Litt. Claus.* 1204–24, 475.
81. E32/145, 187, 227, Foss, Judges, sub nom.
82. Close R. 1242–47, 350–51, 352.
83. 'Letters' (Rolls Ser.) No. CXXIV.
84. ibid., Nos. XXVII, XXVIII, LXXII, LXXXII.
85. E32/267/14; 268.
86. Cal. Close R. 1354–60, 272.
87. E32/41.
88. E32/70; Turner, *Sel. Forest Pleas*, lii.
89. E32/185/1, 12; *Coll. Hist. Staffs*. V i 142.
90. E32/30.
91. E32/139; 251/2d; Cal. Fine R. 1327–37, 206; Turner, op. cit., l–lv.
92. Pipe R. 1166, 1170, 1173, 1175, 1179, 1185, 1190, 1198, 1209, 1212: E32/37, 62, 144, 249.
93. *Rot. Litt. Claus.* 1204–24, 475, 633; Close R. 1227–31, 238.; 1234–37, 344.
94. Cal. Pat. R. 1232–47, 167, 169.
95. Close R. 1237–42, 236: 1247–51, 254; Cal. Pat. R. 1232–47, 462; E32/41, 68, 140, 145, 187, 194.
96. Pipe R. 1240–42; Close R. 1247–51, 356; 1261–64, 127; Cal. Pat. R. 1266–72, 468.
97. R.F. Treharne, 'Baronial Plan of Reform', App. C2., 404–406.
98. Cam. 'Studies in the Hundred Rolls', App. III, p. 113.
99. E32/5, 8, 12.
100. E32/127.
101. E32/132.
102. E32/163/2; *New Forest Documents*, ed. Stagg, 167.

CHAPTER 6

Forest Pleas in the Central Courts

In medieval law the king was the fountain-head of justice: by the twelfth century the King's Court (*Curia Regis*) had established its jurisdiction over a long list of 'pleas of the Crown', among which 'pleas of the Forest' were included by the 'Laws of Henry I'.[1] Pleas nominally heard 'before the King' (*coram rege*) were usually decided by the small body of judges, professionally learned in the law, who accompanied him on his progresses through the realm. It was this body which in the thirteenth century developed into the Court of King's Bench.

From the twelfth century onward, these judges were sent out on circuit, to hear and determine 'all pleas of the Crown' at the General Eyre, or 'pleas of the Forest' at the Forest Eyre. But the *Curia Regis* retained its competence to hear Forest pleas. The king himself on occasion sat with his judges to hear such cases. During his great Forest Visitation in 1175 Henry II held his court in a number of counties and personally gave judgement upon Forest offenders.[2] Edward I, on his return to England in 1289, took an active personal interest in the conduct of an inquiry into the Forest administration:[3] on 24 March he was at Feckenham, and after a sworn inquiry by 'the whole county' of Worcester, he imprisoned foresters and others for trespasses against the venison. Accused persons had subsequently to find six pledges each for their appearance before the king at Woodstock on 5 April 1290, to hear his judgement. The chronicler, a monk of Worcester, recorded bitterly that the Bishop of Worcester was amerced in 500 marks, and the Prior of Worcester in 200, 'since', as he wrote, 'there was no equity in the judgment save the king's arbitrary will.'[4]

Barons and bishops, members of the royal household and other servants of the Crown such as the king's judges, when accused at the Forest Eyre, had the privilege of having their cases referred to the court *coram rege*.[5] Among those so referred by the Justice of the Forest in 1262 were the Archbishops of Canterbury and of Dublin, the Earls of Gloucester and of Leicester, and other magnates.[6] To have one's case transferred from the ordinary Forest courts was a privilege highly esteemed: at the Lancaster Forest Eyre in 1251 'the knights and free tenants of the county of Lancaster who held lands within the bounds of the forest' gave the king a fine of £100 'for having respite to *Coram Rege* of certain articles whereof they claim liberties by charters of the King's ancestors'.[7] A wealthy offender moreover might purchase acquittance directly from the king. In 1207, for example, the sheriff of Essex was informed that Geoffrey de Sackville and Ralph de Marcy had offered King John a fine of a thousand marks for pardon and restoration of their lands of which they had been disseised for a Forest offence. The sheriff was to allow them safe conduct into the county in order to find sureties for payment of the fine before 15 August; otherwise they were to be under the same indictment and in the same condition of banishment as they had formerly been, according to the custom of England.[8] From time to time Edward I made similar grants of acquittance to magnates in return for fines ranging from 100 to 500 marks.[9]

The rolls of the *Curia Regis* for the reign of John contains few cases of Forest pleas. In one such case Simon of Linton accused Roger of Easton of falsely and maliciously indicting Simon's men at the attachment court for a venison trespass. Roger's reply was that the plea was attached before the justices of the Forest, and therefore he did not wish to answer, unless the Court adjudged otherwise.[10] During the next two reigns, however, proceedings *coram rege* related to trespasses against vert and venison;[11] disputes concerning Forest dues, such as cheminage, demanded by the foresters;[12] actions regarding the right to take housebote and haybote and other common rights in the forest;[13] and suits for the possession of hereditary foresterships.[14] Among the 'Pleas before the lord King at

Worcester' in 1237 was an action between the Prior of Kenilworth and William de Beauchamp regarding the latter's claim to take housebote and haybote in the prior's wood of Salford in the royal forest of Feckenham, without permission of the prior, or supervision by the king's foresters. The sheriff was ordered 'to make diligent inquiry by the oath of the foresters and verderers of Feckenham Forest, and by the oath of twelve knights and others of the neighbourhood of Feckenham' into the facts and rights involved. The case was settled out of court by agreement between the parties,[15] but the proposed use of the sworn evidence of the foresters and verderers shows that there was no rigid separation of the Forest law from the common law of England.

Forest revenues were for the most part paid into the Exchequer like other Crown revenues, so that the Barons of the Exchequer acquired jurisdiction in certain Forest cases. On one occasion, for example, the judges at the Forest Eyre called upon the Bishop of Worcester to answer for the crops grown upon certain assarts he had made in the Forest, and enrolled them on the rolls of their eyre. But the Barons decided in January 1231 that the bishop had been given licence to make those assarts by a charter of Richard I, and therefore they pronounced him quit:[16] they appear in this case to have acted as a court of appeal from a decision of the judges at the Forest Eyre.

NOTES

1. art. 17 in *Die Gesetze der Angelsachsen*, F. Liebermann, ed. Halle (1903) I 559.
2. Benedict of Peterborough, 'Chronicle' (Rolls Ser.) I 92–94; *Hoveden,* (Rolls Ser.) II 79; Ralph de Diceto, *'Opera Historica'* (Rolls Ser.) I 402.
3. *Ann. Monast.* (Rolls Ser.) IV Osen. 319–22.
4. ibid., *Wigorn.* 500–501.
5. E32/44/3; 45/4d; 68/4; 144; Turner, *Sel. Forest Pleas*, 9, 34, 130.
6. E32/250B.
7. Pipe R. 35 Hen. III (1251) m. 16; Cal. Lancs. Assize Rolls, ed. Parker, 285–86.
8. Rot. Litt. Pat. 1201–16, 74.
9. Cal. Fine R. 1272–1307, 50; Cal. Close R. 1272–79, 378 etc.
10. *Curia Regis* R. 1210–12, 85–86.
11. *Abbreviatio Placitorum*, (Rec. Com.), 105, 238, 278, 294.
12. ibid., 291.
13. ibid., 197, 206, 302.
14. ibid., 232.
15. ibid., 105.
16. Memoranda R. 14 Hen. III, 50.

CHAPTER 7

The Forest Law in Relation to Other Legal Systems

1
The Common Law in the Forest

Vert and venison were protected within the bounds of the forest by a code of Forest law enforced by Forest courts, but ordinary civil and criminal pleas arising within most forests were dealt with, there as elsewhere, by the ordinary courts of the land, administering the common law of England. The whole county of Huntingdon, for example, was subject to the Forest law, yet the pattern of administration of the common law was similar to that in counties where there were no royal forests. The tenants of lands in the Huntingdonshire forest owed suit to the county court, to the hundred courts, and to the sheriff's tourn. During the thirteenth century justices of Assize and Gaol Delivery frequently sat at Huntingdon, and assizes of novel disseisin and other pleas relating to land in the county were frequently heard in the Court *de banco*,[1] when the procedure followed was the same as for lands outside the Forest. Manors within the forest in Staffordshire, Somerset and other counties appeared by juries at the Assizes, and the forest inhabitants there served as coroners and on coroners' inquests, and were responsible in their hundreds for murder. Crimes such as robbery, rape, theft and homicide committed within the forest were usually tried in the common law courts in the ordinary way.[2]

Inevitably there were uncertainties, disputes and even conflicts between the two systems, especially in criminal cases arising from offences committed in the covert of the forest. At the Gloucester General Eyre of 1221 pleas of the Crown relating to felonies committed within the Forest of Dean were presented, not by coroners, but by verderers, 'because the county records that it used to be done'. The reason for this seems to have been that the thickly wooded parts of the forest were not organized into townships: the verderers said that, 'There is no frankpledge in the forest, and townships ought not to answer for fugitives.' But the judges ruled that that part of the covert which was organized into townships must answer for fugitives, and that the verderers were therefore in default.[3]

In most counties it was exceptional for judges at a Forest Eyre to hear cases of homicide committed within the forest. At the Huntingdon Forest Eyre in 1255, however, it was presented that a certain stranger had been found slain in Sapley Hay, one of the king's demesne woods. The ordinary coroner's inquest – held by the township in which the body had been found, together with the three nearest to it – had not been held, perhaps because Sapley, as a demesne wood, was not included within the boundaries of a manor or township. Richard Leveyse, a walking forester, who had found the body, did not appear, and had not been attached: the verderers declared that it was not the custom for them to do this, or to attach the four neighbours, in cases occurring 'within the metes of the forest, to wit, within the king's demesne wood . . . nor did they present Englishry because of the assize of the forest.' The Forest judges – two of whom, William le Breton and Geoffrey of Lewknor, were common law judges – ruled that 'because the law of the land concerning the death of a man ought not to be abated on account of the assize of the forest, the procedure must be according to the form of the pleas of the crown.' The hundred of Hurstingstone had accordingly to pay a murder fine because they had not produced proof that the dead man was an Englishman.[4] An inquest was ordered, at which the verderers, the four neighbouring townships and the hundred swore that Richard Lenveyse was guilty. He was ordered to be exacted and outlawed, and his chattels were seized by the sheriff.[5]

An attempt to present at a common law court a plea which rightly belonged to a Forest court would involve the presenting jury in amercement. Thus at the General Eyre at Ilchester in 1243 the jury of Carhampton hundred presented that Richard de Wrotham, the warden of the Somerset forests, took herbage dues from them for exercising their rights of common of pasture in the forest: 'and because that plea concerns the Justice of the Forest, the jurors are in mercy for their foolish presentment'.[6]

The New Forest, however, was exceptional in that the two codes were in the thirteenth century administered in the same courts and at the same sessions. It has been suggested that this was because the New Forest was 'ancient royal demesne', and in it prevailed 'a royal, which is also a seignorial justice'.[7] Certainly the Forest records refer to 'the liberty of the New Forest',[8] and references to enfeoffment 'in the full court of the New Forest' indicate that it acted as a seignorial court.[9] This court, for which records are extant for 1299 and 1300,[10] also exercised the jurisdiction of a Forest court of attachment. It heard presentments of 'offences of dry wood' – purprestures; digging turves – 'against the king's prohibition of the forest'; agisting animals in the fence month; receiving 'a hive of bees from the demesne woods of the king'; and even one for 'hunting in the forest without permission'. Fines were imposed at this court, usually six or twelve pence according to the offender's means, though a widow might be let off with a penalty of 3d.[11] But the 'Court of the New Forest' also heard common law pleas, such as would elsewhere have been heard in the county court – actions of debt, detinue, covenant, and trespass; pleas relating to the possession of land; and licences of agreement.[12]

The administration of the civil and criminal law in the New Forest also showed distinctive features. At the Hampshire Forest Eyres in 1257 and 1280 the justices heard, not only presentments of offences against vert and venison, but also separately enrolled 'pleas of Assizes of the New Forest' – i.e., common law actions such as novel disseisin, mort d'ancester and debt.[13] At the same sessions the judges heard separately enrolled 'Crown Pleas of the New Forest' — indictments of homicide, rape, burglary, assaulting and beating, and larceny.[14] Such crimes were investigated in the first instance by the foresters and verderers, and there was a special jury of presentment for them.[15] It was presented at the 1257 Eyre, for example, that a certain Thomas Sweetman had been arrested in the previous year in Hardley with sheep he had admitted to have been stolen. He was brought before the foresters and verderers and committed to gaol at Winchester. Later he was hanged by judgement of Laurence Brook, a judge of gaol delivery. The sheriff of Hampshire, however, declared at the Forest Eyre that this had been an error. He claimed that 'The court of the New Forest had liberty to such an extent that the justices in eyre for all pleas or any other justices, except the justices in eyre for forest pleas, were not to administer pleas touching the court of the New forest.'[16]

At the 1280 Forest Eyre a claim was made on behalf of 'the entire liberty of the New Forest' that 'for some felonies Englishry is not customarily presented in the New Forest'; but the judges did not accept it, and the murder fine was imposed, not on the hundred as elsewhere, but upon 'the community of the New Forest.'[17] At the same eyre a mixed indictment was brought forward. Evildoers were presented for an offence against the venison, and also for having stolen a large cheese from Hartford grange. They were acquitted of the charge of stealing the cheese by the verdict of a jury, but were convicted of the Forest offence.[18] There was clearly no rigid separation of the Forest law and the common law in the New Forest.

The thirteenth-century cases cited show that some wooded districts which formed the nuclei of royal forests were not organised into townships, and so claimed exemption from certain obligations under the common law. The judges strove to limit such exemptions, but failed to extinguish them entirely. As late as the mid-nineteenth century there were still extensive areas of the ancient royal forest which were not contained within the boundaries of any parish. Until an Act of 1857[19] these extra-parochial districts enjoyed virtual exemption from taxation, from the poor and highway rates, and from the militia laws.[20]

These claims for exemption from time to time caused conflict between the representatives of the two legal systems. In 1334 the 'community of the realm' complained by petition to Edward III at the Parliament of York that 'if men are killed in the King's forests or hays, the Wardens and the foresters do not permit the coroners of those places to exercise their office . . . wherefore felonies were often committed there and remain unpunished.' The king ordered the Chief Justices of the Forest to see to it that Forest officers should in future allow coroners to perform their duties 'when accidents happen or felonies are committed in the said forests and hays'.[21]

Judges sitting in the common law courts were on occasion uncertain as to the exact delimitation of the two jurisdictions. In 1293 a plaintiff brought an action of novel disseisin at the Staffordshire General Eyre against the Earl of Warwick, in respect of 100 acres of woodland. The defence was that the wood was within the bounds of the king's forest. Judgement was not pronounced: there was uncertainty whether the judges 'ought to answer here at the common law of a thing that touches vert: inasmuch as pleas of vert belong to the Justice of the Forest in eyre.' The parties later came to terms.[22]

The officers of the forest were exempt from some of the duties imposed by the common law upon the other forest inhabitants. The verderers and foresters of fee were excused from being put on assizes, juries or recognitions, and as a general rule from having to serve as coroner.[23] They were 'quit of suit of the county and hundred courts, because they ought to be assiduously intendant to their baili-wicks',[24] and some of the foresters of fee at least were exempt from the duty of attendance at the sheriff's tourn.[25]

2

The Clergy and the Forest Law

The clerical *privilegium fori* – that is, the claim of the clergy to be tried only in the ecclesiastical courts – was during the twelfth and thirteenth centuries one of the most hotly contested of clerical privileges. Although Henry II attempted by the Constitutions of Clarendon in 1164 to make criminous clerks punishable in his courts,[26] he was forced, after the murder of Thomas à Becket in 1170, to abandon the attempt. But he was determined that the clergy should remain subject to the jurisdiction of the Forest courts. In 1175 he made an agreement with the Papal Legate, Hugo Pierleoni, that clerical privilege should not extend to Forest offences, an agreement bitterly resented by the English clergy.[27] In the next year he wrote to Pope Alexander III that he had conceded:

> That a clerk shall not in future be brought in person before a secular judge for any crime, or for any trespass except a trespass of my forest, and except a lay fee for which lay service is owed to me or another secular lord.[28]

Acting on this agreement, the king did in fact implead English clergy for Forest offences during his great Forest Visitation in 1175,[29] and in 1184 proclamation was made by the Assize of Woodstock that:

> The King forbids any clerk to commit trespass against him in respect of his venison and his forests; he well enjoins his foresters that if they find them trespassing, they shall not hesitate to lay hands upon them, and to detain them, and he himself will well warrant them.[30]

This decree was repeated by Richard I's Forest Assize in 1198.[31]

During the following century the foresters carried out these edicts by arresting clerks and monks for Forest offences, and handing them over to the sheriff for imprisonment.[32] In some such cases the clerical prisoner was delivered on bail to a number of sureties as a layman would have been,[33] or a clerk could be delivered on bail to his bishop,[34] and a monk to his abbot.[35]

Clergy who were indicted for Forest offences were, like laymen, bound to appear or to be essoined on the first day of the Forest Eyre, otherwise they were amerced for default.[36] If a clerk had a lay fee the sheriff would be ordered to distrain him to appear by seizing it.[37] Otherwise the judges ordered his bishop to produce him,[38] or, if the see were vacant, the order was sent to the keeper of the spiritualities.[39] An abbot or prior was responsible for the appearance of any of his monks who had been indicted.[40] If the bishop made no answer to the judges' order, the accused clerk was ordered to be exacted in the county court and outlawed just as if he were a layman.[41] If, however, the accused clerk did appear and were convicted, the judges sentenced him to prison: but there was usually present at the Forest Eyre a representative of the bishop, whose duty it was to claim the prisoner as a clerk, and to whom he was handed over by the judges as a convicted offender against the Forest law. He then had to make a fine before the Forest judges for acquittance of his trespass. Payment was enforced by the sheriff, who levied distraint upon the clerk's lay fee: if he had none, the bishop was responsible for raising the money from the offender's benefice, or from his goods and chattels.[42]

Thus, despite the fact that a distinction was made at the Forest Eyre between lay and clerical offenders, the Forest judges in fact both tried and punished the latter. This was naturally resented with great bitterness: the clergy often offered resistance to the authority of the Forest officers, using spiritual weapons. For example, in 1251 the forester of Huntingdon Forest discovered a band of poachers in the Forest at night time. One of them was identified as Gervais of Dean, a clerk and a member of the household of John of Crakehall, Archdeacon of Bedford. Gervais was arrested by the foresters and committed to gaol at Huntingdon. Then a number of local clergy, including Walter, vicar of St Mary's Huntingdon, with the bailiff of the Bishop of Lincoln, came to the gaol and compelled the foresters to release him by threats of excommunication 'with book and candle'. Gervais had proved his clerical status by displaying his tonsure, which the foresters suspected to have been 'shaved that day in prison'. At the Forest Eyre in 1255 the charges against Gervais and Walter were proved by the testimony of the foresters and verderers, but they refused to answer in a secular court, and were handed over to the Archdeacon of Huntingdon, who was the bishop's representative. But in addition the judges imposed an amercement of 100s. upon Walter, half a mark upon Gervais, and John of Crakehall was adjudged to pay 10 marks for having harboured Gervais.[43]

So in May 1257 the English clergy presented the king with a long list of grievances, including the procedure at the Forest Eyre already described. They complained that, although clerks:

> ought not to be condemned or judged in any way at any inquisition made by laymen . . . they are compelled to pay amercements by their lay possessions, if they have any. If they have none, the bishops are distrained by their baronies to compel the said clerks to pay the amercements from their benefices.[44]

These complaints were repeated at the Convocation of Merton in the following year: clerks who refused to appear before a secular tribunal were banished from the realm. Clerks accused of Forest offences ought to be tried according to canon law in the ecclesiastical courts. If they were found guilty, then they ought to be compelled to make reparation to the king; if innocent, the secular authority should not be allowed to seize their goods, on pain of excommunication.[45]

A case referred to Edward III in 1333 describes the penalties meted out by the courts Christian in such cases. The Bishop of Bath and Wells claimed the right to cut timber for housebote and haybote in the woods of his manors of Axbridge and Cheddar, but Matthew Pecche, hereditary warden of the Somerset forests, and his men, attached the bishop's servants, because they said they could only do so under their supervision. The foresters were then summoned to answer in the bishop's court: one of them, John Champion, was condemned:

> to stand in Wells cathedral while mass is being celebrated, in a prominent place where the congregation can clearly see him; he is to be in the guise of a penitent, with head hung low, bare feet, wearing only a tunic and holding a burning candle in his hand, which he is to offer at the high altar when mass is over.

He was further to swear on the holy relics never to repeat his offence. Matthew Pecche, the warden, was also summoned to answer in the ecclesiastical court, but on 13 March his clerk appeared there on his behalf, and produced a writ from the king. The writ pointed out that the manor of Cheddar, though now held by the bishop in fee farm, was part of 'the ancient demesne of the Crown of England', and therefore still subject to the Forest law.[46] The king declared that the sentences of excommunication pronounced by the bishop against the king's foresters were 'in contempt of Us and the right of Our crown': he ordered them to be revoked.[47]

But these threats of spiritual penalties were not successful in securing any substantial change in the treatment of clerical offenders.[48] During the fourteenth century priests,[49] abbots[50] and even prioresses[51] continued to be imprisoned for offences against vert and venison, and were compelled to obtain royal writs for their deliverance on bail to sureties, just as though they were laymen.

3

The Jews and the Forest Law

In thirteenth-century England, the Jew was regarded as the property of the Crown: as Bracton put it, 'The Jew can have nothing that is his own, for whatever he acquires, he acquires not for himself, but for the King'.[52] He was protected because the wealth he amassed by usury was liable to arbitrary taxation, and formed a valuable source of royal revenue. Owing to his extreme unpopularity, he was not subject to the jurisdiction of the ordinary courts, but to that of the Exchequer of the Jews.

Living as they did in a few selected royal towns, such as York, Lincoln, Norwich, Northampton and Oxford, subject to constant surveillance and hatred,[53] their opportunities to commit breaches of the Forest law must have been comparatively few. Some cases were heard at the Forest Eyre in the ordinary way. At Huntingdon in 1209, for example, Jacob of Chinnock, a Jew, was amerced in 10 marks 'for a hare which he killed in the warren of Cambridge',[54] and at the Essex Forest eyre in 1277 four Jews, townsmen of Colchester, were amerced for joining in the chase after a deer which had run out of the forest into the town.[55]

But the Justices of the Exchequer of the Jews did exercise jurisdiction in at least one case of a Forest offence. In 1268 one Sadekin of Nottingham, a Jew of Northampton, had been arrested and detained in Northampton gaol for a Forest trespass. He obtained a royal writ directing the sheriff of Northampton to hand him over on bail to six Jews, who undertook to produce him a fortnight before Easter before the Justices 'assigned to the custody of the Jews', to stand to right for his trespass. Bartholmew le Jeune, the under-sheriff of Buckinghamshire, and Hagin son of Master Moses, a Jew of London, were subsequently commissioned to inquire by a mixed jury of Christians and Jews as to whether Sadekin were guilty or not. If he were proved innocent, he was to be released from gaol.[56] The employment of a mixed jury of equal numbers of Christians and Jews, as in this case, was usual in causes at the common law in which Jews were concerned.[57]

NOTES

1. The body of king's judges which sat at Westminster, and had by the reign of Edward I become the Court of Common Pleas (Maitland, Constitutional History, 69, 133.)
2. E.C. Wright, *Common Law in the English Royal Forest*. (Philadelphia 1928), 170–73, 177–185: Appendix, 11–13, 34–43.
3. ibid., 189–90; 'Pleas of the Crown for the County of Gloucester, 1221' (London 1894), 47.
4. See Maitland, *Constitutional History*, 46.
5. E32/41/6d; Turner, *Sel. Forest Pleas*, 19.
6. Chadwick Healey, 'Somerset Pleas' (Som. Rec. Soc. XI 302.)
7. *New Forest Documents*, ed. Stagg, p. 4, citing Pollock and Maitland, *History of English Law* (1968) I 384.
8. E32/156/2, 5; 161/21; Stagg, op. cit., 57, 64, 121.
9. E32/156/1; Stagg, 52.
10. E146/1/35; Stagg, 148–64.
11. Stagg, 148–156, 160, 162.
12. ibid., 148–54, 156–59, 160, 164.
13. E32/156/1–2; 161/21–23; Stagg, *New Forest Documents*, 52–57, 126–28, 131, 134.
14. ibid., 58–64, 121–26.
15. E32/156/5; Stagg, op. cit., 63–64.
16. ibid., 64–65.
17. E32/161/21; Stagg, op. cit., 123.
18. E32/161/3; Stagg, op. cit., 98–100.
19. 20 Vict., c. 19.
20. *New Historical Geography of England*, ed. Darby. (C.U.P., 1973), 533.
21. Cal. Close R. 1333–37, 307–308.
22. Wright, *Common Law in the Forest*, 190–91.
23. Close R. 1234–37, 142, 312, 316; 1253–54, 103; Cal. Close R. 1307–13, 108 etc.
24. *Rot. Litt. Claus.* 1204–24, 560.
25. Close R. 1251–54, 98.
26. art. 3 (Stubbs, *Sel. Charters*, 164–65; Maitland, 'Henry II and Criminous Clerks', in *Roman Canon Law in the Church of England*.
27. Abbot Benedict's Chronicle of the reigns of Henry II and Richard I (Rolls Ser.) I 105.
28. Ralph de Diceto, *Historical Works* (Rolls Ser.) I 402–3, 410.
29. ibid.; Benedict of Peterborough, 'Chronicle' (Rolls Ser.) I 92–94; *Hoveden*. (Rolls Ser.) II 79.
30. art. 9 (Stubbs, *Sel. Charters*, 187–88.)

31. art. 10 (*Hoveden*. (Rolls Ser.) IV 64.
32. Close R. 1227–31, 520; Cal. Pat. R. 1281–92, 4; 1301–7, 110; E32/41/5, 6 etc.
33. Close R. 1247–51, 71; Cal. Close R. 1279–88, 218, 342 etc.
34. Turner, *Sel. Forest Pleas*, xcii.
35. Cal. Close R. 1288–96, 207.
36. E32/41/1; 45/1, 1d.
37. E32/41/5; Turner, op. cit., 21.
38. E32/41/6d; 68/2, 4; Turner, op. cit., lxxxviii, 20, 31–32, 35. etc.
39. E32/45/6d.
40. E32/187/5d; *Coll. Hist. Staffs.* V i 146, 160.
41. E32/198/6; Turner, op. cit., lxxxviii–lxxxix.
42. Close R. 1242–47, 512–13; 1247–51, 23.
43. E32/41/6; Turner, op. cit., 12–13.
44. Matthew Paris, *Chron. Maj.* (Rolls Ser.) Add. VI 353ff.
45. *Ann. Monast.* (Rolls Ser.) I Burt. 416–17.
46. pursuant to arts. 1 and 3 of the Charter of the Forest (Stubbs, *Charters*, 345.)
47. *Register of the Bishop of Bath & Wells*, ed. Holmes (Som. Rec. Soc., IX 1895) pp. 117–118, 123–126, 129–130, 210–212.
48. See e.g. E32/45/1, 1d., 4–5, 5d. 6d. 7d. etc.
49. Cal. Close R. 1341–3, 13; 1343–46, 14 etc.
50. ibid., 1318–23, 663; 1341–43, 424.
51. ibid., 1402–1405, 403.
52. quoted Pollock and Maitland, *History of English Law*, I 451.
53. ibid., 452–54, 456; Holdsworth, *History of English Law*, I 45.
54. E32/37/1d.
55. E32/12/3d.; Young, *Royal Forests*, 104.
56. Cal. Pat. R. 1266–72, 278.
57. Pollock and Maitland, op. cit., 456.

CHAPTER 8

The Chief Justices of the Forest

In the twelfth and early thirteenth centuries the Forest administration was headed by a single official – the 'Chief Justice of all the royal forests of England',[1] or, as he was sometimes called, the 'Chief Forester of England'.[2] But the task proved too great for one man, and in 1236 the forests were divided under two Justices. The river Trent was chosen as the dividing line: the two officers were styled 'Justice of the Forest this side Trent' and 'Justice of the Forest beyond Trent',[3] according to where the king was at that particular time. These two Forest Justiceships continued in being until they were abolished by an Act of 1817.[4]

Such was the importance of the Forest Eyre that the Justice of the Forest almost always headed the commission of judges, and usually sat in person. But as the intervals between successive Forest Eyres lengthened, special commissions of *oyer et terminer* were issued to the Justices of the Forest and others.[5] Such proceedings received statutory sanction by the Ordinance of the Forest in 1306: Edward I decreed that:

> Our Justice of the Forest, or his Lieutenant, in the presence of our Treasurer, and by his consent, shall have authority to take Fines and Amercements of those which be indicted for trespasses committed in our forests, and not tarry for the eyre of the Justice.[6]

The Justices of the Forest were also frequently appointed by Edward I to hear and determine pleas of trespasses in private parks and chases.[7]

The Forest Justices were responsible for the enforcement of the Forest law throughout their Justiceships.[8] For this purpose they appointed to serve under them a staff of foresters, carrying bows and arrows, for whom they were personally responsible, and who maintained themselves by levying contributions from the forest inhabitants.[9] The Justices had power to seize for the king the bailiwicks of Forest wardens and foresters of fee who were guilty of misconduct in office,[10] and on occasion removed unpaid Forest officers such as the verderers.[11] Their general responsibility for arresting vagabonds and suspected poachers in the forest[12] sometimes involved organizing and leading an armed expedition, for the Forests were the resort of lawless and desperate characters. In 1238 John Biset, Justice of the southern forests, reported to Henry III that there were 'manifest evil-doers in the forests of Chippenham, Melksham and Braydon', who had hamstrung one of the royal foresters, badly wounded another, killed the Abbot of Stanley's horses, and committed many other crimes. The king therefore sent Nicholas de Bolevill with ten armed men to search for the malefactors, and to inquire who harboured them. Biset was ordered to go to those parts as soon as possible, and summon before him

the foresters and verderers, and the sheriffs of Wiltshire, Gloucestershire and Northamptonshire, with the knights and free men sworn to arms, dwelling in the vicinity of the forests, . . . with their arms.

Under Biset's orders they were to search for the evildoers and those who harboured them, and do whatever was necessary to maintain the king's peace in those parts.[13]

It was the responsibility of the Justices of the Forest to see that the Forest rights of the Crown were not usurped, and for this purpose he made frequent use of sworn inquiries by the foresters and verderers and juries of knights and free men of the neighbourhood. In this way he determined the extent of royal demesne lands and woods within the forest, and revoked encroachment made upon them.[14] He supervised the customary rights of forest inhabitants, and sometimes bore hardly upon them. A petition to the King and Council, dated between 1297 and 1308, stated that 'the men of

Easingwold and Huby are of the king's ancient demesne . . . in the forest of Galtres'. They and their ancestors had 'from time immemorial' been accustomed to have housebote and haybote, that is:

> thirty oaks a year for housebote, without reckoning the small underwood for hedgebote; and now by the command of Robert de Clifford (the Justice of the Forest north of Trent) they are reduced to sometimes ten or fifteen oaks a year.

The Justice of the Forest was ordered to cease these oppressive measures.[15]

When a subject sought from the king some licence or privilege within the forest, the Justice was usually ordered to make a preliminary inquiry *ad quod damnum* – that is, to inquire by means of a local jury as to the extent of the loss which the Crown would suffer if the grant were made. Royal licences to quarry stones, or to cut down and sell timber in the woods of subjects, or to bring such woods into cultivation, or to pasture cattle therein, were frequently preceded by such an inquiry held by the Justice of the Forest or his deputy.[16] To him also was entrusted the general supervision of the economic interests of the Crown in the Forest. He was from time to time ordered to raise money by leasing out assarts and waste lands, and by organizing and supervising sales of timber and underwood.[17] He was responsible for the exploitation of the mineral rights of the Crown – for example, for finding, mining and smelting iron in the forest of Chippenham and in the Forest of Dean[18] and lead in the Forest of the Peak.[19]

The Forest revenues were an important part of the king's income. In the twelfth and early thirteenth centuries they were channelled through the Justice of the Forest. In the reign of Henry II he accounted at the Exchequer for 'the pannage of all the forests of England'.[20] During the reign of John, Hugh de Neville held that office. He and his agents collected very large sums of money to supply the urgent needs of the Crown – mainly Forest amercements, fines paid for privileges in the forest, the proceeds of sales of wood and of the leasing of assarts.[21] He had his own exchequer at Marlborough for this purpose, and accounted at the Westminster

Exchequer for transactions there.[22] Between November 1201 and November 1203 de Neville and his agents paid over 8,000 marks into the king's privy purse at Caen, Rouen and elsewhere[23] to meet the expenses of John's disastrous campaign in Normandy. In 1206 he helped to victual the fleet in preparation for John's campaign in Gascony.[24] His accounts at the Exchequer in 1208 for the past six-and-a-half years showed that he had paid into the royal coffers out of the Forest revenues sums totalling £9,399. 9s. 10d., with outstanding arrears of £5,569. 17s. $\frac{1}{2}$d.[25] De Neville had clearly demonstrated his financial ability to his royal master, who made him Treasurer before January 1209.[26] But by 1212 he had lost the king's confidence and favour, and had to offer an enormous fine of 6,000 marks for acquittances for himself and his staff for all arrears since his first appointment as Chief Forest Justice in 1198.[27]

By the time of Edward I the major part of the Forest revenues was being raised and accounted for by the sheriffs. Although by the terms of their appointment the Justices of the Forest were required to render an annual account at the Exchequer,[28] they did not in fact do so. Between 1270 and 1300, for example, the accounts of the Justices of the Forest north of Trent were presented only four times, and then for comparatively small sums.[29] From the middle of the thirteenth century they were allowed to deduct for themselves a fixed salary out of the Forest revenues they collected – 100 marks a year for the Justice of the Forest north of Trent, and £100 for his colleague south of it.[30]

The Justices of the Forest were for the most part important men who can have devoted a limited amount of time to their Forest duties. Henry III appointed Household officers like his Poitevin favourite Peter des Rivaux: when he became Chief Justice of the Forest for life in 1232,[31] des Rivaux was already Keeper of the Wardrobe, the Chamber and the Treasury of the royal household, and became Treasurer of the Exchequer in the following year.[32] Robert Walerand, appointed Justice of the southern forests in 1256,[33] was Steward of the Household, and was sent to France on diplomatic missions several times during the three years in which he was head of the Forest administration.[34] Edward I nominated magnates like Hugh Despenser the elder, who was absent from

England on the king's service during a great part of the ten years 1297–1307 when he was Justice of the Forest south of Trent.[35] Robert de Clifford, Despenser's colleague for the northern forests, was one of Edward I's greatest soldiers, and was mainly occupied in the Scottish campaigns.[36]

Many of the duties of the Justices of the Forest were therefore performed by deputies. References to them in contemporary documents increased during the second half of the thirteenth century. In 1265, for example, Roger Leyburn, Justice of the Forest north of Trent, received royal approval of his appointment of Roger of Lancaster as his deputy, since he was unable to attend to his duties in person.[37] The absence of Hugh Despenser from England during his Forest Justiceship has already been mentioned. Of the eleven general Forest inquests held during the period 1297–1305 in the forests of Rockingham, King's Cliffe, Whittlewood and Salcey, Despenser presided at only one; the remainder were held before Robert of Harrowden, his deputy.[38]

NOTES

1. *Hoveden*. (Rolls Ser.) II 289–90; IV 63; Pat. R. 1216–25, 123–24, 437.
2. ibid., 1216–25, 285, 423.
3. Cal. Pat. R. 1232–47, 167, 169, 221.
4. 57 Geo. III c. 61.
5. Cal. Pat. R. 1258–66, 228; 1282–91, 42.
6. Statutes of the Realm I 149.
7. Cal. Pat. R. 1281–92, 201, 208, 403 etc.
8. *Rot. Litt. Pat.* 1201–16, 3.
9. Close R. 1234–37, 521–22.
10. ibid., 1237–42, 409, 414; 1242–47, 257.
11. Cal. Close R. 1288–96, 209.
12. Cal. Pat. R. 1292–1301, 447.
13. Close R. 1237–42, 144–45.
14. Pat. R. 1225–32, 325; Cal. Pat. R. 1247–58, 161.
15. SC8/56/2772 (Ancient Petitions No. 2772); N. Riding Records III 234–35.
16. Cal. Pat. R. 1266–72, 14, 76; 1281–92, 427, 468.
17. *Rot. Litt. Pat.* 1201–16, 31; Pat. R. 1216–25, 362 etc.
18. Close R. 1227–31, 260–61, 268–69.
19. ibid., 1251–53, 246.
20. Pipe R. 1170, 64; 1178, 55; 1185, 27–28.
21. ibid., 1200, 175; 1201, 37–38, 46, 253–54 etc.
22. ibid., 1202, 57; *Rot. Litt. Pat.* 1201–16, 70.
23. *Rot. de Lib. regn. Iohann.*, 23; *Rot. Litt. Pat.* 1201–16, 13, 22, 27a., 29, 35.
24. *Rot. Litt. Claus.* 1204–24, 71a.
25. Memoranda Roll 1208, 64.
26. *Rot. Litt. Pat.* 1201–16, 88; Matthew Paris, *Chron. Maj*, (Rolls Ser.) II 532–33.
27. Pipe R. 1212, 157–58.
28. Cal. Pat. R. 1272–81, 443: 1281–92, 388.
29. Pipe R. 6 Edw. I m. 28; 16 Edw. I m. 29; 28 Edw. I m. 29; Chancellor's Roll 8 Edw. I m. 29.
30. Cal. Pat. R. 1247–58, 165; 1258–66, 215.
31. Pat. R. 1225–32, 489.
32. Tout, *Chapters*, I 216–18, 225.
33. Cal. Pat. R. 1247–58, 497.
34. Tout, *Chapters*, IV 40.
35. Cal. Pat. R. 1292–1301, 306; G.E.C. IV 262–63.
36. Cal. Pat. R. 1292–1301, 312, 315, 387, 409.
37. Cal. Pat. R. 1258–66, 471.
38. E32/78, 79, 82, 83.

CHAPTER 9

The Forest Wardens

At the head of the administration of each royal forest, or group of forests, was the officer usually styled 'Warden', or, less frequently, 'Steward' or 'Bailiff' of his bailiwick.[1] He might have the custody of a single royal forest, or of a group of forests: the 'Warden of the King's forests between Oxford and Stamford bridges'[2] kept the forests of Shotover, Bernwood, Whittlewood, Salcey, Rockingham and Huntingdon, in the counties of Oxford, Northampton, Buckingham and Huntingdon.

1
Wardens Appointed by Letters Patent Under the Great Seal

The wardens of a number of royal forests – including Windsor, Clarendon, Feckenham, Galtres, the Forest of Dean and the Forest of the Peak in Derbyshire – were appointed by royal letters patent, usually to hold office during the king's pleasure, but sometimes for a term of years,[3] and exceptionally, as a special mark of royal favour, for life.[4]

Their offices were lucrative, and the king often used them to make provision for those who had a claim upon his bounty. Members of the royal family were provided for in this way. In May 1269 Queen Eleanor, Edward and Edmund the king's sons, and Guy de Lusignan, the king's half-brother, persuaded Henry III to appoint his nephew Henry of Almain to be constable of Rockingham castle and warden of the forests between Oxford and Stamford bridges, as a return for expenses incurred by him in the king's service, and for debts owed by the king to him. The appointment

94

was to be for the life of his father, Richard Earl of Cornwall, the king's brother, with reversion to the Crown. Henry of Almain was to take the profits of the forests and castle for himself, subject only to the duty of maintaining the castle.[5] Some months after the murder of Henry of Almain at Viterbo on 13 March 1271, his father was appointed to the same offices for a term of three years.[6] Shortly before his death in the next year, Henry III granted to his queen, Eleanor, the custody 'of the castle and forest of Windsor and the seven hundreds, and the towns of Old Windsor, Bray and Kempton, during pleasure', provided that she accounted at the Exchequer as Nicholas de Yattendon, the previous constable and warden, had done.[7] In a similar manner Edward I in August 1289 granted to his Queen Eleanor the custody of the royal manor and forest of Feckenham.[8]

Henry III and Edward I made provision in this way for a number of royal servants of different kinds. Among the dozen or so 'King's yeomen' and 'King's serjeants' appointed to Forest wardenships were Robert of Stopham, one of the king's huntsmen, who became warden of the forests of Clarendon and Groveley 1249–59,[9] and Master Walter of Durham, 'the King's serjeant and painter', appointed in 1271 to keep the forest of Galtres, along with John of York, another royal serjeant.[10] When by 1292 John of York had become too old and infirm to perform the duties of his Forest office, Edward I granted him a pension of 'three pence daily out of the issues of the forest, at the hands of the Justice of the Forest north of Trent, and six cartloads of firewood in the said forest by view and delivery of the foresters there'.[11] In 1318 Edward II appointed his cook, Richard of Cleobury, to keep the forest and park of Feckenham, 'as a reward for good service'.[12]

Other Forest wardens were of more exalted rank. Geoffrey Giffard, for example, the curialist Bishop of Worcester, was in October 1270 appointed to keep the royal forest and manor of Feckenham for a term of five years,[13] and Ebulo de Montibus, a Steward of the King's Household, held the offices of constable and warden of Windsor castle and forest from 1266 until his death in 1268.[14] After the Barons' War, a number of feudal magnates with great local estates were appointed as Forest wardens. Philip Basset, the Justiciar, for example, head of a great baronial family, was constable of Devizes castle and warden of Chippenham and Melksham forests, 1263–4 and from 1265 until his death in 1271.[15] Even a woman might secure such an appointment if she were an influential tenant-in-chief: Isabel Countess of Arundel kept the castle and forest of Bere Porchester in Hampshire from 1268 until 1272.[16]

2

The Hereditary Wardens

The Norman and Angevin kings established part of the local Forest administration on an hereditary and territorial basis; the holding of land from the Crown in return for some kind of service was of course the basis of feudal society and government. Robert of Everingham, for example, who was hereditary warden of Sherwood Forest from 1281 until 1287, held:

> ten knights' fees in chief of the lord King, from the service of which he was exonerated on account of his custody of the forest, and in return for finding his foresters at his own cost.[17]

Henry III rewarded his servants on occasion with offices of this kind: in 1265 he granted the wardenship of Cannock Forest to his surgeon, Master Thomas of Weseham, to hold in fee.[18]

Hereditary wardenships of royal forests were grand serjeanties,[19] and therefore subject to the usual feudal incidents of relief, wardship and marriage. King John exacted very large fines from the heirs to these serjeanties for confirming them in their lands and offices – £100 from Philip son of Holgot for the wardenship of Kinver Forest in 1199,[20] a like sum in 1200 from Richard de Munfichet for the forest of Essex,[21] and one hundred marks in 1215 from Michael de Columbars for the forest of Chute.[22] Such excessive fines and reliefs headed the list of grievances which the barons presented to King John in 1215,[23] and Magna Carta made concessions in this respect.[24] Subsequent reliefs were smaller: in October 1241 Adam of Purton, nephew and senior co-heir of Thomas of Sandford, paid ten marks for a grant of seisin of the wardenship of Braydon Forest, which belonged to him by right of primogeniture.[25]

The hereditary Forest wardenship might of course be inherited by women. In July 1221 the sisters and co-heiresses of Philip of Oldcoates, hereditary warden of the forest of Northumberland, paid the Crown a fine of eighty marks for seisin of their inheritance – the wardenship of the forest and the lands at Nafferton and Matfen which were appurtenant thereto.[26] Daniel son of Nicholas of Newcastle, husband of one of the co-heiresses, was appointed by them to perform the duties of Forest warden until he was succeeded in 1226 by Thomas of Stratton, husband of another co-heiress.[27]

King John sold the marriages of such heiresses to the highest bidder. By 1202 he had accepted from William Brewer an offer of a fine of 500 marks for the marriage of the daughter and heiress of Hugh of Morville, late hereditary warden of Inglewood forest, with his son Richard or his nephew Richard Gernon, and for having Hugh's Forest wardenship on the same terms.[28] But in May 1204 Brewer was outbid by Richard de Lucy of Egremont, who paid the king the enormous fine of 900 marks and five palfreys for the inheritance of his wife Ada, Hugh's elder daughter and co-heiress. The wardenship was to be held by him, his wife, and his heirs by her, of the king and his heirs for ever: Brewer handed it over to him at Midsummer 1204.[29]

When the heir to a Forest wardenship was a minor, large fines were also paid for the profitable grant of his wardenship and marriage. John Marshall in February 1218 paid 60 marks for having the wardship and marriage of Richard, son and heir of William of Wrotham, hereditary warden of the forests of Somerset, with the custody of the forests until Richard should be of age.[30] In 1282 Amaury de St Amand paid Edward I 800 marks for a similar grant in respect of the heir of Robert de Keynes, hereditary warden of Braydon Forest.[31]

It was laid down by a judgement of the King's Court in 1205 that 'No one ought or is able to divide up or in any way to alienate a serjeanty'.[32] A hereditary Forest warden had therefore to seek royal confirmation if he wished to grant away his bailiwick. This was done when Hugh Bigod in 1256 purchased from Osbert of Bolbeck the hereditary wardenship of Scalby Forest, with the lands and rents in Pickering appurtenant thereto.[33] Hugh le Despenser acquired the hereditary wardenship of Braydon Forest, with the manors of Somerford and Chelworth, from Robert de Keynes, without such royal licence: consequently in 1300 he had to pay a fine in the presence of the Treasurer in order to keep the wardenship and manors, and to convey a life interest back to Robert de Keynes.[34]

3

The Deputy Wardens

Many Forest wardens could not have performed their duties in person. Hereditary wardenships, for example, were from time to time inherited by priests: in 1207 William of Wrotham, Archdeacon of Taunton, received from King John seisin of the lands he held in chief in Somerset, and the wardenship of the forests of Somerset and Exmoor in Devon. The archdeacon in the king's presence appointed his brother Richard to perform the duties of his Forest office in his place, and agreed to be responsible for him.[35] Such offices were occasionally inherited by women. Avice de Columbars, for example, was amerced in 300 marks at the 1244 Hampshire Forest Eyre: her Forest duties were probably performed by her steward, who was adjudged at the same time to pay 100 marks.[36]

Many of the wardens appointed by royal letters patent, too, can have devoted little personal attention to their Forest offices. Great lay and ecclesiastical magnates, important officers of the king's court and household, busy judges, women of high rank – all appointed deputy wardens to keep the forests on their behalf. Between 1246 and 1255, for example, the wardens of the forests between Oxford and Stamford bridges performed important duties by deputy – by William of Northampton, who was 'bailiff of the forest' from 1246 until 1249, and Hugh of Goldingham, who was 'steward' from 1250 until 1255. It was William and Hugh who led the foresters and verderers to search the houses of suspects for evidence and arrest

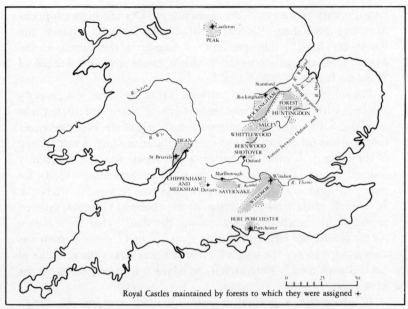

Castleton
PEAK

R. Severn

R. Wye

DEAN

St Briavels

Stamford
Rockingham
ROCKINGHAM
FOREST OF HUNTINGDON
SALCEY
WHITTLEWOOD
BERNWOOD
SHOTOVER
Oxford

R. W. Nene

Forests between Oxford and

CHIPPENHAM AND MELKSHAM
Devizes
Marlborough
R. Kennet
SAVERNAKE
Windsor
WINDSOR
R. Thames

BERE PORCHESTER
Porchester

0   25   50

Royal Castles maintained by forests to which they were assigned +

Castles and Forests – The Defence of the Realm

offenders, and who presided at special inquests on Forest offences,
and at the local Forest courts.[37]

4
Duties and Perquisites of the Forest Wardens

Many royal forests were 'assigned to the maintenance' of royal castles
in or near them. In April 1305 Edward I granted the forest of
Savernake to Queen Margaret to hold in dower, as appurtenant to
the castle and town of Marlborough, because the forest was
'necessary for the frequent repairs of the castle and town'.[38] For this
reason the constables of many royal castles were appointed at the
same time to be wardens of neighbouring forests: the constable of
Rockingham castle was usually warden of the forests between
Oxford and Stamford bridges;[39] the constable of Porchester kept

Bere Porchester Forest;[40] the constable of Devizes kept Chippen-
ham and Melksham Forests;[41] the constable of St Briavels the
Forest of Dean;[42] the constable of Castleton the Forest of the
Peak;[43] and the constable of Windsor castle was also warden of
Windsor Forest.[44]

The constable/warden had to see to it that the castle was properly
stocked with provisions and munitions of war, and to pay the
garrison. Substantial payments were made out of the Forest revenues
for these and other purposes relating to the maintenance and upkeep
of the castle.[45] Timber for building and repair was very frequently
ordered to be taken from the forest.[46] In September 1231, for
example, John le Malemort, a smith, was sent to make quarrels[47] at
St Briavels castle, and the warden of the Forest of Dean was ordered
to supply him with 'wood for making the shafts, charcoal and iron
for the heads, and lard for greasing them'.[48] In 1255 the warden was
commanded to pay the smith 25 marks a year out of the revenues of
his bailiwick for 25,000 quarrels, which he was to keep safely for the
king's use.[49]

Wardens had a general responsibility for keeping the king's
peace within his bailiwick,[50] and in times of rebellion or disturbance he was naturally an important buttress of royal authority.[51]
On occasion he took measures for the safety of the king's subjects
travelling through the forest. In July 1231 Henry III wrote to
Gilbert Basset, warden of the forests of Chippenham and
Melksham:

> We have been given to understand that our forest of Chippenham around the
> place called 'Holloway' is so dense that malefactors are able to lie hid in those
> parts, and so travellers are threatened with frequent losses, and some incur
> peril of lives and goods there. Therefore we command you to cause trees to be
> felled in that dense part, and a ride to be made to the least possible damage
> of the forest, so that henceforth a way through those parts may be open for
> travellers, without danger.[52]

It was the warden's duty to see that the deer in the forest were
supplied with sufficient food in times of scarcity,[53] and that they
were not hunted by anyone without authority from the king or the
Chief Justice of the Forest.[54] He had the right to arrest all poachers

found within his bailiwick, and to raise the hue and cry upon them.[55] The sheriff could be called upon to assist him with armed men when he raised the hue,[56] and to arrest men of whose names the warden informed him.[57] The warden was responsible for the safe keeping in the castle gaol of ordinary prisoners and political prisoners, as well as Forest offenders,[58] and for delivering them on bail on receipt of the appropriate writ.[59]

The warden or his deputy presided at Forest inquests into venison trespasses, and at the attachment courts. In some forests he took for himself the profits of the minor pleas: a thirteenth-century Cumberland jury swore that if any man 'furtively' felled an oak in Inglewood Forest, then the warden's duty was 'to attach his body according to the law of the forest' to answer before the Justice of the Forest at the Forest Eyre. The king had 'the attachments and the amercements', but the warden took the oak.[60]

The prevention of purprestures was his responsibility: he threw down houses, sheepfolds and other buildings and enclosures erected without licence in his bailiwick,[61] and attached those who made them to appear at the next Forest Eyre. He also seized assarts together with any crop grown on them.[62] He supervised the exercise of common rights by the forest inhabitants, seeing to it, for example, that cattle were not pastured in the forest beyond the period allowed by the Forest law, and seizing animals illegally pastured there.[63] There were constant complaints by the forest landowners and inhabitants in the thirteenth century of interference with their rights. In 1220, for example, the lepers of St Leonard at Lancaster petitioned the Crown. King John, they said, had granted them by charter the right to pasture their animals and to take housebote and firebote in Lonsdale Forest without payment, but they had lost the charter during the disturbances at the end of his reign. Roger Gernet, hereditary warden of the royal forests of Lancaster, had seized this opportunity to exact from them an ox for winter pasture and a cow for summer pasture, and had prevented them from taking housebote and firebote in the forest. The sheriff of Lancaster was ordered to see that their rights were restored to them.[64] Before the king made a grant of new privileges in the forest, the warden was often ordered to summon a jury to hold an inquest *ad quod damnum*, to ascertain the extent of the loss the Crown would incur by making the grant.[65]

When the king commanded deer to be taken for his use in the royal forests it was usually the warden's responsibility to see that this was done in the proper manner. Sometimes he was called upon to take the deer with his own men, hounds and equipment,[66] while on occasion he called upon the forest inhabitants to help him.[67] At other times the king sent his own huntsmen and hounds to the forest.[68] On these occasions the warden was informed of the number and kind of game they were to take, and it was his duty to keep a check on the number of deer taken, and to inform the king.[69] He was at times ordered to aid and supervise the royal huntsmen by leading them to those parts of the forest where the game was most plentiful,[70] supplying them with trained hounds,[71] and seeing that they did not drive the deer out of the forest[72] or continue their hunting longer than their instructions warranted.[73] He often had to pay the wages and expenses of the royal huntsmen out of the issues of his bailiwick.[74] He then was responsible for salting the venison and packing it in barrels, and keeping it safe until required, or sending it wherever the king wanted it.[75]

The warden had also to effect royal gifts of venison, and sometimes of live deer from the forest for the stocking of private parks.[76] Some of these royal gifts presented the warden with a formidable task: in December 1238 the sheriff of Essex and Richard de Munfichet, warden of the forest of Essex, were ordered to take alive in the forest 120 bucks and does for the Count of Flanders, put them in cages, and transport them in carts to the Thames, where Raymond Ruffus, a yeoman of the king, was to have a ship ready to take them to Flanders.[77] Sometimes the king allowed subjects to take deer for themselves in his forests; the warden's duty was to see to it that they had a proper writ of warranty when they came to his forest, that they did not take more than the specified number, and that they took them in the prescribed manner.[78]

The warden frequently received orders from the king to take timber in the forest for building operations, for firewood and charcoal for the king's needs, and as gifts for subjects.[79] So on 13 December 1230 Henry III wrote to the warden of Bere Forest:

> We are sending you Hurtard our serjeant, to cause 40 oaks to be cut down in
> the said forest and carried to Winchester against Christmas, for our hearth.
> We order you to cause the said oaks to be delivered to him in the place which
> is most suitable for transporting them, and to assist him to find men to cut
> them down and carry them, at our expense.[80]

To keep a check on the quantities taken, tallies were cut and kept by
the warden who delivered the timber and the Household official who
received it.[81]

The revenues collected and the perquisites enjoyed by the wardens
of the various royal forests show a general similarity. First, there was
cheminage, a toll on carts and pack-animals passing through the
forest. The foresters used this customary toll as a pretext for
extortion: the Charter of the Forest therefore conceded in 1217 that
henceforth cheminage might be exacted only by foresters of fee
paying the king a farm for their bailiwicks. They might take it only
from those who came into their bailiwicks from outside, with their
permission, to buy underwood, timber, bark or charcoal, to carry it
elsewhere to sell it, and from no others. Two pence per half-year
might be taken for each cart, and one halfpenny for each pack-horse.
Cheminage might be levied only 'in the places where it is
accustomed and ought to be taken by ancient usage', and only for
wood from the king's demesne woods. 'Moreover, those who carry
upon their backs brushwood, bark or charcoal to sell, though that be
their livelihood, shall henceforth give no cheminage.'[82] But in fact
the Forest wardens in the thirteenth century exacted cheminage
from all who carried wood and charcoal through their bailiwicks.
The Franciscan friars of Reading found it necessary in 1234 to obtain
from the king a letter ordering the warden of Windsor Forest not to
exact cheminage in respect of the timber given them in the forest for
their buildings at Reading.[83] In the Forest of Dean the warden
levied cheminage, not only on loads of wood, but also on sea coal
and iron ore carried 'through the forest towards Gloucester'.[84]

'Herbage' was often included in the warden's farm; that is, the
dues collected for cattle and horses on the king's forest pastures. In
1251 Geoffrey of Liston, warden of Windsor Forest, was granted as
part of his farm the herbage of the whole forest, including 'the
herbage and hay of Kempton park, saving maintenance for the

King's deer there'.[85] In the same way the perquisites of the hereditary wardens of Cannock Forest included all the herbage of the king's hays of Alrewas, Hopwas and Gailey, except during the fence month and the pannage season.[86]

In the forests of Dean, Windsor and Clarendon the wardens took the pannage dues, and in Cannock, Sherwood and Inglewood Forests they had the profits of after-pannage – that is, money paid for the agistment of pigs in the king's demesne woods after 11 November.[87] The warden of Galtres Forest had 'the profits of pigs entering the forest during the fence month; to wit, one halfpenny from each pig'. This payment was a fine for disturbing the deer when they were supposed to be fawning.[88] The wardens of Inglewood took 'escapes' – or fines paid by the owners of animals which had strayed into forbidden parts of the forest. This they took for 'all animals except swine, and swine all the year round in the hay of Plumpton, and during the fence month . . . in the rest of the forest'.[89]

Many of the wardens had the right to take 'cablish' or windfallen wood. In Cannock Forest the warden might take ten oaks from those blown down in the hays of Alrewas, Hopwas and Gailey, and in 'the wood called Hockley'.[90] In Rutland Forest he had 'dead and dry wood which can be collected in the demesne woods of the lord King with the hand alone, without any iron instrument'.[91] In Inglewood Forest he took:

> all dead wood standing and fallen, all dry wood and barren trees, stumps, twigs and bark (of trees cut down), wood of alders and willows, and all cablish and branches . . . except in the hay of Plumpton.[92]

In the forests of Dean, Windsor, Cannock, Sherwood, Essex, Inglewood and Galtres the warden took the lop and top, and sometimes the bark, of oaks given by the king, or felled for his use.[93]

Some Forest wardens had the right to hunt certain animals and to take certain birds of prey used in hawking. Thomas of Milton, warden of Inglewood Forest from 1222 until 1265, had the right to hunt 'hare, fox, wild cat, wolf, badger, otter, marten, squirrel and all woodland beasts save hart and hind, fallow buck and his doe, wild boar and sow, which are the king's'. He also had 'all falcons, sparrow-hawks, muskets,[94] and eyries except hawk's, which are the king's', and all honey and wax in the Forest.[95]

The warden usually had under him foresters of fee, whose hereditary offices were subject to the usual feudal incidents. In 1355 Roger Mortimer, Earl of March, claimed as warden of Clarendon Forest

> to have after the death of every forester of fee of the bailiwick by way of a heriot, the said forester's best riding-horse, and a saddle with a bridle, a cloak, cap and sword, leggings with spurs, a horn, a bow and barbed arrows, and his dog called a 'bercelet'.[96]

In the forests of Chippenham and Melksham, Dean, Feckenham, Peak and Windsor the warden had also the custody of royal manors in the forest,[97] and he had to see that they were properly stocked and managed.[98] He was often directed to see to the ploughing, tilling and sowing of assarts, waste and other lands belonging to the king in the forest,[99] and cattle were sometimes sent to him to be fattened on the forest pastures.[100] From time to time he was instructed to raise money by conducting sales of wood from the king's demesne,[101] and he carried out the king's policy regarding mining in the forest, which wavered between a desire to increase the Forest revenues and concern lest the vert be destroyed.[102]

Some wardens accounted for the revenues of their bailiwicks directly at the Exchequer.[103] In such cases they were often allowed to take for themselves an annual salary out of those revenues. Bernard of Savoy, in December 1241 appointed constable and warden of Windsor castle and forest, was granted a salary of £10 a year by the hands of the bailiffs of Windsor, and one tun of wine.[104] The warden of Clarendon and Groveley Forests was likewise allowed £20 a year.[105] More usually, however, the wardens paid a fixed annual sum into the Exchequer for the rights to collect for themselves certain forest revenues. This arrangement naturally resulted in frequent complaints by the forest inhabitants about illegal extortion by the foresters. Furthermore, many wardens presented their accounts very irregularly, and left office heavily in debt. In 1250, for example, Peter de Neville, warden of Rutland Forest, owed the king the large sum of £324, which included 'the arrears of the annual revenue of the same forest'. He promised to pay off his debt at the rate of 20 marks a year.[106] Other wardens were from time to time granted leave by Henry III to postpone their accounts at the Exchequer,[107] and he remitted the debts of others.[108] It seems clear therefore that the central administration was unable at this time to exercise effective financial control over the Forest wardens.

5

Administrative Conduct of the Forest Wardens

Complaints of irregular and oppressive conduct by local Forest officers were frequent during the thirteenth century. At the Rutland Forest Eyre in 1269 the verderers, regarders and other jurors presented a long list of indictments of this kind. The warden, Peter de Neville, and his foresters, bailiffs and vendors of wood were accused of having taken great quantities of timber from the king's demesne park and woods during the preceding thirteen years, for Neville's own use, for sale and for making lime and charcoal. The damage done to branchwood and underwood could not be estimated. Neville had defrauded the Crown by unlawfully taking for himself the dues for after-pannage, the agistment of cattle, and the escapes of beasts into forbidden enclosures in the forest. He had also taken the profits of minor pleas of the vert, and 'pleas of taking hares, foxes, rabbits and cats, and of having dogs and greyhounds in the forest', which pleas rightfully belonged to the king. Prisoners arrested for Forest trespasses ought to have been handed over to the sheriff of Rutland for imprisonment in Oakham castle, but Neville put them in his own gaol at Allexton, which was 'full of water at the bottom', and bound them with iron chains. Some of these unfortunate prisoners were later found innocent at the Forest Eyre. Others had their cattle seized by Neville's men until they paid extortionate fines, although their cases should have been heard before the king's judges.

Forest townships were compelled to pay the warden large sums of money if they did not attend Forest inquests at his summons. He had set a forester on the road between Stamford and Casterton bridges, who exacted four pence for cheminage from every cart carrying wood or timber from Lincolnshire to Stamford, contrary to custom and the Charter of the Forest.[109] When Geoffrey son of Sarah of Empingham resisted this illegal demand, the forester raised the hue and cry upon him, and distrained him until he gave him two shillings and found sureties for appearing at the attachment court. There the warden arrested him, imprisoned him in his gaol at Allexton, and afterwards released him for a fine of half a mark. Finally, Neville had abused his power of appointing foresters by appointing an excessive number of them, with boys under them: they levied contributions from the forest inhabitants and were an intolerable burden on the countryside. In thirteen years de Neville had misappropriated Crown revenues and wasted Crown property, besides imposing a regime of grave oppression, extortion and injustice upon the unfortunate people of Rutland.[110] Peter de Neville lost his wardenship, and in February 1272 both he and his son Theobald were still in prison charged with these offences.[111] But in 1300 Theobald recovered his father's wardenship in fee simple,[112] presumably by paying a substantial fine.

Sometimes the sheriff, that medieval 'maid-of-all-work', was called in to restrain the oppressive conduct of the Forest wardens. In 1222 it was reported to the Council of Regency that Thomas of Milton, hereditary warden of Inglewood Forest, had under him twelve riding foresters with their underforesters, who were maintained at the expense of the Crown and the men of the king's demesnes. He had imposed heavy and illegal exactions upon the forest dwellers, prevented the men of the royal demesnes from having their customary rights of housebote and haybote, and taken for himself the dues for escapes of cattle and other animals in the forest, which rightly belonged to the king. The Council commanded the warden to cease these unlawful practices, and to reduce his foresters to six, which he was to maintain himself. The sheriff of Cumberland received orders to see that the Council's commands were carried out in all respects.[113]

Many other Forest wardens were accused of peculation, oppression or neglect. The most frequent complaint was that, although the warden ought to have maintained the 'stewards, clerks and foresters' who kept the forest under him, yet in practice he appointed an excessive number of them; he compelled them to pay for their appointments, and in some cases to make annual payments to him afterwards. The foresters recouped themselves by illegal exactions from the forest inhabitants, and by committing waste and destruction in the forest. The Charter of the Forest had tried to stop this abuse by enacting in 1217 that the number of foresters necessary to keep the forests should be determined 'by the view and oath of the twelve regarders when they make the regard'[114] – that is, every three years. But this safeguard was ignored or was ineffective, for the complaints continued. Wardens were also accused of levying illegal or excessive dues for the lawing of dogs and for common of pasture in the forest, and for non-attendance at Forest courts and inquests, besides illegally taking the king's deer and timber, and conniving at offences in return for bribes.[115]

Many Forest wardens were deprived of their offices after conviction of such malpractices at the Forest Eyre. But the principal purpose of the Forest system was by this time the raising of revenue: in most cases the wardenships were restored to the offenders or their heirs on payment of a fine to the king.[116] In many other cases the warden for the time being escaped indictment at the Forest Eyre; the verderers, regarders and jurymen, fearing his retribution, preferred to wait until he was out of office and harmless. By that time it was difficult to punish the offender, and the Crown frequently abandoned the attempt to exact fines and arrears from ex-wardens.[117]

NOTES

1. See e.g. Close R. 1242–47, 442, 453.
2. Cal. Pat. R. 1247–58, 402, 418.
3. ibid., 1232–47, 51; 1292–1301, 356; 1301–7, 75.
4. Pat. R. 1225–32, 489; Cal. Pat. R. 1307–13, 183, 206.
5. ibid., 1266–72, 342–43.
6. ibid., 581.
7. ibid., 684.
8. ibid., 1281–92, 320.
9. ibid., 1247–58, 40; Close R. 1247–51, 150.
10. Cal. Pat. R. 1266–72, 534.
11. ibid., 1281–92, 479.
12. Cal. Fine R. 1307–19, 353.
13. Cal. Pat. R. 1266–72, 469–70, 507.
14. Cal. Pat. R. 1258–66, 543; 1266–72, 215; Tout, *Chapters*, VI 40–41.
15. Cal. Pat. R. 1258–66, 264, 279, 574; *Ex. e Rot. Fin.* II 551–52; and see Bazeley, *Forest of Dean*, 184.
16. Cal. Pat. R. 1266–72, 204, 496, 626.
17. E32/132/9d; Turner, *Sel. Forest Pleas*, 67.
18. Cal. Pat. R. 1258–66, 450.
19. Cal. Inq. Misc. I pp. 74, 493–94; Cal. I.P.M. II p. 232.
20. *Rot. de Ob. temp. Iohann.*, 7.
21. Pipe R. 1200, 48.
22. *Rot. de Ob. temp. Iohann.*, 567.
23. art. I (Stubbs, *Sel. Charters*, 285.)
24. art. 2 (ibid., 293).
25. *Ex e Rot. Fin.* I 357.
26. ibid., 67; Pat. R. 1216–25, 296.
27. *Rot. Litt. Claus.* 1224–27, 101.
28. Pipe R. 1202, 256.
29. ibid., 1204, 143–44; Rot. Chart. 1199–1216, 132.
30. *Ex. e Rot. Fin.* 1, 5.
31. Cal. Fine R. 1272–1307, 177.
32. Book of Fees II 1163–65.
33. Cal. Close R. 1302–7, 140–41; Yorks. Arch. Assoc., Record Series XII 45–46.
34. Cal. Pat. R. 1292–1301, 536.
35. *Rot. Litt. Pat.* 1201–16, 68.
36. Close R. 1242–47, 314.
37. E32/39a, 63, 65; Turner, *Sel. Forest Pleas*, 75–108.
38. Cal. Pat. R. 1301–7, 362.

39. ibid., 1232–47, 474; 1247–58, 59, 63 etc.
40. Pat. R. 1225–32, 198; Cal. Pat. R. 1232–47, 141 etc.
41. ibid., 51, 234 etc.
42. ibid., 55, 160, 175 etc.
43. ibid., 140; 1281–92, 61.
44. ibid., 1258–66, 300, 543.
45. ibid., 1232–47, 433; 1258–66, 91; Bazeley, *Forest of Dean*, 252.
46. Close R. passim.
47. 'Quarrel – a short, heavy, square-headed arrow or bolt formerly used with the crossbow' (*S.O.D.*, s.v.)
48. Close R., 1227–31, 564.
49. ibid., 1254–56, 97.
50. Cal. Pat. R. 1232–47, 165.
51. ibid., 1258–66, 627.
52. Close R. 1227–31, 537.
53. E32/30/17; Bazeley, *Forest of Dean*, 188.
54. *Rot. Litt. Claus.* 1204–24, 417; Close R. 1247–51, 47.
55. E32/41/6; E32/65; Turner, *Sel. Forest Pleas*, 11–12, 95–96.
56. Close R. 1237–42, 439.
57. Cal. Pat. R. 1232–47, 62.
58. Bazeley, op. cit., 187, 232–33.
59. *Ex. e Rot. Fin.* I 293; Close R. 1231–34, 36 etc.
60. Cal. Inq. Misc. I 156.
61. *Rot. Litt. Claus.* 1204–24, 407; Close R. 1242–47, 445 etc.
62. *Rot. Litt. Claus.* 1204–24, 93.
63. Close R. 1231–34, 63.
64. *Rot. Litt. Claus.* 1204–24, 414.
65. Cal. Pat. R. 1258–66, 303, 354, 396, 394 etc.
66. Close R. 1237–42, 95; 1242–47, 333 etc.
67. ibid., 1251–53, 186.
68. ibid., 1227–31, 196, 206–7, 288 etc.
69. ibid., 1237–42, 200; Cal. Close R. 1272–79, 287.
70. Close R. 1227–31, 77.
71. ibid., 1237–42, 2.
72. *Rot. Litt. Claus.* 1224–27, 53–54.
73. Close R. 1234–37, 534; 1237–42, 210.
74. Cal. Lib. R. 1226–40, 288; Close R. 1251–53, 127.
75. ibid., 1227–31, 546; 1234–37, 398; Cal. Lib. R. 1226–40, 47, 233, 431.
76. *Rot. Litt. Claus.* 1204–24, 138 etc.
77. Cal. Lib. R. 1226–40, 354.
78. Close R. 1234–37, 203, 483; 1237–42, 385.
79. ibid., 1227–31, 6, 569; 1234–37, 36–37, 102, 107 etc.
80. ibid., 1234–37, 403.
81. ibid., 1231–34, 270; 1234–37, 429.

82. art. 14 (Stubbs, *Sel. Charters*, 347.)
83. Close R. 1231–34, 415.
84. Bazeley, *Forest of Dean*, 194, 223; and see Fisher, *Forest of Essex*, 128.
85. Cal. Pat. R. 1247–58, 109–110.
86. Cal. Inq. Misc. I 74, 493–94.
87. Cal. Pat. R. 1247–58, 109–110, 450; 1354–58, 198–199; Cal. Inq. Misc. I 74, 156, 493–94; Cal. I.P.M. II 390.
88. Close R. 138 m. 25; Turner, *Sel. Forest Pleas*, xxi n. I.
89. Cal. Inq. Misc. I 156.
90. ibid., 74, 493–94.
91. E32/140/3; Turner, op. cit., 46–47.
92. Cal. Inq. Misc. I 156.
93. Cal. Pat. R. 1247–58, 109–110, 450; 1354–58, 198–99; Cal. Inq. Misc. I 74, 156, 493–94; Cal. I.P.M. II 390; Fisher, *Forest of Essex*, 126.
94. a kind of sparrow-hawk.
95. Cal. Inq. Misc. I 156.
96. Cal. Pat. R. 1354–58, 198–99.
97. Pat. R. 1216–25, 55; 1225–32, 317; 1247–58, 39, 109–10, 450 etc.
98. Close R. 1227–31, 302; Bazeley, 'Forest of Dean', 188.
99. Close R. 1247–51, 413–14; Cal. Fine R. 1272–1307, 12.
100. Close R. 1234–37, 148.
101. Pat. R. 1216–25, 360, 361–62 etc.
102. See Bazeley, *Forest of Dean*, 236–37.
103. Cal. Pat. R. 1232–47, 141; 1258–66, 436, 498 etc.
104. ibid., 1232–47, 268, 269.
105. ibid., 1247–58, 40.
106. Close R. 1247–51, 209–10.
107. ibid., 305; 1251–53, 12.
108. Cal. Pat. R. 1258–66, 472–73, 639; and see Bazeley, op. cit., 226–33.
109. art 14. (See above, p. 103.)
110. E32/140/3, 3d., 4; Turner, *Sel. Forest Pleas*, 44–53.
111. Cal. Close R. 1272–79, 6, 7.
112. Cal. Pat. R. 1292–1301, 560.
113. *Rot. Litt. Claus.* 1204–24, 513.
114. art. 7 (Stubbs, *Sel. Charters*, 346.)
115. *Rot. Litt. Claus.* 1204–24, 433–34, 436; C99/101; E32/184/9d; Turner, op. cit. xxi, n. 4, 125–28; Bazeley, op. cit., 189–91.
116. Pat. R. 1225–32, 325; Cal. Pat. R. 1292–1301, 17; 1301–1307, 341; Pipe R. 1230, 258.
117. Bazeley, op. cit., 190–91.

CHAPTER 10

Foresters of Fee, Foresters and Woodwards

1
Foresters of Fee

Many of the Forest wardens had under them Forest officers who held their office by hereditary right – the foresters of fee. They performed their duties within wards or subdivisions of the forest. They were subject to the warden's authority,[1] and in some forests swore fealty to him.[2] There were nine of them in the Forest of Dean,[3] five in the New Forest,[4] and five in Savernake.[5] By the reign of Henry III their offices were of considerable antiquity. A jury swore in 1266 that John son of Nigel and his ancestors had been foresters of fee of Bernwood Forest 'from the Conquest of England':[6] another jury declared that the ancestors of William son of Adam had been granted the manor of Hutton-in-the Forest by Henry I, to hold by the serjeanty of keeping the bailiwick of Plumpton in Inglewood Forest.[7] William of Dean, one of the foresters of fee of the Forest of Dean, held in chief in Great Dean two carucates of land and 6 marks of rent, and paid to the king an annual farm of 10s. He was bound to provide at his own cost one riding forester and two walking foresters to keep his bailiwick, and to perform the military service of 'going in the army at the King's cost wherever the King goes'.[8]

Foresters of fee usually paid a farm to the warden of the forest: Hugh of Stratford, forester of fee of Wakefield in Northamptonshire, paid to John de Neville, warden of the forests between Oxford and Stamford bridges, 1234–1244, as a farm for the aforesaid bailiwick, $2\frac{1}{2}$ marks a year . . . and two quarters of nuts . . . 30 geese . . . 30 hens . . . and 200 eggs'.[9] Some foresters of fee, however, paid no farm: Henry son of Aucher, forester of fee of Waltham in the forest of Essex, was in 1292 bound only to make 'wanlace' – that is, bring the quarry to bay, whenever the king came to hunt in his bailiwick.[10] By the terms of their appointment many foresters of fee were supposed to provide underforesters at their own expense, but in practice some took money from them for their appointment. In the reign of Henry III Simon son of Norman, forester of fee of Kingswood in the forest of Essex, had under him five walking foresters, each guarding his own ward: they paid him annually sums ranging from 5s to 2 marks for their perquisites, which included the right to levy cheminage.[11]

These hereditary Forest offices were subject to the usual feudal incidents of wardship, relief and marriage, which involved periodic payments of substantial fines to the Crown.[12] When the heir had done homage to the king, it was usual for the Justice of the Forest, on receipt of the appropriate writ, to take from him security for the payment of relief, and then to give him seisin of his Forest bailiwick; the king's escheator was ordered at the same time to hand over his lands to him, those appurtenant to his forestership, and whatever others he might hold in chief by other service.[13]

Foresterships of fee might be inherited by women: in such cases the duties of the office were usually performed by their guardians, husbands or sons. In March 1239 Agnes de Amundeville, a forester of fee of Feckenham Forest, gave the king an annual payment of one mark at the Exchequer for recovery of her bailiwick: it had been seized because of a venison offence by her son Ralph, committed when he was keeper of that forest. Richard, Agnes's younger son, was to find the Justice of the Forests south of Trent twelve 'free and law-worthy men' who would guarantee that he would well and faithfully keep the said bailiwick on Agnes's behalf: the Forest Justice was then to admit him to the custody in Agnes's place.[14]

Foresterships of fee, and the lands appurtenant thereto, were grand serjeanties, and therefore ought not to have been divided or alienated except by the king's licence. But a commission appointed in June 1246 found that a number of foresters of fee had in fact disposed of all or part of the lands they held by service of keeping their forest bailiwicks. Thomas son of Adam, who had held the manor of Hutton-in-the-Forest by the serjeanty of keeping the king's hay of Plumpton in Inglewood Forest, had by 1244 alienated the manor entirely to several tenants.[15] In 1250 it was discovered that the lands which Aubrey, a forester of fee of Whittlewood Forest, held by serjeanty in Northamptonshire, had been alienated in part,[16] and that 'the serjeanty of Peter of Minton in Shropshire, for which he ought to keep the forest of Long Mynd and the hays of Bushmoor and Haycrust' had been 'alienated in part by divers parcels'.[17] Foresters of fee who held no land of the king[18] relied on the dues they exacted from the forest inhabitants as their recompense for guarding vert and venison: the temptation to extortion was great.

The foresters of fee usually had the right to take 'cablish' – that is, dead and dry wood, and trees or branches blown down by the wind within their bailiwicks:[19] in Bernwood Forest, if the wind felled ten trees 'in one night and one day', the king took them all, but if there were less than ten, the forester of fee took them.[20] In many forests they took the lop and top, and in some cases the stump, of all trees given by the king from the woods in their bailiwicks, or taken there for his use. In the Forest of Dean they also took housebote and haybote and a tree trunk at Christmas, under the supervision of the verderers and other Forest officers: they employed men to make some of this wood into charcoal and to operate travelling forges for the smelting of iron, and were answerable to the Crown when these workmen took wood in the forest to which they were not entitled.[21]

The foresters of fee had rights of pannage and common of pasture in the forest for themselves and their men, and some of them took the nuts gathered in the king's demesne woods.[22] They exacted various dues from the forest inhabitants, such as cheminage, pannage or afterpannage, and the dues for having dogs unlawed in the forest[23]. In the reign of Henry III Hugh of Stratford, forester of

fee of Wakefield in Northamptonshire, took from the forest townships in his bailiwick:

> one quarter of wheat for every virgate of land, in return for their having
> housebote and paling for their corn, and for collecting dead wood for their
> fuel in the King's demesne wood . . . and from every house a goose and a
> hen every year.[24]

The main duty of the foresters of fee was of course the safe keeping
of vert and venison: the Forest rolls show them searching for,
arresting and attaching offenders, and indicting them at the Forest
Eyre. At the Gloucester Forest Eyre of 1282 the judges ruled that
every forester of fee was to have his own roll of attachments of vert
and venison to present before them.[25] In times of civil disturbance
they were also called upon to help in maintaining the king's peace,
as when in June 1234 the foresters of fee of all the royal forests of
England were commanded to aid the sheriffs in arresting the
malefactors who were roaming over the countryside as a result of the
disturbances created by the Earl Marshal and his adherents.[26]

The warden was responsible for the conduct of the foresters of fee:
on a number of occasions he seized their bailiwicks because of their
misconduct.[27] But the Forest wardens in many cases held office
during the king's pleasure and for relatively short periods: many
were important and busy persons who performed many of their
Forest duties by deputies. On the other hand, foresters of fee were
often landowners of some local importance,[28] and of course held
office for life. The intervals between Forest Eyres were too long to
maintain effective control over such men: nevertheless when the
Forest Eyres were held they frequently resulted in the conviction of
the foresters of fee of serious misconduct, and in their amercement,
forfeiture of office, and even imprisonment.[29] The Gloucester Forest
Eyre rolls of 1270 and 1282 record long lists of offences of which the
foresters of fee of the Forest of Dean were convicted. They had kept
in their service underforesters who were habitual poachers, cut down
trees and underwood in large quantities, and kept the proceeds of
sale for themselves. They had allowed others to commit waste and
make assarts; they had embezzled fines which rightfully belonged to

the king, taken large sums for the agistment of animals in the Forest pastures so as to overburden them, and illegally kept unlawed dogs. The regarders accused one of them, Ralph of Abinghall, of having impounded in Walmore Green the animals belonging to the men of the district, extorted sixty geese from them as an amercement, and kept the beasts for himself, although all profits of such attachments belonged to the king.[30] But the Crown was primarily concerned at this time with the raising of revenue, and not with the punishment of offenders, who in many cases were able to recover their forfeited offices on payment of a fine.

2

The Riding and Walking Foresters

The larger forests were divided into wards, each policed by a forester who kept vert and venison under the warden. Some were appointed by letters patent under the Great Seal: in 1299, for example, Gervase of Holloway, King's yeoman, was granted for life, as a reward for long service:

> the bailiwick of the custody of the forest of Brigstock and Geddington [in Rockingham Forest in Northamptonshire] . . . since it appears . . . that this is one forest kept by one man appointed by the King.[31]

Some subordinate foresters appointed by the king were paid wages: in 1228 Hubert de Burgh, as warden of Windsor Forest, was paying 6d. a day to Osbert and Robert, King's serjeants, for keeping the forest of Odiham,[32] and in 1233 2d. a day to each of six serjeants on foot for keeping the forest of Windsor by the king's command.[33]

The Chief Justices of the Forest, the wardens and the foresters of fee also appointed subordinate keepers, called 'riding foresters', 'walking foresters' or 'serjeants'. In the forest of Essex towards the end of the thirteenth century there were six riding foresters, all appointed by the warden, and removable at his pleasure. Each had a defined territorial bailiwick or ward. The riding forester of Becontree paid an annual farm of 5 marks a year to the warden, and the others 40s. apiece. Each riding forester had under him two or three walking foresters, who made annual payments to him equal to the amount of the farm which he paid to the warden.[34]

All foresters had to take an oath in the local Forest court, in the presence of the verderers, to perform their duties conscientiously, to keep the Forest law, and not to oppress the forest landowners and the other inhabitants of the forest.[35] No attachment might be made except by a sworn forester. At the Essex Forest Eyre of 1277 it was presented that Alexander Not of Havering had entered the Abbess of Barking's wood and felled an oak. He had been discovered by the abbess's steward, Richard of Bernstead, who, when he resisted attachment, seized and bound him, took him to Barking, imprisoned him for three days and afterwards delivered him to the forester and the verderer. The judgment of the court was that because Richard was not a sworn forester, he was liable to amercement.[36]

In the execution of their duties the foresters often had to contend with armed bands of desperate men; in many cases they were beaten and even killed while attempting to arrest Forest offenders. In 1351 Edward III granted John the woodward of Raskelf a pension of 3d. a day 'for good service and especially because his eyes were torn out and his tongue and his fingers cut off by malefactors in the Forest of Galtres in the time when he was one of the King's foresters there'.[37] For self-defence therefore the sworn foresters were allowed to carry bows and arrows in the forest.[38] The statute *De malefactoribus* of 1293 created a statutory defence in cases of homicide by foresters:

> If any forester do find any trespasser wandering within his liberty . . . within the forest . . . and after hue and cry made to him to stand unto the peace, will not yield himself, but flee or resist . . . if the forester do kill any such offender, he shall not be impeached for this felony.[39]

When foresters raised the hue and cry, the men of the neighbouring townships were bound to come and help them. Neglect of their duty involved severe penalties. On 1 August 1245, for example, foresters discovered poachers in Rockingham Forest with bows and arrows, and raised the hue upon them, but the township of

Wadenhoe refused to come and follow the hue. Men from Wadenhoe who were present at the next Northamptonshire Forest Eyre in 1255 were committed to prison, and the whole township was adjudged to be 'in grievous mercy'.[40]

Complaint was frequently made that excessive numbers of underforesters were appointed, and that they levied oppressive exactions to maintain themselves and the grooms or pages by whom they were accompanied. The judges at the Rutland Forest Eyre in 1269 ordered that they should be reduced to the customary and reasonable number, which was five walking foresters and one riding forester with one page, and that no walking forester in that forest was in future to have pages under him.[41]

In 1279 the 'people of the forest of Somerset' presented to Edward I a long list of abuses, including 'scotale'.[42] They complained that, contrary to the Charter of the Forest:[43]

> the foresters come with horses at harvest time, and collect every kind of corn in sheaves within the bounds of the forest, and outside near the forest. Then they make their ale from what they have collected, and those who do not come there to drink and do not give money at the foresters' will are sorely punished at their pleas for dead wood, although the King has no demesne; nor does anyone dare to brew when the foresters brew, or to sell ale so long as the foresters have any kind of ale to sell; and this every forester does year by year to the great grievance of the country. Besides this they collect lambs and sucking pigs, wool and flax; from every house where there is wool, a fleece; and in the fence month, from every house a penny, or a farthing for each pig. And when they brew, they fell trees for their fuel in the woods of the good people without leave, to wit, oaks, maples, hazels and thorns, felling the best first, whereby the good people feel themselves aggrieved on account of the destruction of their woods.

The foresters attached the forest dwellers every year if their dogs were not lawed, although the Charter of the Forest had promised that this should be done only every three years.[44] They also made illegal exactions in the name of cheminage, and in return permitted waste of the vert. In the forests of Mendip and Selwood they took, again contrary to the Forest Charter:[45]

> from every poor man who carries wood upon his back, six pence, and from

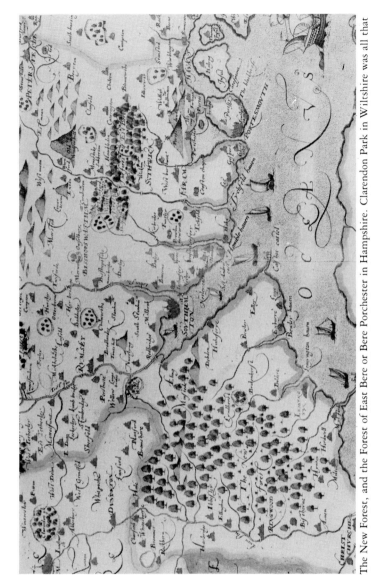

The New Forest, and the Forest of East Bere or Bere Porchester in Hampshire. Clarendon Park in Wiltshire was all that then remained of the extensive royal Forest of Clarendon in the south-east corner of that county. (Detail from Christopher Saxton's map of Hampshire, 1575. By permission of the National Library of Wales.)

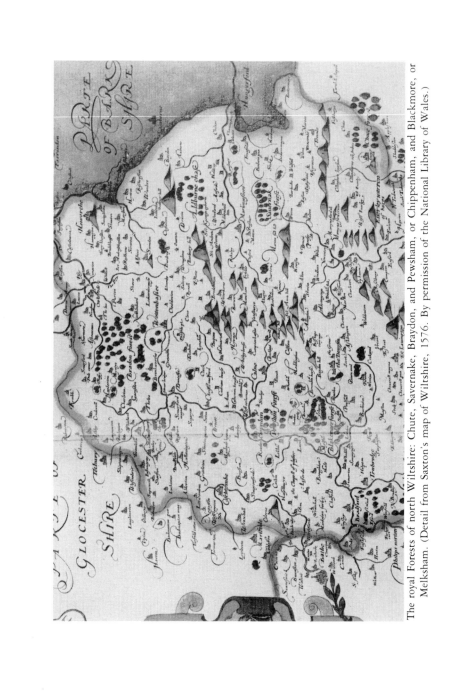

The royal Forests of north Wiltshire: Chute, Savernake, Braydon, and Pewsham, or Chippenham, and Blackmore, or Melksham. (Detail from Saxton's map of Wiltshire, 1576. By permission of the National Library of Wales.)

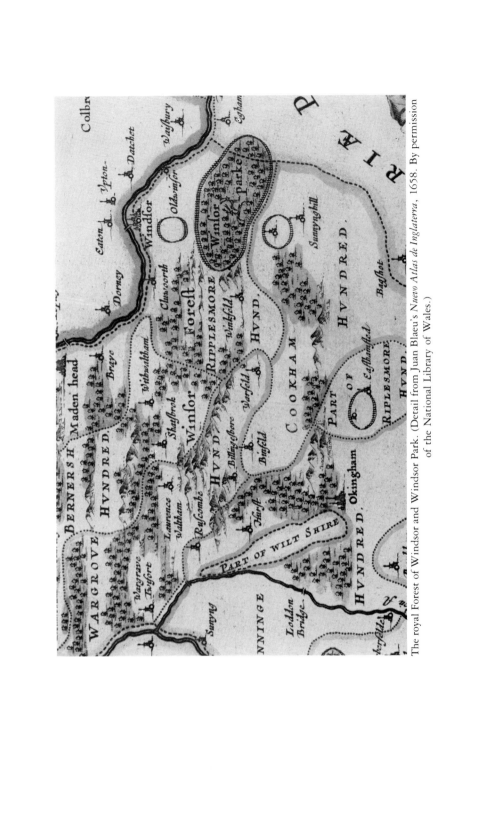

The royal Forest of Windsor and Windsor Park. (Detail from Juan Blaeu's *Nuevo Atlas de Inglaterra*, 1658. By permission of the National Library of Wales.)

The royal Forests of Rockingham in Northamptonshire and Lee or Leighfield in Rutland. (Detail from Saxton's map of Northamptonshire, 1576. By permission of the National Library of Wales.)

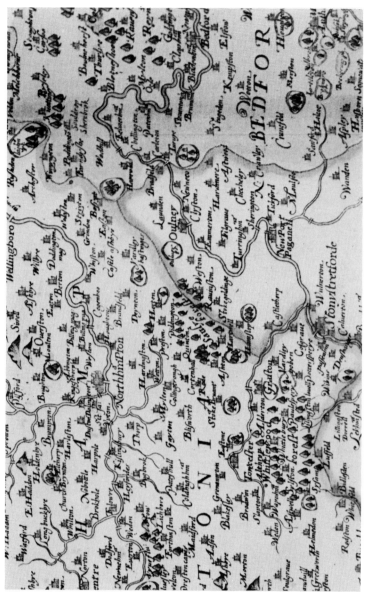

The royal Forests of Whittlewood and Salcey. (Detail from Saxton's map of
Northamptonshire, 1576. By permission of the National Library of
Wales.)

The royal Forest of Dean. (Detail from Saxton's map of Gloucestershire, 1577. By permission of the National Library of Wales.)

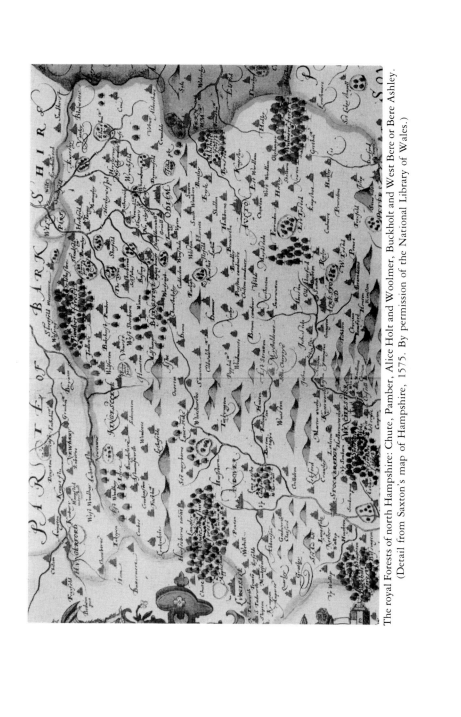

The royal Forests of north Hampshire: Chute, Pamber, Alice Holt and Woolmer, Buckholt and West Bere or Bere Ashley. (Detail from Saxton's map of Hampshire, 1575. By permission of the National Library of Wales.)

The royal Forests of north-east Yorkshire: Pickering and Galtres. (Detail from Saxton's map of Yorkshire, 1577. By permission of the National Library of Wales.)

the rich as much as they are able to pay. The foresters, both riding and walking, and their pages take for a cart two, three or four shillings, from some more and from others less according to their means, and for a pack-horse twelve, sixteen or eighteen pence, to raise their fine which they have made with the warden [for their appointment]; this to the great destruction of the King's forest and the grievance of those who have woods in the forest, for they suffer the carriers to go quit all through the year without attachment, and yet the King has no profit . . . Where the people rest with their wood or timber and unload it from carts outside the close of the franchise of the Charterhouse among the towns, and afterwards take up their loads of the same wood or timber, the Foresters attach them and amerce them grievously at their will without right.

The inhabitants of Exmoor Forest also complained that:

the foresters attach likewise the good folk of their demesne woods and lands, and amerce them grievously; and the small folk they attach at their homes and in their enclosures and in their crofts among the towns. The foresters attach to come before them men who work in their own ground, making 'hoes' to sow corn, although the King had no demesne there: and they say that they have made waste and purpresture if they do not their will for having peace; from each man holding land they will have the skin of a lamb or a farthing, and they say that is their fee.

Although the king from time to time forbade 'puture' – the contributions in money and in kind exacted by the foresters[46] – the levying of puture seems to have become a general practice at least by the fourteenth century.[47] In the reign of Edward III, for example, a forester of Inglewood Forest, in a suit against the Abbot of St Mary's, York, claimed to have food and drink at the table of the abbot's grooms every Friday, together with the right to carry away, whenever he pleased, a flagon of the best ale in the abbot's cellar and two tallow candles from the abbot's chamber, a bushel of oats for his horse, and a loaf of black bread for his dog.[48]

The foresters were frequently convicted at the Forest Eyres of trespasses against vert and venison,[49] and of oppressive conduct towards the forest inhabitants. At the Huntingdonshire Eyre in 1255, for example, Norman Sampson, a riding forester, was convicted of having extorted money from a man in his bailiwick by making him sit upon a harrow.[50] At the Staffordshire Forest Eyre in

1271 Hugh of Evesham, another riding forester, was indicted because he had taken

> with him a certain clerk, who he said was the clerk of the Justice of the Forest, and made a view of dogs which were not lawed throughout his bailiwick. He thus unjustly extorted a great sum of money from the men of the bailiwick, not being content with any mode of lawing, saying, if the right leg was lawed, the left leg ought to be lawed, and vice versa, and if all the feet were lawed, saying falsely that this was against the assize and the tenor of the king's Charter.[51]

But the intervals between Forest Eyres were too long for effective control. The conduct of the foresters made them a by-word for oppression and extortion. Boroughs within the royal forests were prepared to pay for exemption from their hated authority. In 1256 Henry III granted by charter to the burgesses of Scarborough that 'no forester may enter the borough to make attachment for trespasses within the Forest [of Scalby]'[52] and in 1348 Edward III made a similar concession to the burgesses of Penrith for Inglewood Forest.[53]

A case heard at the Essex Forest Eyre in 1277 illustrates the conflict between municipal privileges and Forest jurisdictions. The foresters gave evidence that two townsmen of Colchester had been seen hunting in the forest, but had evaded attachment. The bailiffs of the town were ordered by the court to produce them, but did not do so. The sheriff was then ordered to arrest one offender, who had been recognized. Subsequently two foresters had attempted to arrest a townsman in Colchester and had accidentally killed him, whereupon the bailiffs and townsmen had arrested and imprisoned the foresters. The townsmen produced at the Forest Eyre a charter of Richard I conceding that no forester was to have power of attachment within the bounds of the borough. The court finally decided that the Justice of the Forest should confer with the king about this dispute.[54]

3
The Woodwards

All subjects who had demesne woods within the royal forest were bound to appoint sworn woodwards to keep vert and venison in them. The owners of the woods were bound to present their woodwards to the Justice of the Forest on their appointment, and at every subsequent Forest Eyre, to take an oath to perform their duties faithfully.[55] If the Justice of the Forest discovered that a wood was without a woodward, or that a woodward had not taken the oath or had not appeared at the Forest Eyre to be sworn, or neglected his duty, or committed trespasses in the forest, the wood in question was seized for the king,[56] but the owner was usually allowed to recover it on payment of a fine.[57]

The woods kept by the woodwards were as a general rule also subject to the authority of the king's foresters; if the latter discovered a Forest offence there which had not been reported by the woodward, the wood was seized and the woodward attached to answer for his default.[58] But some forest landowners were able from time to time to obtain from the Crown a grant of partial exemption from this supervision. A royal charter granted in 1257 to Roger de Merlay for his lifetime, that his own woodwards should have exclusive custody of the vert in his woods, provided however that the king's foresters should still have custody of the venison there, and that de Morlay's woodwards should be answerable to the Justice of the Forest, or at the Forest Eyre for any waste of those woods.[59]

Only sworn foresters of the king were allowed to carry bows and arrows in the forest: woodwards, according to a fourteenth-century judgement of the Court of King's Bench, 'ought . . . to carry an axe . . . in order to make presentments regarding the vert and the venison'.[60] Roger de Merlay, however, interpreted his charter to mean that his woodwards might carry bows and arrows within their bailiwicks, and in September 1259 obtained judgement in his favour on appeal to the king. The Justice of the Forest was ordered to take the oath of fealty from his woodwards,

and to permit them to carry bows and arrows for the defence of themselves and their custody, as is the custom of the King's foresters, and the foresters of others elsewhere in England.[61]

The Court of King's Bench likewise ruled in 1338 that Henry Percy's woodward might carry a bow and arrows in the woods of his manor of Seamer, by prescriptive right.[62]

NOTES

1. Close R. 1237–42, 149; Pat. R. 1216–25, 428.
2. Cal. I.P.M. II p. 489; Cal. Close R. 1288–96, 210.
3. Bazeley, *Forest of Dean*, 191.
4. E32/160/1; C47/12/2/1; *New Forest Documents*, ed. Stagg, 77, 84–85.
5. *Rot. Litt. Claus.* 1204–24, 539.
6. Cal. Pat. R. 1266–72, 15.
7. Book of Fees, I 198.
8. Cal. I.P.M. I 119.
9. Cal. Inq. Misc. I pp. 51–52.
10. Fisher, *Forest of Essex*, 140–42.
11. ibid., 140.
12. *Ex. e Rot. Fin.* I 172, 240, 289, 375 etc.
13. Cal. Fine R. 1272–1307, 376, 394, 486–87.
14. *Ex. e Rot. Fin.* I 321.
15. Book of Fees, Introduction, II 1149.
16. ibid., 1223–24.
17. ibid., 1184–85.
18. See e.g. Cal. I.P.M. II pp. 94, 489.
19. *Rot. Litt. Claus.* 1204–24, 533, 539.
20. Cal. Inq. Misc. I pp. 104–105; Turner, *Sel. Forest Pleas*, 122.
21. *Rot. Litt. Claus.* 1204–24, 442–44; Close R. 1234–37, 5, 50; Cal. Inq. Misc. I 51–52, 104.
22. Close R. 1227–31, 354; Cal. Inq. Misc. I pp. 51–52.
23. Cal. Pat. R. 1266–72, 119; Cal. I.P.M. I 149.
24. C47/11/2/14; Turner, op. cit., 123–24.
25. E32/30/33; Turner, op. cit., xxxvii n. I.
26. Close R. 1231–34, 565–66.
27. ibid., 1237–42, 26, 409; Cal. Close R. 1272–79, 386.
28. Bazeley, *Forest of Dean*, 195, 205–206.
29. Pipe R. 1199, 32; Close R. 1234–37, 414; 1237–42, 457 etc.
30. E32/29, 30; Bazeley, op. cit., 200–201.
31. Cal. Pat. R. 1292–1301, 405.
32. Cal. Lib. R. 1226–40, 69.
33. ibid., 19–20, 227.
34. E32/13, 14; Fisher, *Forest of Essex*, 137–39.
35. Assize of Woodstock 1184, art. 6 (Stubbs, *Sel. Charters*, 187); Forest Assize of Richard I 1198 (*Hoveden*. IV 64).
36. E32/12; Fisher, op. cit., 74.
37. Cal. Pat. R. 1350–54, 38.
38. E32/65; Turner, *Sel. Forest Pleas*, 109–110.

39. Statutes of the Realm, I p. III.
40. E32/68/3; Turner, op. cit., 27.
41. E32/140/4; Turner, op. cit., 52.
42. C99/101; Turner, op. cit., 125–28.
43. art. 7, (Stubbs, *Sel. Charters*, 346).
44. art. 6 (ibid., 345–46).
45. art. 14 (ibid., 347).
46. *Rot. Litt. Claus.* 1204–24, 489; Close R. 1227–31, 493 etc.
47. Cal. Close R. 1343–46, 186–87; 1346–49, 482 etc.
48. Year Book 11–12 Edw. III (Rolls Ser.) xxiv, 269–75.
49. E32/41/5d, 6d; 68/4d; 194/3d. 4; Turner, op. cit., 20–21, 25, 37, 55, 56, 58.
50. E32/41/6d; Turner, op. cit., 20.
51. E32/184–186; *Coll. Hist. Staffs.* V i 150–151.
52. Cal. Chart. R. 1300–1326, 190–191.
53. Cal. Pat. R. 1348–50, 248–49.
54. E32/12/15d., 22; Young, *Royal Forest*, 95.
55. Assize of Woodstock 1184, art. 4 (Stubbs, *Sel. Charters*, 187); E32/152/2; Turner, *Sel. Forest Pleas*, lxvii–lxviii.
56. Cal. Close R. 1279–88, 18, 270; 1288–96, 181.
57. E32/72,6d; Turner, op. cit., 38–40.
58. Statutes of the Realm I 244; E32/2/1; E32/65; Turner, op. cit., xxv, 113–4.
59. Cal. Charter R. 1226–57, 468; Close R. 1256–59, 437.
60. KB 27/315/106; Turner, op. cit., xi, xxv n. I.
61. Close R. 1256–59, 437.
62. KB 27/315/106; N. Riding Records, N.S., III 167–171.

CHAPTER 11

The Unpaid Officers of the Forest: Verderers, Regarders and Agisters

A characteristic feature of the English Forest was the appointment of knights of the locality to act as unpaid officers. Henry II decreed by the Assize of Woodstock that in every Forest county four knights should be appointed as agisters to agist his woods, and twelve knights 'to keep his vert and venison'.[1] The latter were the forerunners of the verderers and the regarders. By the thirteenth century these officers were elected in the county court from among the knights who resided in the neighbourhood of the forest and held land within it; they took an oath in the county court or in the attachment court faithfully to perform the duties of their office.[2] Since they were chosen by the landowners of the county, the latter were held responsible for their conduct in office. At the Staffordshire Forest Eyre in 1286 John of Pendeford, a verderer of Cannock Forest, was convicted of a trespass against the venison. He had, however, sold all his possessions and left the county. The Court ruled that:

> as the said John was elected verderer by the knights and others of the county

of Stafford, in full county court, faithfully to serve the King in his office of
verderer, therefore judgment shall be pronounced on them on that account.[3]

Verderers and agisters were on occasion, however, appointed
directly by the king[4] or by the Justice of the Forest;[5] at other times
the warden of the forest was ordered to see that vacancies were
filled.[6]

During the thirteenth and fourteenth centuries the verderers,
regarders and agisters usually held office for life, provided that they
discharged their duties faithfully and well,[7] but in the fifteenth
century the authority of the verderer, like that of the coroner, was
brought to an end by the death of the king, and the sheriffs were
ordered to hold new elections.[8] Verderers might also be removed
from office on a report by the Justice of the Forest to the Chancery
that they were incapacitated by old age or sickness, or occupied with
other duties, or were insufficiently qualified in that they held no
land within the forest and did not dwell there, or had committed or
connived at trespasses of vert or venison, or had become a paid officer
of the forest,[9] or, in one case, had 'entered the priestly order'.[10] It
was considered too onerous for a man to serve both as coroner and
verderer, and verderers were often excused from serving in the
former office.[11]

The verderers, regarders and agisters were of course unpaid, and
there were no perquisites attached to their offices, apart from one
or two special privileges. These offices involved exacting duties in
the enforcement of a system which was considered hateful and
oppressive by the forest inhabitants; default in any particular
resulted in heavy amercement at the Forest Eyre. Therefore all
landowners who were able to secured, by influence or by purchase,
a royal grant of exemption from such appointments. In June
1252, for example, Henry III granted to Alexander de Montfort
exemption from

being put on assizes, juries or recognitions, and from being made sheriff,
justice of gaol delivery, Steward of the Forest, forester, vendor of the King's
wood, escheator, coroner, verderer, regarder, agister, or one of the knights
to elect the grand assize.[12]

126

1
The Verderers

Verderers are mentioned by that name at least as early as Richard I's Forest Assize of 1198. [13] Numbers in the thirteenth century varied: there were eighteen in the extensive forest of Essex, [14] and only two in the small forest in Rutland. [15] They shared with the foresters a general responsibility for the safe keeping of vert and venison, the sheriff could seize their lands if they failed in their duty. [16] They supervised and assisted the foresters in finding, arresting, questioning and attaching Forest offenders, and in holding the attachment courts and the special inquests upon beasts of the forest. They kept under their seals the rolls of presentments of Forest offences committed within their wards, for production at the Forest Eyre. In 1287 William de Vescy, Justice of the Forest north of Trent, ruled at the Nottingham Forest Eyre that:

> All verderers are in future to make answer before the justices in eyre by a single roll of the vert and venison, and are not to have, each one for himself, rolls of the different bailiwicks for production before the Justices. [17]

If the verderers (or their heirs, if the verderers had died in the mean time) [18] failed to present their rolls to the judges on the first day of the Forest Eyre, or if their rolls were deficient in any material particular, they were liable to amercement. At the Huntingdonshire Forest Eyre of 1255 the foresters and verderers presented a clerk and his page for a trespass against the venison. The judgment of the court was that

> because the verderers . . . and . . . the Steward of the Forest made no mention in their rolls of the name of the said page, nor of his delivery, nor of his escape, and the business of the King so far as it relates to the said boy is entirely undone, therefore they are in mercy.

But the verderers were finally acquitted,

> because the verderers ought not and are not able to enroll anything in their rolls except a presentment of the foresters, and the foresters presented nothing of the matters aforesaid. [19]

The verderers were closely examined at the Forest Eyre as to the facts to which they deposed in their rolls of presentments, and even minor contradictions in their evidence might result in their committal to prison and subsequent amercement. At the Northampton Forest Eyre of 1255 John Lovet, a verderer, had to pay the substantial fine of twelve marks 'for mendacity and conceal-ment': he had contradicted his roll by saying that the deer which had been taken in the forest by the men of the parson of Eaton Maudit 'was a certain sheep'.[20] At the Gloucester Forest Eyre of 1282 two of the verderers were convicted of falsifying their rolls of presentments 'in that they took out the names of the living, and put in the names of the dead'.[21]

The verderers also co-operated with the foresters in supervising the exercise of customary rights within the forest, such as taking wood for fuel, fencing and house-repair;[22] in making arrangements at the swanimote for the agistment of the king's demesne woods; and in carrying out various inquiries in the forest into such matters as the rights of the Crown and the perquisites of the Forest officers.[23] The verderers were intended to act as a check upon the paid Forest officers in the interests of the Crown, but the numerous instances already cited of peculation and extortion on the part of the latter seem to indicate that the verderers were in many instances overawed by the authority and influence of the wardens and foresters of fee. From the evidence of the Forest rolls, however, they seem to have discharged their duties with reasonable efficiency as far as ordinary poachers were concerned.

2
The Regarders

The principal duty of the knights elected as regarders was of course the making of the triennial regard. In addition they were bound, according to the Ordinance of the Forest of 1306, to attend the attachment courts, along with the foresters, verderers and agisters, to make presentments of Forest offences.[24] They were also employed in making various inquiries in the forest. In 1292, for example, the king ordered an inquiry to be made in the forest of Essex by the foresters, verderers and regarders of the three regards of Colchester, Ongar and Chelmsford, together with a jury of thirty-six knights and others, into a complaint by the Abbess of Barking that the foresters had interfered in her woods, which she claimed to be exempt from the regard and from the jurisdiction of the king's Forest officers.[25]

The regarders, like the verderers, were frequently amerced at Forest Eyres for failure to carry out their duties to the satisfaction of the judges – for failing to appear with the other regarders to make the regard, or to take the regarders' oath, or to present their rolls of the regard on the first day of the Forest Eyre, or for losing their rolls, or for incompleteness in their returns.[26] In such cases the sheriff might be ordered to seize the chattels of defaulting regarders.[27]

3

The Agisters

The agisters were responsible for the agistment of the king's demesne woods in the forest. In the reign of Henry III they accounted for the agistment dues at the Exchequer,[28] but made substantial payments into the Wardrobe from time to time,[29] and paid out sums locally for such purposes as the maintenance of a neighbouring royal castle, building operations, the enclosure of a royal park, and the expenses incurred by the Forest officers in taking venison for the king.[30] In all such cases the agisters received a writ of Allocate for the purposes of their account at the Exchequer.

NOTES

1. art. 7 (Stubbs, *Sel. Charters*, 187); and see E32/38/2.
2. Close R. 1231–34, 31, 50, 145, 456; Cal. Close R. 1279–88, 442, 455.
3. E32/188/4d; *Coll. Hist. Staffs.* V i 162.
4. *Rot. Litt. Clause.* 1204–24, 603; Close R. 1234–37, 143.
5. Ordinance of the Forest 1306 (Statutes of the Realm I 147–49).
6. Close R. 1231–34, 33; 1247–51, 313, 473.
7. Ordinance of the Forest 1306 (Statutes of the Realm, loc. cit.)
8. Cal. Close R. 1422–29, 1, 13, 35, 38 etc.
9. Close R. 1234–37, 410–11; Cal. Close R. 1279–88, 47; 1288–96, 184; 1330–33, 256.
10. ibid., 1354–60, 34.
11. ibid., 1307–13, 108; 1313–18, 259 etc.
12. Cal. Pat. R. 1247–58, 198.
13. *Hoveden.* IV 63.
14. Fisher, *Forest of Essex*, 130.
15. Turner, *Sel. Forest Pleas*, xx.
16. Close R. 1227–31, 188.
17. E32/127/10d; Turner, op. cit., 62–63.
18. E32/41/4d; Turner, op. cit., 26.
19. E32/41/5; Turner, op. cit., 22.
20. E32/68/4; Turner, op. cit., lxiv, 35.
21. E32/30; Bazeley, *Forest of Dean*, 211.
22. Forest Assize 1198 (Hoveden IV 63).
23. Cal. Pat. R. 1247–58, 524–25; E32/132/9d; Turner, op. cit., 66.
24. Statutes of the Realm I 147–49.
25. Fisher, *Forest of Essex*, 155.
26. Pipe R. 1199, 33; E32/41/5; 187; 188/14; *Coll. Hist. Staffs.* V i 137, 139, 169; Turner, op. cit., 25.
27. Close R. 1234–37, 113.
28. Close R. 1251–53, 56.
29. ibid., 43, 46, 49 etc.
30. ibid., 1251–53, 47; 1261–64, 266, 320; Cal. Lib. R. 1240–45, 277, 281.

SECTION THREE

Disafforestment and Decline

CHAPTER 12

The Struggle for Disafforestment in the Thirteenth and Fourteenth Centuries

1
Causes of Popular Hatred of the Forest System

The Forest law was universally hated because of the penalties and restrictions it imposed on all classes of the king's subjects. Land-owners within the forest regarded the restraints imposed upon them as an arbitrary intrusion upon the rights of property which was contrary to natural law and justice. They resented the Forest law which forbade them to hunt over their own lands and woods on pain of heavy penalties. Some landowners were from time to time able to obtain, by favour or by purchase, a royal grant of the right to hunt the lesser beasts of the forest, such as fox, wild cat and hare,[1] but rarely the deer; the general prohibition remained. Reference has already been made to the heavy penalties imposed for waste, assart and purpresture, and in respect of agistment, escapes and the lawing of dogs. Forest landowners could not even erect fences or hedges unless they were low enough to allow the deer to enter and leave, consequently crops were often destroyed by them.[2] In 1365 Edward III granted John of Appleby an annuity of 20 marks for good service 'and in recompense, of the loss which he sustains year by year by the King's deer in respect of his land in Bernwood Forest, then lying uncultivated on account of the said deer'.[3]

Lesser folk were aggrieved by the foresters' interference with their rights of common in the Forest; the Forest officers for their part reported that privileges they claimed had no warrant. Consequently inquiries were frequently ordered by the Crown. In 1251 the Chief Justice of the Forest was ordered to make inquiry by sworn juries into common rights in a number of royal forests, including those in Shropshire, Pickering and Galtres in Yorkshire, and Rockingham in Northamptonshire.[4] The returns show that the men of the royal manors in the forest generally had common of pasture in the king's demesne woods for all their animals, except goats, throughout the year. In the forest of Galtres, however, they had no such right for their sheep within the covert. Pigs were excluded in all forests during the fence month. They usually had in addition the right to gather firewood which could be collected without the use of an edged instrument, and in some cases the right to take housebote and haybote under the supervision of the foresters and verderers. The men of the royal manors of Claverley and Warfield, for example, had from Morfe Forest in Shropshire one oak a year for each virgate of land they held.[5] These privileges were enjoyed by the king's grace, and not of right;[6] various payments in money, produce or labour service were made for them. The free and unfree tenants of the royal manors of Geddington and Barford, for example, did three plough-ings each year for the king or the king's bailiff who farmed the manor of Geddington. Each tenant had to mow three days in autumn, and gather nuts for one day; each gave a hen at Christmas and ten or twelve eggs at Easter to the warden of the forests between Oxford and Stamford Bridges, to make up his farm.[7] These common rights were enjoyed only by those who dwelt and held land within the forest bounds.[8] But constant complaints were made by the forest inhabitants that the Forest officers did not allow them to exercise these common rights unless they paid illegal and extortionate dues.

The Forest courts themselves were a cause of general complaint. Attendance at attachment courts and the Forest Eyre, the unpaid duties imposed upon verderers, regarders and agisters, the multifarious penalties inflicted on those who broke the Forest law, all constituted a heavy burden upon the forest inhabitants, especially when the Crown exploited the Forest system as a significant source of revenue, largely through fines and amercements. The Forest law moreover clashed with other legal systems. The monastic chroniclers especially recorded with high indignation the resolute enforcement of the Forest jurisdiction over clerical offenders.

Little wonder then that the Forest system was heartily detested by all classes of the king's subjects, and that from the twelfth century onward a bitter and determined struggle was carried on between Crown and people for its abolition.

2
Disafforestments Before the Great Charter of 1215

The royal forests of England had almost certainly reached their widest extent by the end of the reign of Henry II. Thomas fitzBernard as Chief Justice of the Forest heard Forest pleas in twenty-nine counties between 1178 and 1180, and his successor Geoffrey fitzPeter did the same between 1184 and 1185.[9] Henry II's successors, however, sought to raise money for their pressing needs by granting the disafforestment of large areas in return for substantial fines. Richard I in 1190 needed funds for his forthcoming crusade. Consequently the knights of Surrey obtained, for a fine of 200 marks, the disafforestment of all their county from the river Wey eastward to the Kent boundary, and from the Guildford road southward 'as far as Surrey extends';[10] thus only the north-western corner of the county remained within the royal forest of Windsor. At about the same time the barons of Bedfordshire paid £200 'for the disafforestment of that part of Bedfordshire which Henry I first afforested'[11] – a definition which was to be the subject of future contention. And £100 was paid for a like concession for the wapentake of Anstey in Yorkshire.[12]

His successor King John sold charters to a number of his barons which freed named woods and manors from the Forest law. In 1200, for example, Hubert fitzRalph paid 30 marks in respect of his manor and wood of Crich, and William fitzWakelin 60 marks for his manor of Stainsby, all in Derbyshire;[13] in 1205 William of Eynesford obtained a similar charter for his manor of Stockton,[14] and in 1209 Henry Biset owed the king £100 for the disafforestment of his wood of Borley and manor of Kidderminster, according to the metes and bounds declared under the eye of the Chief Justice of the Forest and the knights of the county of Worcestershire.[15]

But the financial burden of the war with France compelled John to make much more sweeping concessions. In March 1204 the men of Cornwall agreed to pay a fine of 2,000 marks and 20 palfreys worth 10 marks each for the disafforestment of the whole of the county, with the exception of two moors and two woods, and for having a sheriff chosen from their own nominees.[16] During the same month the men of Essex agreed to pay 500 marks and five palfreys for the disafforestment of Essex north of the 'Stanestreet'.[17] Other royal charters freed from the Forest law Ryedale Forest in North Yorkshire, Brewood Forest in Shropshire, the New Forest in Staffordshire, and Wyresdale Forest in Lancashire.[18] In May the men of Devon agreed to pay the enormous fine of 5,000 marks for the disafforestment of their county outside the bounds of Dartmoor and Exmoor Forests,[19] and the men of 'Hertfordlythe' (Hartforth) in North Yorkshire owed 100 marks and two palfreys for a similar charter in respect of their forest.[20] Such was John's desperate need of money that substantial sums were ordered to be paid by the 'collectors of the fine' directly to the king's servants and into the king's Chamber.[21]

In 1207 the 'barons, knights, free tenants and all the men of the rape of Hastings' agreed to pay 60 marks and one palfrey for a grant 'that they and their heirs should be quit in perpetuity of suits, summonses and pleas of the forest'.[22] At the end of the reign John's desperate situation produced a further crop of charters of disafforestment in 1215 – for the remainder of Cornwall in return for a fine of 1,200 marks and four palfreys paid by the men of that county; for Nassaburgh hundred in Northamptonshire, for which the Abbot of Peterborough paid 1,220 marks; and for the Abbot of Abbey Dore's lands in Treville Forest, for which the abbot paid 600 marks and ten palfreys.[23]

The charters defined the rights to be enjoyed by the inhabitants of the disafforested areas. The men of Devon were in 1204 granted the right to 'assart, impark, take all kinds of venison, have dogs, bows and arrows and all kinds of weapons, and to make deerleaps', except on the outskirts of the forests of Dartmoor and Exmoor, where neither deerleaps nor enclosures might be made. They were to be punishable under the Forest laws, however, if their dogs coursed in the royal forest. Only the barons, knights and free tenants were to enjoy these rights.[24] In Cornwall, only those who had contributed to the fine made in 1204 were to be allowed to hunt and take the deer within the disafforested districts. If anyone else did so, his horses and dogs were to be forfeited to the contributaries, and he was to pay an amercement to the king.[25] Such a condition was obviously inserted to encourage Cornishmen to make their contributions to the royal coffers, but its enforcement against individual landowners would appear to have been impracticable once disafforestment had taken place.

3

Concessions in the Great Charter 1215 and the Charter of the Forest 1217. The Forest Perambulations of 1218 and 1219. The Re-issue of the Charter of the Forest and the Perambulations of 1225

When opposition to John's misrule came to a head in 1215, the forest figured prominently among the grievances which the barons presented to him.[26] He sought refuge in vague and ambiguous promises. In the Great Charter he undertook to put out of the forest 'at once' the districts which he himself had afforested, and the rivers he had placed 'in defence'. But he only promised to 'do justice' regarding the forests created by Henry II and Richard I. An inquiry was to be made in every county by an elected jury of twelve knights into 'evil customs' of forests, warrens and rivers, and these customs were to be abolished within forty days, provided that the king, or, in his absence, the Justiciar, were first informed.[27] A 'revolutionary committee' of barons seemed about to take control of the central government:[28] the forest would have had short shrift from them. In desperation the king and his advisers persuaded the Archbishops of Canterbury and Dublin and six other bishops to subscribe to a declaration that the article of the Great Charter regarding 'evil customs' was not to be construed as abolishing any customary laws essential to the continued existence of the forest.[29] The outbreak of civil war and the death of King John saved it: when the Great Charter was re-issued on 12 November 1216, after the accession of the infant Henry III, article 48 regarding 'evil customs' was one of the 'difficult and doubtful' clauses which were omitted and postponed for further consideration.[30]

Some concessions were, however, inevitable, and on 6 November 1217 the Earl Marshal issued the Charter of the Forest in the king's name. No one was henceforth to suffer death or mutilation for taking the king's deer: the penalties were to be limited to amercement, imprisonment or exile. A royal pardon was granted to all men outlawed for such offences before the king's coronation in 1216, and also for all assarts, purprestures and waste in the forests before then. All lands afforested by Henry II or his sons were to be disafforested. Owners of lands in the forests were henceforth to be allowed to bring them into cultivation and to make mills, fishponds and other constructions outside the covert, to agist their pigs in their woods at their pleasure, and to have all the eyries and honey in them. Forest dwellers were not to be compelled to attend the swanimotes, nor those who lived outside the forest to attend the Forest Eyre, unless they were accused of an offence, or were sureties for someone else. The number of foresters was to be limited under the supervision of the regarders: no warden or local Forest officer was to hold pleas of the forest, which were reserved for the Forest Eyre. The dues exacted for unlawed dogs and for cheminage were defined and limited, and the foresters were forbidden henceforth to make scotale or to exact contributions from the forest inhabitants. Bishops and barons were to have the right to take one or two deer when passing through the royal forest.[31]

In pursuance of the Forest Charter, the Council of Regency on 24 July 1218 ordered twelve law-worthy knights to be chosen in each Forest county by the sheriff and four worthy knights. They were to make perambulations, distinguishing between those districts which ought to remain in the forest, and those which ought to be put out. The sheriff was then to send the record to the king.[32] But in some counties the forest dwellers had not waited for these instructions. On 3 July the men of Huntingdonshire had made a perambulation in their county, which had until then been entirely forest, a perambulation which was declared to be 'in accordance with the Charter of the Forest'. The perambulators swore that Henry II had afforested the whole of Huntingdonshire, with the exception of the demesne hays of Weybridge, Sapley and Harthay; the county ought therefore to be disafforested, except those hays and the king's demesne woods of Brampton and Alconbury.[33] In Rutland the jurors swore on 25 July that a great part of the county had been afforested by Henry II,[34] though there is evidence that this had been done by Henry I.[35] Subsequent returns for Leicestershire, Nottinghamshire and Somerset also demanded extensive disafforestments.[36] The regents were not prepared to accept such returns. In January 1219 the sheriff of Huntingdon was ordered to see that the Forest was kept as it was in the time of King John: the perambulating jury was summoned before the Council, amerced and imprisoned.[37] On 20 July another perambulation of the Huntingdonshire Forest was ordered to be made.[38] But the men of the county stood firm: their perambulation, made ten days later, exactly repeated the assertions made the year before.[39]

The perambulations of the other forests were as little to the liking of the regents, and in December 1219 they ordered fresh perambulations to be made in all the forest counties. All districts afforested by Henry II and John were to be disafforested after examination of the returns by the Justiciar and the Council of Regency.[40] Perambulations which appear to have been made pursuant to these instructions are extant for the counties of

Buckingham, Cumberland, Huntingdon, Oxford, Shropshire, Yorkshire and Wiltshire. Once more they claimed the disafforestment of extensive areas.[41] The regents were still unwilling to accept verdicts of such dubious historicity.[42] In some instances they temporised: in May 1221 they conceded that 'the knights and free tenants of the forest of Berkshire' should elect 'two law-worthy and discreet knights' of their number to keep the forest, under the Chief Justice of the Forest, until Henry III came of age, when a final decision would be made about disafforestment. In the mean time, the Forest administration was to be carried on as usual.[43] But on 30 October the regents once more affirmed the rights of the Crown: they ordered Hugh de Neville, the Chief Justice of the Forest, to cause the royal forests to be kept by the same metes and bounds as they had been in the time of King John before the war between him and his barons.[44]

The perambulating juries contended that only the 'ancient demesne' of the Crown should remain subject to the Forest law. They relied on oral tradition, a doubtful guide concerning such a hated institution as the forest. Moreover, they undoubtedly claimed the disafforestment of districts which had been put out of the forest during the reign of Stephen, and subsequently reclaimed by Henry II. But the Angevin kings regarded Stephen as a usurper: they considered that such districts were not covered by the disafforestment clauses.

Further gestures of conciliation, however, had to be made in 1224. Louis VIII of France overran Poitou and attacked Gascony, and money was needed to finance Richard of Cornwall's campaigns to recover and defend these possessions of the English Crown. On 1 February of the following year, therefore, the Great Council granted the king an aid of a fifteenth of all moveables, and in return the Charter of the Forest was re-issued. Five days later Hugh de Neville, and eight other commissioners were appointed to supervise the making of yet another series of perambulations. They were to be made in each Forest county by an elected jury of twelve knights, two or more knights nominated by the Crown, and the foresters of fee and verderers. But no woods were to be felled or venison taken in the districts claimed to be disafforested until the perambulations had been notified to the Council, which would decide what was to be done.[45]

The resulting verdicts amounted, once again, to a demand for the abolition of the Forest jurisdiction outside the king's demesnes. On 3 April 1225 the Huntingdonshire jurors exactly repeated the earlier perambulations of 1218 and 1219.[46] In Surrey, Staffordshire, Sussex, Leicestershire, Rutland, Nottinghamshire, Lancashire and Dorset the jurors declared that all the forests there had been established since the accession of Henry II, and that only those lands and woods held by him in demesne – the 'ancient demesnes of the Crown' – could, according to the Charter of the Forest, remain in the Forest.[47] In Wiltshire even one of these, Boreham Wood in Savernake, was put out.[48] In Essex there were to remain in the Forest only the half hundred of Waltham and parts of the hundreds of Ongar and Becontree, said to have been afforested before 1154, and the royal demesnes of Havering, Hatfield, Chelmsford and Kingswood near Colchester.[49] Such verdicts caused controversy and bitter illwill between the people and the Forest officers. In 1226 Roger Gernet, hereditary warden of the royal forest of Lancaster, and one of his foresters were accused of causing the death of Hugh of Wyresdale. The accusation was declared to have been made by Hugh's widow and family 'from ill will and hatred, because Roger was reproached concerning the perambulation of the forest in those parts not properly performed'.[50]

The regents were nevertheless compelled to accept these verdicts for the time being. In August 1225 they ordered the disafforestment of the whole of the forest of Rutland, with the exception of the royal demesne woods of Oakham and Ridlington,[51] and confirmed the perambulations in Surrey, Staffordshire and Sussex.[52] Private chases created by tenants-in-chief since 1154 outside their own demesnes were likewise abrogated, in accordance with the provisions of the Forest Charter.[53]

Roger of Wendover says that the inhabitants of the disafforested districts made full use of their newly acquired liberties, by cutting and selling timber from their woods, making assarts and bringing suitable waste land into cultivation, and hunting the deer. 'The very dogs', he says, 'who had formerly been used to have their paws cut, rejoiced in their freedom'.[54] But the king's advisers were merely temporizing. In May 1225 they had written to Hugh de Neville:

> You have signified to us . . . that the perambulators of the forest in the county of Dorset . . . wish to disafforest the whole of that county, except the wood of Hartley, the 'broil' (or wood) of Watmoor, and the park of Gillingham, to our loss and injury . . . You are strictly to forbid them to deprive us of anything which ought of right to belong to us. But if they nevertheless persist in making that perambulation in the manner aforesaid, we must endure it for the present, and await an opportune time to amend it.[55]

The king's advisers decided in 1226 that the opportunity had arrived. On 26 October they ordered the sheriffs of Shropshire, Hampshire, Yorkshire and Huntingdonshire to make public proclamations forbidding anyone to make waste, sales or gifts of wood, assarts or purprestures in their woods within the royal forest by reason of the perambulations, until further orders.[56]

4

The Revision of the Perambulations by Henry III. The Exploitation of the Forest by Household Officials During Henry III's Personal Rule: 1227–59

On 9 January 1227 Henry III declared himself to be of full age, and immediately began measures to reclaim the Forest rights of his crown. Beginning on the very next day, orders were sent to the sheriffs of Shropshire, Rutland, Nottingham, Leicester, Hampshire, Berkshire, Oxford, Huntingdon, Surrey and Warwick.[57] The foresters of fee were to be summoned to appear before the king to show by what warrant they held their bailiwicks: likewise everyone who had assumed any liberty in the forest since 1217, to produce his authority. The jurors who had made the perambulations in 1225 were summoned to explain why they had put out of the forest districts which had been forest before 1154, and also royal demesnes. Lands disafforested during the reign of the usurper Stephen and

142

subsequently reclaimed by Henry II were not within the terms of the Charter of the Forest.

The jurors, having appeared before the king, were induced, probably by threats of amercement and imprisonment, to acknowledge their error and to modify their perambulations; they then received the king's pardon.[58] The Gloucestershire jury, for example, in 1228 re-defined the boundaries of the Forest of Dean at their widest extent – that is to say, the rivers Severn and Wye, and a northern boundary running from Goodrich castle in the west through Ross and Newent to Gloucester castle in the east. They swore that the forest had existed by these bounds from ancient times.[59] In nine counties the forests were ordered to be kept by the same bounds as before the war between King John and his barons; on 27 October 1228 the juries who had made the perambulations of the Yorkshire forests of Galtres and Farndale, and the forest between Ouse and Derwent, obediently amended their verdicts.[60] In the counties of Nottingham, Hampshire, Essex, Northampton, Somerset and Wiltshire large areas were likewise reclaimed into the forest.[61] Boreham Wood in Savernake was reclaimed as a royal demesne wood by the warden, Geoffrey Esturmy,[62] and there were similar reversals in the Dorset forests of Gillingham and Bere.[63]

The revised perambulations did, however, make extensive concessions in Derbyshire, Northamptonshire and Wiltshire; the hundred of Tendring in Essex was disafforested,[64] as was the whole of Sussex with the exception of two demesne woods – the 'broils of Chichester' and 'Falconer's Wood'.[65] The men of Leicestershire gave the king £100 to have yet another perambulation: he finally conceded in 1235 that that county should be put out of the forest with the exception of the manor of Withcote, which was ancient demesne of the Crown.[66] To ensure freedom from the Forest law the inhabitants of the districts disafforested in Nottinghamshire paid 20 marks in 1228 for exemption from suit at the Forest courts.[67]

During the period of his personal government, however, Henry III was compelled by shortage of money to follow the practice of Richard I and John of selling charters of disafforestment. In May 1227 he granted such a charter for the greater part of Berkshire,[68] and in June 1228 for most of the forest in Gloucestershire east of the

Severn;[69] in October 1229 for Ombersley and Horewell in Worcestershire;[70] and in April 1230 for Kesteven in Lincolnshire.[71] On 16 July 1232 the king confirmed a perambulation which substantially reduced the extent of Sherwood Forest,[72] and in July 1234 he disafforested the forest 'between Ouse and Derwent', with the exception of the hay of Langwith.[73] In November 1251 Henry III granted to the men of Archenfield in Herefordshire freedom from the Forest jurisdiction, and in the next year he ordered the sheriff:

> to distrain by their lands and chattels all those who shared in that liberty, and have lands within the bounds of the disafforested districts, to contribute towards the payment of the 200 marks to the King, in proportion to the lands they had in the said district, and the advantage they gained from the disafforestment.[74]

The extent of the royal forests was also diminished by Henry III's grants to members of his family. In 1239 he gave the Forest of Dartmoor to his brother Richard, Earl of Cornwall, and his heirs,[75] and in 1267 Amounderness and Lonsdale Forests in Lancashire and Pickering Forest in Yorkshire to his second son Edmund, Earl of Lancaster and his heirs.[76] Edmund later received from Edward I the right to appoint Forest justices of his own whenever the King's judges went on eyre in the royal forests, and to receive the fines and amercements therefrom.[77] On the accession of Henry IV, these Lancastrian forests of course came once again into the hands of the Crown.[78]

Henry III was also 'lavish in grants of liberties scarcely to be distinguished from complete disafforestments',[79] such as the grant of right of chase in all his lands, within and without the forest, to the Bishop of Winchester.[80] Other districts were illegally withdrawn from the Forest jurisdiction by magnates to make their private chases – such as the Earl Marshal's chase near Chepstow, carved out of the Forest of Dean early in Henry III's reign;[81] the Bishop of Coventry and Lichfield's chase of Cannock;[82] and the Bishop of Ely's chase of Somersham. The king's foresters and verderers complained at the Huntingdon Forest Eyre in 1286 that they had gone to Benwick to make an inquest of the venison. The Bishop of Ely claimed Benwick as part of his chase: they had been met by the bishop's bailiff, leading three priests in full vestments, with Bible, cross and candle, 'so that they could make no inquest there that day'.[83]

Despite all these inroads into the royal forest, the hated system was enforced after 1227 over a large part of England. Henry III's interpretation of the Charter of the Forest was rejected by his subjects, who thought him guilty of a flagrant breach of the promises made by the Charter. The chronicler Roger of Wendover wrote that at the Council of Oxford in 1227, 'the King caused to be cancelled and annulled all the charters of liberties of the forest, although they had already been in force in the whole realm for two years': the earls who rebelled in July were said to have compelled the king to restore the charters by the threat of armed force.[84]

It was the policy of Henry III, moreover, to dislodge ecclesiastical and lay magnates from the great offices of state, and to replace them by Household officials who would make the central administration a more pliant instrument of his will. Poitevin favourites were appointed to key positions;[85] the Household clerk, Peter des Rivaux, was in 1232 appointed for life to be Chief Justice of the Forests of England, and also warden of the Forests of Clarendon, Gillingham and Dean.[86] Even after the fall of the hated Poitevins in 1234, 'Henry III in no wise gave up the policy of making his household the centre of the administration of the State'.[87] Foreign dependants of the Court continued to be appointed to important Forest wardenships – such as Amaury de St Amand, Steward of the Household 1233–40, who was also warden of the Forest of Dean during the greater part of that time,[88] and Peter Chaceporc, the able Poitevin Keeper of the Wardrobe 1241–54, who was appointed to the same wardenship in May 1248.[89]

But it was an English Household clerk who in 1244 persuaded his royal master that his financial difficulties would be solved by making rigorous inquiries into encroachments on the Forest rights of the Crown, and imposing heavy amercements on those who made them.[90] Robert Passelewe was a Household clerk who after 1228 had been attached to the Poitevin party, shared in their downfall in 1234, and was restored to favour in 1236;[91] his appointment in 1246 as Justice of the Forests south of Trent[92] therefore brings the administrative history of the forest into line with that of the Household and the great Departments of State. The employment of clerks in the Forest administration was anathema to the leaders of the English clergy: they successfully opposed Passelewe's preferment beyond the archdeaconry of Lewes. In April 1244 he was elected Bishop of Chichester on the king's nomination, but Boniface of Savoy, the Archbishop of Canterbury, rejected him as ignorant, and declared his election void; his rejection was confirmed by Innocent IV.[93] When he was presented to the church of Northampton, Robert Grosseteste, the saintly Bishop of Lincoln, refused to admit him. The bishop declared that for a clerk in holy orders to sit as a justice in eyre for forest pleas was contrary to the canons of the Church, and rendered him ineligible for an office involving the cure of souls. What particularly incensed the good bishop was that Passelewe as a Forest judge had ordered the arrest and imprisonment of clerks as well as laymen, and had thus flouted clerical privileges.[94]

Passelewe's unpopularity was due in large measure to his energy and zeal in the royal service. Between December 1244 and December 1249 he and his colleagues heard pleas of the Forest in thirteen counties south of Trent.[95] Concurrently two commissions were sent out to conduct a searching investigation into the condition of the southern forests; the articles of their inquiry[96] followed the usual pattern of those of the Forest Eyre. Passelewe seems to have used these inquiries as proceedings preliminary to the Forest Eyre itself, as when he sat at Gloucester in January 1248.[97] He pursued his task of raising money for the king with vigour and severity. The chroniclers as usual were hostile. Matthew Paris says that he convicted innumerable monks and laymen, nobles and commoners, on a multitude of indictments for breaches of the Forest law, and, in order to enrich the king, imposed such heavy penalties on the offenders that many were flung into prison, many were despoiled of all their goods and were forced to eke out a bare existence in misery, and many others became exiles and wandering beggars.[98] Many forest landowners were in fact heavily amerced by Passelewe: in 1264 the Abbot of Bruern paid 500 marks for acquittance of all the trespasses of which he had been convicted at the Oxford Forest Eyre in 1245.[99] Passelewe rigorously investigated encroachments on the Forest rights of the Crown. Jurors were required to restate the Forest bounds, for example in the counties of Dorset and Huntingdon,[100] under the baleful eyes of this new team of royal servants. Woods belonging to subjects which had been unlawfully withdrawn from the forest – such as the Abbess of Romsey's woods of Ashton Steeple and Edington in Wiltshire,[101] and a wood belonging to Stratford Mortimer in Berkshire[102] – were once again reclaimed into it. Men of the king's demesnes, as in Rodley in the Forest of Dean, were required to show by what warrant they exercised their rights of common and estovers of dead and dry wood in the forest, and if they could produce none they were required to pay for them.[103]

Many Forest officers fared ill at Passelewe's hands. John de Neville, an important English baron and a former Chief Justice of the Forest, who held for life the wardenship of the forests between Oxford and Stamford bridges,[104] was convicted of grave offences, amerced in the enormous sum of 2,000 marks, and deprived of his wardenship, which Passelewe in 1246 secured for himself.[105] Neville only escaped utter ruin by the intercession of his peers with the king. Yet, says Matthew Paris with relish, he did not deserve to be rescued in this way, for he had shown no mercy to others when he himself had been an officer of the Forest.[106]

Many others forfeited their bailiwicks for breaches of the Forest law: they included John of Monmouth, who lost the custody of the New Forest,[107] Richard de Munfichet, the forest of Essex,[108] and the wardens of the forests of Aliceholt and Woolmer, Wychwood and Braydon.[109] The wardens of the forests of Chute, Porchester and Dean were mulcted in large sums at Passelewe's Forest Eyres.[110] Many foresters of fee in the forests of Clarendon, Essex, Dean and New Forest were likewise removed from office or fined.[111] Hugh of Stratford, for example, forester of fee in Whittlewood Forest, was ejected from his office:

> by Robert Passelewe, Justice of the Forest . . . for the destruction of underwood in the King's demesne wood by his customary tenants, and for a little assart made by him at Brede, and a purpresture at Pollesley on which he built houses.[112]

Robert Passelewe placed a number of Household officials in charge of the forfeited wardenships. He no doubt intended to bring the local Forest administration more closely under his control: he certainly used his opportunities to promote his own relatives. William Passelewe, another King's clerk,[113] Hugh Passelewe and Simon Passelewe were among those appointed as Forest wardens at this time.[114] Under the new regime the farms paid by the wardens and foresters of fee of the New Forest, the Forest of Dean and the forests between Oxford and Stamford bridges were substantially increased.[115] William Passelewe, for example, accounted directly at the Exchequer for £224. 14s. 11½d. of the revenues of the New Forest from January 1246 until Michaelmas 1247, and by then had paid most of it in. His predecessors had farmed these revenues for less than £50 a year, and in some years failed to make any payment at all.[116] These new accounting procedures do not appear to have lasted long, however. In most cases the hereditary wardens and foresters of fee, or their heirs, were able within a few years to recover their bailiwicks by payment of substantial fines to the Crown.[117]

In 1250 Robert Passelewe was supplanted in the king's favour by Geoffrey of Langley — by sycophantic arts, according to his severe critic, Matthew Paris.[118] Langley was a Household official who had assisted Robert Passelewe in carrying out the great series of Forest Eyres and inquests south of the Trent between 1244 and 1249. In March 1250 he was appointed Chief Justice of 'all the forests of England on both sides of the Trent',[119] so that the Forest administration was once again united under a single head. Early in 1250 he went on Eyre in some of the southern Forest counties.[120] He subjected the perambulations made at the beginning of the reign to searching investigation, and re-afforested the forest of Bere in Dorset.[121] He turned his attention mainly to the northern forests, however; he examined the local juries as to the way in which they had been kept,[122] and held Forest Eyres in all the northern Forest counties.[123] Matthew Paris says that he performed his duties with cunning, shamelessness and violence, and extorted from the northern landowners an 'incredible' and 'stupefying' amount of money. His large entourage were all animated by a spirit of hostility towards the northerners: any nobleman who murmured against them was instantly thrown into gaol. Langley spared neither blood nor fortune – he would beggar a nobleman for taking a fawn or a hare wandering on the road. He 'miserably impoverished all the forest districts, without reason or pity.'[124]

The violence of the language used by the chronicler of St Albans shows his hatred of the Forest system, which was so often used to extort money from the monasteries. But Chancery and Exchequer records provide corroboration. The issues of Langley's Forest Eyres in Cumberland and Northumberland amounted to about five times as much as previous eyres had brought in.[125] Among the barons amerced were Robert de Muscamp, adjudged to pay £100 at the Northumberland sessions, Ralph de Amundeville, fined 80 marks at York, and Ralph Bigod 40 marks at Nottingham.[126] Other sources of Forest revenue were vigorously exploited. On 2 September 1251 Langley was commissioned 'to cause the king's demesne parks and hays to be agisted by the king's agisters in those parts, throughout England, wherever there is mast.' The agisters were ordered to pay the agistment dues into the Wardrobe or into the Exchequer, and the sheriffs were commanded to compel them to do so by distraint where necessary.[127] These energetic measures produced unusually large sums.[128] At the same time, the king, at Langley's suggestion, appointed four knights in each county to sell underwood belonging to the Crown, and in March 1252 the sheriffs of nine Forest counties were ordered to distrain them to carry out their duties.[129] Such vigour and severity helped to relieve the financial problems created by Henry III's improvidence, but it also increased the hostility of barons and people against the Forest system, and against the personal government of Henry III himself.

At the end of 1252, however, Geoffrey of Langley was relieved of his Forest office, and was sent to Scotland to act as counsellor to Henry III's daughter Margaret, Queen of Scotland.[130] Two Forest Justices were once more appointed, one for the forests north of the Trent, and the other for those in the south.[131] For the southern forests Henry III continued to appoint Household officials as Justices – men like Robert Walerand, who held office from 1256 until 1259,[132] and who enjoyed the confidence and even the friendship of the king. But such men neither exercised the extreme severity, nor attracted the bitter odium, of Passelewe and Langley. Henry III continued to be in desperate need of money, however, and resorted yet again to the expedient of ordering large-scale sales of forest timber. He had returned from Gascony at the end of 1254, after disastrous and expensive enterprises in France and in Sicily: in the following March commissioners were appointed for the sale of timber in the royal forests 'for the relief of the King's debts', with the assistance of two or three knights and the local Forest officers.[133] In May the warden of the Forest of Dean was ordered to pay 300 marks into the Wardrobe out of the proceeds, and in September to repay a royal debt of 200 marks to Robert Walerand.[134] In July 1256 James Fresel, a royal clerk, was sent to this forest to raise 1,000 marks, to be paid into the Wardrobe, by the same means, and as Henry III's financial difficulties increased he appointed Adam Grenville in April 1257 to raise another 3–4,000 marks by selling wood in the royal forests of England.[135]

5

Growth of Opposition to the Forest System: 1232–59; the Forest and the Baronial Plan of Reform: 1259–65

In 1232 the Waverley annalist noted that it was now eight years since the king had confirmed the Great Charter and the Charter of the Forest and the bishops had pronounced sentence of excommunication against those who violated them. He continued sadly, 'But alas! the yoke of slavery is now become more burdensome, and conditions worse than before, especially with regard to the forests.'[136] His financial difficulties, however, compelled Henry III in 1237 and yet again in 1253 to repeat his confirmation of the Charters in return for an aid from the magnates.[137] In 1238 he ordered the Charter of the Forest to be read out in full county court, and the concessions contained therein to be observed; but he was careful to add the proviso that 'if any dispute or doubt arise regarding the articles of the Charter' the Chief Justice of the Forest was to 'seek the counsel of the King and his Court before anything

The Royal Forests of England North of the Trent, at their Greatest
Extent, in the Twelfth and Thirteenth Centuries

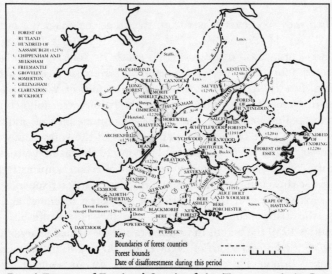

The Royal Forests of England South of the Trent, at their Greatest
Extent, in the Twelfth and Thirteenth Centuries

be done in regard thereto'.[138] The Archbishop of Canterbury and the bishops renewed the sentence of excommunication against the violators of the Charters in 1239 and in 1253;[139] in the latter year they secured its confirmation by Pope Innocent IV.[140] But Henry III had no intention of surrendering the Forest rights of the Crown: demands for reform made at the Councils of 1254, 1256 and 1257 were fobbed off by royal promises which were never carried out.[141]

Grievances relating to the forests therefore figured prominently in the 'Petitions of the Barons' brought forward at the Parliament of Oxford in June 1258. The barons complained that Henry III had arbitrarily re-afforested woods and lands which had been put out of the forest by the perambulations of 1225; that he claimed the wardship of heirs to assarts made within the forest, to the detriment of the overlords in whose lands such assarts had been made; and that he made frequent grants of the right of free warren in disafforested areas, thereby restricting the free rights of hunting which ought to have been enjoyed by landowners in such districts.[142]

When they took over power from the king, the 'magnates of the Council' on 11 September 1259 appointed Thomas Gresley, a reformer baron, as Justice of the southern forests, and later confirmed John d'Eyville, also a reformer baron, as Justice of the northern forests.[143] The articles of the Provisions of Westminster, issued in October, show however that the barons were following a cautious policy regarding the forest. Commissions of inquiry regarding the state of the forests and abuses of the Forest law were appointed,[144] but never sat, probably owing to the disintegration of the party of reform early in the next year. Certain administrative changes at this time appear designed to effect a stricter supervision by the Exchequer over the collection of the Forest revenues, and to lessen the temptation to extortion by the Forest officers. In November 1259 the barons in Council raised the annual salary of the Justice of the Forests south of Trent from 100 to 200 marks a year, and his colleague for the northern forests was in August 1260 granted an annual salary of 60 marks,[145] instead of having to pay an annual farm of the same sum as he had previously done.[146] Also, the wardens of the Forest of Dean, and of the forests between Oxford and Stamford bridges, were required to account directly at the Exchequer for the revenues of their bailiwicks, instead of farming them as had been the previous practice.[147]

During the war between Henry III and Simon de Montfort from 1263 until 1265, the central administration was of course unable to enforce the Forest law, and the forest inhabitants were able to take the deer and cut wood at their pleasure. But after the defeat and death of de Montfort at the battle of Evesham, the king on 2 September 1266 wrote to Roger Leyburn, Justice of the Forest north of Trent:

> As the Earl of Leicester is now dead, in whose keeping the King was by reason of the disturbance in the realm, and now by the favour of God the King is snatched out of his hands and raised again to his former estate, whereby with the common consent of the realm the King has caused all things attempted by the Earl for the diminution of the King's right, honour and royal dignity to be revoked; and whereas the forests north of Trent, which before the war in the time of the Earl were preserved whole and uninjured, have been disafforested and destroyed to the King's disherison, the King commands the said Roger to re-afforest all the forests in his bailiwick as they were . . . before the war; and if any part thereof ought of right to be disafforested, the King is prepared to do full justice.[148]

The Justices of the Forest were once more sent out on eyre to hear pleas of the Forest,[149], and to re-establish the Forest system in any districts which had been lost. To this end local juries in Dorset, Hampshire, Surrey and Rutland were required to make sworn statements of the forest bounds in the presence of the King's judges.[150] The policy of appointing Household officials to the highest Forest offices was however abandoned. Henceforth the Justices of the Forest were for the most part great barons, who often held extensive estates in or near the forests they administered. Such was Roger de Clifford the Elder, who presided over the southern forests 1265–81,[151] and his grandson Robert de Clifford, 'one of the greatest barons of the age',[152] who headed the northern Forest administration 1297–1308.[153]

6

The Struggle for Disafforestment Under Edward I: 1272–1307

Edward I enforced the Forest law with great energy and severity: he himself sat in judgement upon offenders against the venison. The intervals between successive Forest Eyres became longer, but fines and amercements grew in number and amount. Under the menacing eyes of Edward's Forest judges, juries in Essex, Hampshire, Gloucestershire, Derby, Staffordshire, Huntingdonshire and Northamptonshire restated the bounds of the forests in their counties at their widest extent.[154] In 1280, for example, 'the metes and bounds of the New Forest from the first time that it was afforested' were said to extend from the Test westwards to the Avon, and from the Solent northwards to the Wiltshire county boundary.[155] These bounds included extensive districts on the east, west and south-west claimed to be disafforested by the perambulations of 1217–18, 1298 and 1300.[156] When Charles I's Attorney-General sought to reclaim the long-lost Forest rights of his master's Crown, this group of returns was among the documents he triumphantly dug out of the records of the Exchequer.[157] Searching investigations were made by Edward's judges into all liberties exercised within the forest. At Gloucester in 1282, for instance, Roger Bigod's chase near Chepstow was ordered to be seized into the king's hand.[158] After the Stafford Forest Eyre of 1286 the Bishop of Coventry had to pay the enormous fine of £1,000 to recover his 'free chase' within the royal forest of Cannock.[159] Important Forest officers did not escape. In November 1286 Robert of Everingham, hereditary warden of Sherwood Forest, and ten others were released on bail from prison in Nottingham, to which they had been committed for venison offences. At the Forest Eyre in January the judges deprived Robert of his wardenship, which was henceforth to be at the disposal of the Crown.[160]

Such a policy intensified opposition to the Forest system: as early as 1277 the king was compelled to offer certain concessions. On 1 March he published his intention of inviolably observing the

Charter of the Forest in all its articles: he appointed four commissioners to supervise the making in each forest county of 'a true perambulation, namely that which was made in the time of the lord King Henry our father, which has not yet been challenged'. The perambulations were to be made by juries of twelve law-worthy men in each county, in the presence of the commissioners and the foresters and verderers. But no steps were to be taken to put them into effect until they had been communicated to the king, who, when he had satisfied himself that they had been made without prejudice, would decide what was to be done.[161]

In Essex there was no modification of the forest bounds. The jurors at the Forest Eyre, under the watchful eye of the judges, declared that the whole county south of the 'Stanestreet' should remain within the forest.[162] But in other counties desire to shake off the burden of the hated Forest law had fostered the growth of traditions which sought to justify its abolition. In Somerset a jury declared that only a corner of north-west Somerset ought to remain within Exmoor Forest:[163] another Somerset jury made the startling statement that King John had afforested all England![164] In Hampshire, Wiltshire and Dorset also the jurors demanded the disafforestment of extensive areas.[165] Edward made a few concessions. The forest of Blackmoor, the largest of the Dorset forests, was disafforested in 1279,[166] and in the next year the forest of Northumberland, in return for an annual payment of 40 marks, was apportioned among the Forest landowners.[167] But the perambulations made between 1277 and 1279 in most cases came to nothing.

'Hostility to the Forest system grew rapidly in the next twenty years.'[168] The king sailed for Flanders on 22 August 1297 to conduct the war with France. In his absence the regents made concessions to the magnates in return for grants of taxes in aid of the war with Scotland. The Charters were once again confirmed. Copies were to be sent to all sheriffs, who were to publish them to the people; others were to be kept in all cathedral churches and read twice a year. Sentence of excommunication was once again to be pronounced against those who violated them. Yet another series of perambulations was ordered to be made,[169] which once again

claimed disafforestment of large areas, such as the whole of the
Oxfordshire portion of Bernwood Forest, and part of the
Buckinghamshire portion,[170] and many vills, hamlets, woods and
heaths in the Somerset forests outside the royal demesnes.[171] But
these perambulations were nullified by the king's determination not
to surrender his Forest rights.

Upon his return to England on 14 March 1298, the battle for
disafforestment was fairly joined. The barons demanded fresh
confirmation of the Charters and a revision of the Forest boundaries
in accordance with their interpretation of their provisions: this as a
condition of their service in the Scottish campaign.[172] Edward still
prevaricated, but at the Parliament of March 1299 the magnates
extorted further concessions by the threat of armed force. New
perambulations were promised, but Edward reserved his coronation
oath, the rights of his Crown, and his right and that of all others to
challenge the perambulations.[173]

The baronial leaders were incensed by these continued tergiver-
sations: when the king's ordinance was read at St Paul's in London,
there was uproar,[174] and the terms of Edward's proclamation issued
on 25 June showed that he realized the extent and intensity of
hostility to the Forest. He was beset by difficulties; it was
impossible to carry out the perambulations during the harvest
season. He asked his people not to believe those who went about
saying that he was not going to keep his promises. This proclamation was to be read out in towns and other places without delay, in
the presence of some 'good religious' who could read and so bear
witness to its authenticity.[175] This proclamation was in fact made in
the English language in Worcester on 4 July.[176] During the
following months five judges presided over a new series of perambulations in the counties of Northampton, Huntingdon, Rutland,
Oxford and Surrey.[177] The returns followed the familiar pattern.
The Rutland jurors swore on 7 December 1299 that all the vills and
lands outside the bounds they then set out had been afforested in the
time of King John.[178] In the Surrey part of Windsor Forest the
verdict on 5 March 1300 was that 'the whole county of Surrey was
forest in the time of Henry II, who died seized of it.' Richard I had
disafforested the southern half, but they did not know whether

Henry II had afforested any district which had not been forest in the time of Henry I.[179]

At the Parliament on 6 March 1300 fresh concessions were obtained. The 'Articles concerning the Charters' ordained that they were to be observed in full, including those regarding disafforestment, and read out in every county court four times a year. The appointment in every county of three elected commissioners to hear and determine pleas relating to breaches of the Charters, however, was rendered illusory by Edward's reservations and exceptions.[180]

On 1 April 1300 six groups of justices were commissioned to conduct Forest perambulations in eighteen counties not covered by the commission of 1299. The forest bounds were to be determined by a local jury in each county, in the presence of the justices, the Justice of the Forest or his deputy, and the foresters, 'according to the tenor of the Forest Charter of Henry III, saving always the King's oath, the right of his Crown, and the actions and claims of the King and all others'.[181] Once again the declarations of the jurors reflected the wishes and interests of the forest inhabitants rather than the facts of recorded history. The Warwickshire jurors, on being asked on what authority they had returned that ten townships 'with their woods, wastes and fields' had been afforested by King John, and that in 1154 there had been no royal forest in their county, replied that they knew by what their ancestors had related and by the common talk of the country.[182] In Staffordshire the jurors said that they knew 'by the evidence of old people, and by those who best know the truth of the matter, and by perambulations previously made'.[183] The reliability of such evidence is shown by the fact that jurors in other counties swore that John had afforested Hewelsfield in the Forest of Dean, and the wood of Ross in Herefordshire, both of which are recorded in Domesday Book as being then within the royal forest.[184] It was on 'evidence' such as this that a Gloucestershire jury on 22 May 1300 reduced the Forest of Dean to the king's demesne lands and woods. Twelve manors, a vill and four hamlets held by subjects on the west side of the Severn from Newent in the north to Lydney, Alvington and Aylburton in the south were named: they were said to have been afforested by John, and so were claimed to be free of the Forest law.[185] These were the 'Seventeen

157

Towns' disputed by counsel at the Gloucester Forest Eyre of 1634, when Charles I's ministers attempted to re-assert the ancient bounds of the forest.[186]

In Staffordshire Cannock Forest was reduced to seven scattered demesne hays,[187] and in Kinver Forest twenty-three vills and parts of six others were put out,[188] despite the evidence of Domesday that Chasepool, Enville and Kidderminster were already in the forest in 1086.[189] The Rutland jurors again asserted that King John, who seems to have been cast by popular tradition as the villain of the piece, had afforested the greater part of the forest in that county,[190] whereas it seems in fact to have been a creation of Henry I.[191] In Exmoor, the Buckinghamshire part of Bernwood, Cumberland, Worcestershire and Wiltshire the perambulations of 1300 demanded more extensive disafforestments than ever before:[192] more than half the forest area that remained in England was declared to be outside the ancient bounds.[193]

Edward remained unwilling to surrender the Forest rights of his Crown. On 20 January 1301 he met his Parliament at Lincoln, which had been summoned to consider the reports of the commissioners for disafforestment,[194] and asked from the magnates a declaration that he could ratify the perambulations without injuring the Crown or violating his coronation oath. They refused, and by the threat of armed rebellion they extorted from him once again the confirmation of the Charters, and the ratification of the perambulations made in 1299 and 1300.[195] But Edward was determined to avoid honouring these concessions, made under duress; in October 1301, when he appointed commissioners to make a perambulation in the Devon forests, he once again reserved the rights of his Crown.[196] In 1305 he found it expedient to issue an Ordinance of the Forest recognizing the disafforestments already carried out, but he declared that the inhabitants of such districts had forfeited their rights of common within the forest, and that the royal demesne should be kept *in statu quo*.[197] On 20 December Pope Clement V was persuaded to issue a Bull, declaring that the concessions Edward had made had been unjustly extorted from him by force, were incompatible with his coronation oath to defend the honour and rights of the Crown, and were therefore null and void.[198] Edward then on 27 May 1306 promulgated another Ordinance of the Forest, revoking the disafforestments. He recognised that there was general resentment of the oppressive conduct of the Forest officers, and made provision for regular inquiries into it, and for presentment of Forest offences to be made at the attachment courts, as a procedure preliminary to the Forest Eyre.[199] But Edward's subjects can have had little faith in these oft-repeated promises of reform: they continued to regard disafforestment as the only effective remedy for their grievances. They were once again disappointed in their hopes, however. The royal demesne vills, fields and woods in Sherwood Forest, for example, which had been put out of the forest by the perambulation of 1300, were now 'entirely put back into the forests by the said King Edward'.[200]

7
The Struggle Continued Under Edward II: 1307–1327

During the early years of Edward II's extravagant and oppressive personal rule, his unpopular favourites were placed at the head of the Forest administration. Hugh Despenser the Elder was re-appointed Justice of the Forests south of Trent in March 1308,[201] and, shortly after the king went north in September 1310 to escape the Lords Ordainers, he appointed Piers Gaveston to be Justice of the northern forests for life, with wide powers to enclose and arrent the forest wastes and audit the agisters' accounts, and unprecedented authority to remove verderers and appoint his own men in their places.[202]

The forests continued to figure prominently among the grievances of the English people. The famous Ordinances which Edward II was compelled to accept in October 1311 once again denounced the oppressive conduct of Forest officials who secured the conviction of innocent persons by means of irregular and unlawful procedures. It was decreed that they were all to be suspended from their duties: commissioners were to hear complaints against them, and those found guilty were to be permanently removed from office. The Forest Charter of 1217 and the Forest Ordinance of 1306 were to be strictly observed.[203] The Lords Ordainers removed Gaveston and

Despenser from their Forest offices, and replaced them by members of the baronial opposition. [204]

Edward II, however, had no intention of keeping the promises which had been extorted from him. In January 1312, as soon as he felt himself to be beyond the reach of the barons, the favourites were restored. On 3 April Gaveston was again appointed Justice of the northern forests, but in May he was captured at Scarborough by the Earl of Lancaster and hostile barons. He was beheaded by them, and replaced by an adherent of the Lords Ordainers. [205] The elder Despenser, however, was re-appointed in June 1312 as Justice of the southern forests, [206] and took part in the efforts by the king and his advisers to have the Ordinances set aside as invalid and illegal.

Humiliating defeat at Bannockburn in 1314, again placed the king in the hands of the baronial opposition. A general parliament was held from January to March 1315: Hugh Despenser was removed from the Council, and replaced as Justice of the southern forests by Ralph de Monthermer, Earl of Gloucester, [207] one of the Ordainers. Parliament granted taxes in return for the king's promise to grant the 'requests of the Commons' for the observance of the Charters and the Ordinances, and the appointment of commissioners to make perambulations of the forests. On 20 April the sheriffs were ordered to make proclamation that the king intended to fulfil his promises, and that he had already appointed the commissioners. [208] But the inhabitants of Galtres Forest did not wait. They at once proceeded to make a perambulation without authorization, and publicly proclaimed in the city of York that any forester who entered the forest would lose his head. On 4 May Edward ordered the Justice of the Forest to examine this perambulation, and the sheriff to arrest those who had made it. [209] On 10 May he himself appointed five commissions of judges to make Forest perambulations in twenty-three counties 'pursuant to the Ordinances, so that the Charter of the Forest may be observed'. [210] But his subjects evidently doubted his good faith, for in June the tax collectors in Staffordshire and Shropshire were resisted on the ground that the king had not carried out his promises regarding the forest. [211]

At the Lincoln Parliament in January 1316 the baronial opposition, led by Thomas, Earl of Lancaster, the king's cousin, seized control of the central government. In response to a petition by the 'prelates, earls, barons and commonalty of the realm', Edward II was compelled to agree that the Forest perambulations made in his father's reign should be enforced in accordance with the provisions of the Charter of the Forest, provided that:

> if it shall appear by the record of the books, rolls and memoranda of his court, or by ancient perambulations, or by any other sufficient evidence, that any royal demesnes, or lands or woods which were in the forests before the time of Henry II, had been excluded by the late perambulations, then they shall be re-afforested. [212]

The Treasurer and barons of the Exchequer were ordered to examine Domesday Book and other records and documents in the Exchequer and Treasury which might throw light on this question, and to report to the Council: former officers of the Forest, such as Hugh Despenser, were to deliver up to the Chancellor and Treasurer all relevant documents in their possession and custody. The foresters of fee were to bring their rolls before the Council, and were 'to be there in person, to propound the King's claim'. Two knights were to be elected in each county court to appear before the Council 'with full power to assent for the community of the county as to what shall be ordained . . . concerning the forests': all landowners who wished to claim the disafforestment of their lands and woods were to be there to substantiate their claim. [213]

The knights met the Council at Lincoln in July 1316, and the king's officers drew up for them a list of 'divers errors' contained in the perambulations of 1300. In Somerset, for example, they showed by the evidence of Domesday that Dulverton and Winford were of the 'ancient demesne' of the Crown of England, and therefore ought to remain in Exmoor Forest, according to the provisions of the Charter. The long list of townships claimed for disafforestment had in fact remained in the Forest since the beginning of Henry III's personal rule, and had been acknowledged and treated as such by judges and juries at successive Forest Eyres. [214]

But these objections were swept aside. Parliament granted a tax of a sixteenth, and in return it was promised that the perambulations of Edward I should be confirmed, and that new perambulations should be made before Christmas in the forests where they had not been made in the previous reign. The Justices of the Forest were to drive the deer from all disafforested districts into the remaining forests during the forty days after disafforestment: after the expiration of that time places put out of the forest were to be exempt from the operation of the Forest law.[215] Commissioners to make the new perambulations were appointed – for example in Somerset, Dorset, Devon and in Rutland, but it is doubtful how far they proceeded: no perambulation had been made in Devon by November 1318, and fresh commissioners were appointed to perambulate the Devon and Nottinghamshire forests before Whitsun 1319.[216] During this period of weakness and confusion, in any case, the inhabitants of large districts cast off the Forest law, without scrupulous consideration of the reservations in the king's grant of disafforestment. By June 1318 the forest of Selwood in Wiltshire had been so much reduced in size that the warden's farm of £10 a year could no longer be paid,[217] and the Forest of Dean had been reduced by a quarter before the end of the reign.[218]

In October 1321 the king took up arms to restore his personal authority. On 11 February 1322 he recalled his favourites; on 14 February he called upon Aymer de Valence, Earl of Pembroke, Justice of the Forest south of Trent, to arm a 'suitable number' of foresters and bring them to Coventry.[219] They must have played their part in the overthrow of Thomas of Lancaster and the Lords Ordainers at the battle of Boroughbridge on 16 March. After his triumph Edward appointed the elder Despenser as Justice of the Forest south of Trent for life, repealed the Ordinances, but republished the Ordinance of the Forest of 1306.[220] He soon turned his attention to the districts which had been put out of the forest earlier in the reign. In 1323 the Justices of the Forest were ordered to recall all the royal demesne woods which had been disafforested contrary to the Charter of the Forest:[221] Henry Scrope, appointed Justice of the Forest north of Trent on 10 September,[222] reafforested thirty-three townships in the Forest of Galtres alone.[223] The king himself took a hand in the vigorous re-enforcement of the Forest law. He was at Pickering castle from 8 to 22 August 1323: an inquiry was held regarding venison trespasses in Pickering Forest 'since that forest had been forfeited to the Crown by the treason of the Earl of Lancaster'.[224] Over a hundred offenders, including Northern magnates like Sir John Fauconberg and Sir Robert Capon, were indicted by the sworn evidence of the Forest officers and other jurors. The king instructed the sheriff to arrest them, and they were to be kept in prison until further orders. Sir John Fauconberg was only released after undertaking to pay a fine of 100 marks.[225]

This renewed severity was bitterly resented by the king's subjects. At the Parliament of November 1325 'the King's liege men' complained that:

> the ministers of the forest . . . have taken again into the forest lands and woods as entirely as they were at any time, contrary to the Charter . . . and cause ditches to be thrown down, and interfere with their cultivation, and take from them grievous and excessive ransoms.

Numerous disputes arose between the Forest officers and the owners of lands and woods they had re-afforested. The Abbess of Barking complained that her wood of Alderfen, belonging to her manor of Tollesbury, had been recalled into the Forest of Essex, 'although she says the wood is not in the forest and ought not to be'. Humphrey of Bassingbourn's wood of Bamfield, and the dowager Countess of Pembroke's manor of Thorpe Waterville had likewise been adjudged to be part of the forest of Rockingham; the Prior of Kenilworth complained that his wood of Wolverton, pertaining to his manor of Salford Priors in Warwickshire, and Robert Burdet that his wood of Arrow had been re-afforested as part of the forest of Feckenham. The king ordered these disputes to be heard and decided by the King's Council on 28 June 1326.[226]

But there followed the downfall and deaths of the Despensers and of their royal master. Queen Isabella and Mortimer sought to gain popular support by a conciliatory policy regarding the forest. At the first Parliament of Edward III, held in February and March 1327, charges were brought against William of Claydon, the elder Despenser's deputy as Justice of the southern forests. He was alleged to have recalled into the forest without warrant 'vills, lands and woods' which had been put out by Edward I's perambulations and confirmed by Edward II: he had, in breach of the Charter of the Forest, amerced men living outside the forest for not attending the Forest Eyre. By heavy amercements and by imprisonment he had compelled the regarders to make their regard in the 'purlieus' – that is, in districts which had been disafforested; he had prevented the forest inhabitants from exercising their rights, even those conceded by royal charter and writs, unless they paid fines therefor before the Forest justices, and at Forest inquests he had compelled Forest officers and juries, under threat of imprisonment, to indict persons whom they knew to be innocent.[227] Parliament further complained that Edward II's confirmation in August 1316 of the Forest perambulations made in the previous reign had never been carried into effect. To remedy these grievances it was enacted that the Charter of the Forest was to be kept in all its articles, that the perambulations made in the time of Edward I were to be observed, that those perambulations which still remained to be made should be made as quickly as possible, and that the forest boundaries in each county should be confirmed by royal charters, as laid down in the perambulations.[228] Commissioners were accordingly appointed to make perambulations in the forests of Devon and Surrey: they were to be returned into the Chancery before Christmas, but were not to be put into effect until the officers of the central administration had had an opportunity of comparing them with the earlier perambulations of Edward I's time.[229]

Once more the inhabitants of the northern forests showed their impatience of these delays. In the 'free chase' of Knaresborough, which had been assigned to Queen Isabella for life, they made an unauthorized perambulation and acted upon it by felling trees, planting hedges, and hunting the deer without warrant. On 10 May 1327 the steward of the castle and honour of Knaresborough was ordered to go and reclaim any encroachments made upon the chase in this way.[230]

Pursuant to the promises made to Parliament, four commissioners were appointed on 30 March 1327, and sat at Chertsey to decide the fate of the Surrey part of Windsor Forest. The deputy warden, John of Swynnerton, urged that consideration should be given to a perambulation made at Lambeth in 1282 before Roger Brabazon and other judges. But the perambulating jury dismissed these proceedings as having been made under duress of Hugh Despenser, then Edward I's Justice of the Forest. They followed instead the verdict of 1225, and declared that all Surrey was out of the forest. After repeated petitions by the 'commonalty of the county', charters confirming the disafforestment of Surrey were finally granted on 26 December 1327: they were to be proclaimed in the county court, and the warden of Windsor forest was ordered to drive out all game from the disafforested areas into the remaining forest within the next forty days.[231] In like manner the claim of a Staffordshire jury that a large part of Cannock Forest had been created by Henry II was proved false by earlier records; nevertheless their verdict was accepted and Cannock Forest much reduced in extent.[232]

On 5 April 1329 Isabella and Mortimer appointed as Justice of the Forest south of Trent Sir John Maltravers, who had been one of the gaolers, and probably one of the murderers of Edward II:[233] when Edward III assumed personal authority in the following year, Maltravers saved himself by flight to France. The queen and Mortimer, however, persisted in their policy of concession to the end. On 12 July 1330, during the last months of their rule, the perambulations made during the reigns of Edward I and Edward II were ordered to be observed in every particular, and the Forest officers in Shropshire were forbidden to take any action against the owners of lands within the disafforested districts who had taken the deer or cut timber there.[234]

8
Partial Restoration of the Forest by Edward III

When Edward III grasped the reins of government in November 1330, he was as determined as any of his predecessors to vindicate the Forest rights of his Crown. In some counties, however, he was compelled to accept the bounds of 1300. In Wiltshire, after the declaration of the Forest bounds at the Salisbury Forest Eyre in 1330, scattered areas of demesne lands and woods alone remained in the forest: Savernake was reduced from an estimated ninety-eight square miles to a mere thirteen, and by 1331 the forest of Chute in that county had been 'almost disafforested'.[235] By 1341 the Forest of Dean had been diminished by a quarter, and the warden's farm was reduced from £160 to £120.[236] But many districts which had secured their freedom from the Forest law during Edward II's reign were once more made subject to it. In August 1333 the king declared that divers woods and other places in Surrey had been unjustifiably disafforested under colour of the Statute of 1327: there was evidence in 'divers inquisitions taken in the time of his progenitors and . . . other memoranda in the Exchequer' that they ought to remain in the forest. The Justice of the Forest was accordingly ordered to re-afforest them.[237] By 1347 Edward III had re-afforested also the royal forest of Bere Porchester in Hampshire. Landowners were, however, allowed to retain the rights of pasture and of cutting wood which they had previously enjoyed, subject to the customary payment of 'puture' to the foresters, and 'saving always to the king his deer and pasture for the same'.[238]

The officers of the Forest felt the weight of a new hand. In 1331 John Cromwell, Justice of the Forest south of Trent, William Ayet, warden of Galtres Forest, and a number of subordinate Forest officers, were convicted of trespasses of vert and venison, and were ordered by the King's Council to be dismissed.[239] The ponderous machinery of the Forest Eyre was once again set in motion – in Berkshire and in Surrey for Windsor Forest, and in Wiltshire, Hampshire and Somerset. Ralph de Neville in 1334 heard pleas of Sherwood Forest in 1334, and eyres were also held in the Earl of Lancaster's forests of Amounderness, Lonsdale and Pickering in Lancashire and Yorkshire. These counties had not seen a Forest Eyre for more than thirty years.[240] At these eyres hundreds of persons were convicted of Forest offences. But long intervals had elapsed since many of these offences were committed. Many offenders had died in the mean time, and the sheriff failed to produce others, so that the sessions were adjourned time and time again during the next few years.[241] Of 223 defaulters at the Pickering Forest eyre of 1334, only nineteen finally surrendered themselves at the York county court in August 1338; the remainder, who had no lands or chattels by which they could be distrained, were outlawed.[242]

By this time, therefore, the Forest Eyre was found to be a cumbersome and ineffectual engine, and was allowed to fall into desuetude: only two short eyres were held in the southern forests during the remainder of the century – in Northamptonshire and Buckinghamshire in 1348, and in Hampshire and Wiltshire in 1355.[243] More effective means had to be devised to enforce the Forest law to protect vert and venison, and to raise revenue. Commissions of *oyer et terminer* were appointed to deal with specific Forest offences as they were reported to the king. In November 1341, for instance, Robert Parning the Chancellor, Bartholomew Burghersh, Justice of the Forest south of Trent, and two other judges were appointed to inquire into, hear and determine and punish 'trespasses, wastes and excesses' committed by the officers of the Forest and other royal officials in Northamptonshire. Subsequently the 'community of the officials of Northamptonshire, both of the forest and elsewhere' made fine before the judges by 4,000 marks 'for certain trespasses committed by them'.[244]

The other effective procedure was the general commission of inquiry into the condition of the forests. During the last two decades of the reign the Justice of the Forest or his deputy went on circuit every year to hold such inquests.[245] Forest wardens, verderers, regarders, foresters and sworn jurors made presentments before them of offences against vert and venison. The sessions were short, and the Justice completed his circuit of the forests in a single county in a matter of weeks. In the month of May 1372 John of Foxley, the Justice of the southern forests, and his deputy held ten consecutive sessions in the counties of Hampshire, Wiltshire, Worcestershire, Staffordshire and Northamptonshire, and heard presentments regarding fifteen forests.[246] These commissions were more flexible and effective procedures than the ponderous engine of the Forest Eyre.

Edward III's Forest policy met with widespread opposition from his subjects, who took advantage of his absences from England to make wholesale depredations upon the deer in his forests and parks.[247] At times the officers of the Crown were worsted by large and desperate bands of armed malefactors. In 1356 a commission of *oyer et terminer* for the counties of Gloucester and Hereford was issued to Richard of Willoughby and five other judges, on information that John Gayner of St Briavels and a large number of others, banded together by oath, had committed many trespasses against vert and venison in the Forest of Dean, assaulted the foresters, and:

> prevented the King's officers from levying his rents and the amercements incurred by the King's tenants in the Forest courts, or executing the orders of the King and of the King's Justices and other ministers.

The people of the neighbourhood dared not indict these malefactors before the Justices of the Forest, 'because of their power and malice, and the poor of those parts cannot obtain justice for injustice inflicted upon them unless they first make ransom to the same evil-doers'. In July of the same year John Gayner and many others resisted arrest at Lydney, killed a number of the king's servants and those of the warden of the forest, and chased the others 'as far as the Forest and would not surrender to the King's peace'.[248]

Numerous petitions concerning the forest were presented at the Parliaments of this reign and the beginning of the next. Complaint was made in 1383 that persons accused of Forest offences were being imprisoned without indictment in due legal form, and detained by the Forest officers until they paid fines for their release.[249] The Commons asked at various times that the perambulations should be observed, that new perambulations should be made, and that charters should be granted defining the forest limits.[250] The king promised redress, but did not keep his promises. In 1347 he promised that the grievances of the Commons should be remedied by Chancery writs against Forest officers, but next year 'the commons of the county of Surrey and of other counties' complained that although they had sued for a writ in the Chancery, they had not been able to obtain the promised remedy.[251]

The 'purlieus', or areas put out of the forest by the perambulations,[252] were a special bone of contention. Mounted officers called 'rangers' were appointed to drive back into the forest deer which had strayed into the purlieus. The Commons wished the purlieus to be completely free from the Forest law, so that every landowner should have the right of free chase in his own lands and woods.[253] But the Forest officers continued to attach and imprison men for Forest offences within these districts, and to take money from them for their deliverance from gaol, often compelling reluctant juries to make presentments against their will, and obtaining indictments in other irregular ways.[254] The Parliament of January 1377 asked that the common law remedies of False Imprisonment and Trespass should be granted against foresters who made attachments within the purlieus.[255] Complaint was also made that the deer destroyed crops and pastures within the forest, and that the foresters illegally compelled the forest dwellers to attend the swanimotes.[256] To all these petitions the Crown returned empty promises of redress.

9
Decline of the Forest: 1377–1485

During the century following the death of Edward III the power of the Crown was diminished by lavish grants to the great magnates. Many of the royal forests were granted to them to hold in fee. In 1391 the castle of St Briavels and the Forest of Dean were given to Thomas, Duke of Gloucester to hold in tail male,[257] and in 1398 the forest of Rutland to Edward, Duke of Albermarle:[258] by 1405 the Somerset forests of Neroche, Exmoor, Mendip and the park of North Petherton had been granted away to the Earl of March.[259] Humphrey Duke of Gloucester held the forests of Savernake and Feckenham in chief of his brother Henry V,[260] and in 1444 Henry VI granted the reversion of Feckenham Forest to Henry, Duke of Warwick in tail male.[261]

The principal Forest offices were held by the great barons as life appointments. In the north the Nevilles established a strong claim to the Justiceship of the forests north of Trent. In 1331 Ralph Neville was appointed to that office, and several of his descendants secured a like appointment, culminating in the grant in 1443 to Richard Neville, Earl of Gloucester, of the northern Forest justiceship to hold as an hereditary office for himself and 'the heirs male of his body', with certain Forest rents and revenues and 'power to appoint at will all foresters and officers in Inglewood Forest'.[262] In the south, Humphrey, Duke of Gloucester was Justice of the Forests south of Trent from 1416 until his death in 1447; his successors were all great barons.[263] During the Wars of the Roses each party appointed leading magnates to the principal Forest offices during their periods of ascendancy. The Lancastrians appointed Henry Percy, Earl of Northumberland, to be Justice of the northern forests in 1459 and again in 1471, and William FitzAlan, Earl of Arundel to be Justice of the southern forests. Both these appointments were expressed to be rewards 'for assistance against the rebels'.[264] Yorkist appointments included John Mowbray, Duke of Norfolk, in 1461, and Henry Bourchier, Earl of Essex, in 1462, successively as Justices of the Forests south of Trent, and Richard, Duke of Gloucester, the future Richard III, in 1472 as Justice of the northern forests.[265]

The weakness of the Crown and the internecine strife of the barons plunged England into anarchy. 'Riots, robberies and forcible entries were prevalent', and 'the enforcement of law under such conditions was scarcely attempted.'[266] During this period control of the Crown over what remained of the Forest administration dwindled away. Writs for the holding of the regard in forests such as Sherwood, Galtres, Pickering, Inglewood and Rutland continued to be sent out from the Chancery during the fifteenth century,[267] but the Forest Eyre, which would have punished offences revealed by the regard, had now almost fallen into desuetude. The Chief Justice of the Southern forests from 1462 until 1483, Henry Bourchier Earl of Essex, held only four Forest Courts – in 1464 at Marlborough for Savernake Forest, in 1465 at Headington for Shotover and Stowood, and, after an interval, in 1468 at Chelmsford for the forest of Essex.[268] Commissions of *oyer et terminer* for Forest pleas were rarely issued at this time.[269]

The records of attachment courts held every forty days in Pickering Forest in 1407 and 1408 show that the Forest townships were still bound to send the reeve and four men to attend them. But the frequency of fines for non-attendance indicates the declining authority of the Forest administration.[270] In the forest of Inglewood attachment courts continued to impose small amercements for vert offences during the reign of Henry VI, and pannage fees and fines for agistment during the fence month were also being collected.[271] 'Swainmotes' were held at Weybridge in Huntingdon Forest at Midsummer, Michaelmas and Martinmas in the middle of the fifteenth century, but only a few presentments of venison trespasses by husbandmen were presented by the foresters before the verderers between 1451 and 1455. Moreover, at four of the sessions the foresters swore that they had no presentments to make.[272] The Forest administration in Huntingdonshire was patently in full decline.

On his accession in 1461 Edward IV was clearly determined to restore the Forest. The authority of the verderers, like that of the coroners, had ended with the previous reign,[273] so the king sent out orders to the sheriffs to make arrangements for the election of 'as many verderers as there ought to be and used to be' in nineteen forests south of Trent, and in Sherwood Forest north of it, 'as no verderer is as yet elected therein by command of the King'.[274]

Nevertheless the Forest fell into the background of national history: there are infrequent glimpses of how it was affected by the general lawlessness and violence of the times. The clerks and scholars of the University of Oxford were reported to have gathered 'to them great numbers of evil-doers in unlawful assemblies, with no small power by night and by day'. They were wont to enter the neighbouring royal forests of Shotover, Stowood and Bernwood, and the king's warren of Woodstock and park of Beckley, and were said to:

> have hunted, slain and carried away deer, hares, coneys, pheasants and partridges . . . threatening the King's officers in life and limb, so that they . . . for a long while have not dared openly to pass and do their business there.

In 1413 and again in 1460 the Chancellor of the University was ordered, 'under pain of the King's wrath and of forfeiting the liberties and privileges of the University', to issue a proclamation forbidding these practices, and to 'arrest any man under his rule offending in that behalf . . . and imprison them until he shall have special order of the King for their deliverance'.[275]

As the power of the king declined, so the privileges of substantial landowners increased. At the Parliament of 1389 the gentry complained that 'Artificers and Labourers' kept greyhounds and other dogs, and destroyed the game in their parks and warrens. As a result the right of hunting and taking game was reserved by statute for the upper classes. Laymen who did not hold land worth forty shillings a year, and clerks who did not have a benefice worth ten pounds a year, were forbidden to keep a greyhound or other dog, on pain of one year's imprisonment.[276] It is significant that the insurgent peasants of Essex in 1381 demanded the abolition of the hunting privileges of the landowners, and made no mention of the Forest laws of the Crown.[277]

NOTES

1. Cal. Pat. R. 1272–81, 78, 283, 423 etc.
2. Matthew Paris, *Hist. Minor* (Rolls Ser.) II 119; *Rot. de Ob. temp. Iohann.* 292–93.
3. Cal. Pat. R. 1364–67, 60.
4. Cal. Inq. Misc. I pp. 37, 39–41, 43.
5. Close R. 1247–51, 514.
6. ibid., 496: 1251–53, 43.
7. Cal. Inq. Misc. I pp. 40–41.
8. Cal. Close R. 1318–23, 197.
9. Pipe R. 1179–80, 1185–86; 1188 p. 87.
10. ibid., 1190, 155.
11. ibid., 145.
12. ibid., 67; Rot. Chart., 40b. The wapentake covers 'the low-lying land along the Ouse adjoining York and between the lower reaches of the River Wharfe and the River Nidd' (P.N.S. xxxIII, Part Four, p. 216)
13. ibid., 42b., 43 a-b.
14. ibid., 153b.–154a.
15. Pipe R. 1209, 64.
16. ibid., 1204, 40; Rot. Chart., 122b.
17. ibid., 123a. For the 'Stanestreet' see above, p. 6, 13n.
18. *Rot. Chart.*, 121a–123a.
19. ibid., 132; Pipe R. 1204, 85.
20. ibid., 189.
21. *Rot. Litt. Claus.* 1204–24, 2b., IIa., 15b., 33a., 36b.
22. Pipe R. 1207, 41.
23. *Rot. Chart.*, 206, 381; *Rot. Litt. Claus.* 1204–24, 197a., 227. The old Nassaburgh hundred 'forms a promontory between the Welland and the Nene'. [EKWALL, *C.O.D. Placenames*, s.v.]
24. *Rot. Chart.*, 132 a–b.
25. *Rot. Litt. Pat.* 1201–16, 40.
26. Petit-Dutaillis, *Supplementary Studies*, I 118.
27. arts. 47 and 48 (Stubbs, *Sel. Charters*, 298–99.)
28. *Rot. Litt. Pat.* 1201–16, 145; McKechnie, *Magna Carta*, 440.
29. Close R. 17 John m. 27d. (printed Foedera I 134.)
30. Petit-Dutaillis, op. cit., II 185–86.
31. Stubbs, *Sel. Charters*, 345–48.
32. Pat. R. 1216–26, 162.
33. E32/38/3d; Wright, *Common Law in the Forest,* App., 6, 10–13.
34. E32/102/8; C47/11/1/7; C99/8; Turner, *Sel. Forest Pleas*, xciv–xcv.
35. See above, p. 4.

36. C47/11/1/5, 6; C47/12/1/1; and see maps, *Sherwood Forest Book*, 35, 36.
37. *Rot. Litt. Claus.* 1204–24, 386.
38. Pat. R. 1216–25, 197.
39. DL 39/1/11; C47/11/1/9; Wright, op. cit., App., 8.
40. *Rot. Litt. Claus.* 1204–24, 434b.
41. C47/11/1/10, 14, 16, 19; E32/38/2; 225/10; B.M. Stowe MSS. 798 fo. I; Bazeley, *Extent of the Forest*, 166–67; *V.C.H. Wilts.* IV 399, 428, 431.
42. *Rot. Litt. Claus.* 1204–24, 417.
43. Pat. R. 1216–25, 288–89.
44. ibid., 491.
45. Pat. R. 1216–25, 567–70, 575; *Rot. Litt. Claus.* 1224–27, 70a., 72b.
46. ibid., 209; Wright, *Common Law in the Forest*, App. 9; and see above, pp. 139–40.
47. *Rot. Litt. Claus.* 1224–27, 56b., 80 a–b., 169, 207b.–208a; Cal. Close R. 1227–31, 100–101.
48. *V.C.H. Wilts.* IV 399, 428.
49. Fisher, *Forest of Essex*, 23–24, and map opp. p. 20.
50. *Rot. Litt. Claus.* 1224–27, 163b., 166a.
51. ibid., 80a.
52. ibid., 56b., 80 a–b.
53. art. 7 (Stubbs, *Sel. Charters*, 348); Pat. R. 1216–25, 575–76.
54. *Chronica* (Rolls Ser.) II 286.
55. *Rot. Litt. Claus.* 1224–27, 73. The Dorset perambulation of 1225 is printed in Hutchin's *History of Dorset* III 662–63.
56. *Rot. Litt. Claus.* 1224–27, 156–57.
57. *Rot. Litt. Claus.* 1224–27, 206; Close R. 1227–31, 90.
58. Pat. R. 1225–32, 109–10, 184.
59. Close R. 1227–31; E32/284; Hart, *Verderers and Forest Laws of Dean*, 80.
60. C47/11/1/22.
61. *Rot. Litt. Claus.* 1224–27, 167–70; Close R. 1227–31, 102–104; E32/154/1; *V.C.H. Wilts.* IV 399, 402, 407, 418; Bazeley, *Extent*, 168–69: Greswell, *Forests of Somerset*, 171–73.
62. *V.C.H. Wilts.* IV 418.
63. C47/12/2/2/; Bazeley, op. cit. 150.
64. Cal. Chart. R. 1226–57, 8; Rot. *Litt. Claus.* 1224–27, 80; Close R. 1227–31, 102–104.
65. *Rot. Litt. Claus.* 1224–27, 80b.
66. Close R. 1234–37, 51, 82, 304–305; Cal. Chart R. 1226–57, 193.
67. Pipe R. 1230, 81; Close R. 1231–34, 86.
68. Cal. Chart. R. 1226–57, 39.
69. Close R. 1227–31, 58, 293.
70. Cal. Chart. R. 1226–57, 102; Pipe R. 1230, 71.
71. ibid., 312; Cal. Chart. R. 1226–57, 122.
72. Close R. 1227–31, 238; C47/11/8/3; E32/76, ff. 4v.–6v; *Sherwood Forest Book*, 33–38.

73. Close R. 1231–34, 477; 1234–37, II.;
74. ibid., 369; 1251–53, 130.
75. Cal. Chart. R. 1226–57, 247.
76. ibid., 1257–1300, 78.
77. Cal. Pat. R. 1281–92, 167.
78. DL 42/1 ff. 1, 6, 58d., 257d.; *Rot. Parl.* III 428.
79. Bazeley, *Extent*, 154.
80. Cal. Chart. R. 1257–1300, 274–75.
81. Bazeley, *Extent*, 145.
82. E32/188/8, 8d; *Coll. Hist. Staffs.* V i 166–68.
83. E32/45/6d.
84. *Chronica* (Rolls Ser.) II 318–19, 322.
85. Tout, *Chapters*, I 186, 215, 244–89.
86. Cal. Pat. R. 1225–32, 487, 489, 491–92, 505; Cal. Chart. R. 1226–57, 169.
87. Tout, *Charters*, I 240.
88. ibid., IV 39; Bazeley, *Forest of Dean*, 181–84; Cal. Pat. R. 1232–47, 55, 160, 175, 252.
89. Cal. Pat. R. 1247–58, 13.
90. Matthew Paris, *Chron. Maj.* IV 400.
91. Treharne, *Baronial Plan of Reform*, 40.
92. Close R. 1242–47, 379, 396.
93. *Flores Historiarum* (Rolls Ser.) II 278.
94. Grosseteste, *Letters*, (Rolls Ser.) 353–55.
95. E32/37, 135, 249; Cal. Pat. R. 1232–47, 462; Close R. 1242–7, 350–542; 1247–51, 23, 96, 209–210.
96. Matthew Paris, *Chron. Maj.* (Rolls Ser.) VI 94 ff.
97. Close R. 1242–47, 542.
98. *Chron. Maj.* (Rolls Ser.) IV 400–401, 426–27.
99. Close R. 1261–64, 339–40.
100. E32/11/1/1d; E32/38/2; Cart. Ramsey Abbey (Rolls Ser.) 195, 209; Hutchin, *History of Dorset* IV 79; Bazeley, *Extent*, 170.
101. Cal. Inq. Misc. 1216–1307, No. 401.
102. C47/11/3/2; C47/12/10/2; Bazeley, *Extent*, 153.
103. Cal. Close R. 1323–27, 441.
104. Close R. 1231–34, 472; *Ex. e Rot. Fin.* I 260.
105. Cal. Pat. R. 1232–47, 474; 1247–58, 59.
106. *Chron. Maj.* (Rolls Ser.) IV 563–64.
107. Pat. R. 1216–25, 47; Cal. Pat. R. 1232–47, 471.
108. ibid., 1247–58, 58.
109. Rot. Litt. Claus, 1204–24, 347; Close R. 1247–51, 129; Pat. R. 1216–25, 369, 469; Cal. Pat. R. 1232–47, 472; 1247–58, 58.
110. Cal. Pat. R. 1232–47, 451; Close R. 1242–47, 314; Bazeley, *Forest of Dean*, 189.
111. *Ex. e Rot. Fin.* II 108, 109, 234, 236, 369; Cal. Chart. R. 1226–57, 351,

364, 455; Cal. Pat. R. 1247–58, 67; 1258–66, 472, 525; Close R. 1247–51, 256, 392; 1251–53, 278, 367; 1261–64, 64, 338.

112. Cal. Inq. Misc. I 31–32.

113. See e.g. Cal. Pat. R. 1232–47, 482.

114. Cal. Pat. R. 1232–47, 471; 1247–58, 58; Close R. 1247–51, 87.

115. Cal. Pat. R. 1232–47, 252, 446, 474; 1247–58, 13, 59, 63, 529; Close R. 1242–47, 542; Cal. Chart. R. 1226–57, 236, 362, 364; *Ex. e Rot. Fin.* I 260; II 108.

116. Pipe R. 1199, 2–3; 1200, 191–192; 1201; Pipe R. 31 Hen. III m. 14*D*.

117. Cal. Pat. R. 1232–47, 472; *Ex. e Rot. Fin.* II 91–92, 234, 236.

118. *Chron. Maj.* V 85, 94, 137.

119. Cal. Pat. R. 1247–58, 61.

120. C47/12/2; Close R. 1247–51, 254, 318, 527.

121. C47/12/2/10.

122. Close R. 1247–51, 359.

123. Cal. Pat. R. 1266–72, 468.

124. *Chron. Maj.* V 136–37, 340.

125. Pipe R. 1231–33, 1241–42, 1252 (printed Hodgson, *History of Northumberland*, III iii 167–68, 226; Parker, Pipe R. for Cumberland, 37–39, 92, 158–59).

126. *Ex. e Rot. Fin.* II 87, 158, 333.

127. Close R. 1247–51, 497; 1251–53, 53, 56, 190.

128. Pipe R. 1252 (printed Parker, op. cit., 159); Close R. 1251–53, 43, 46, 49.

129. ibid., 1247–51, 563; 1251–53, 201.

130. Matthew Paris, *Chron. Maj.* V 340.

131. Cal. Pat. R. 1247–58, 154, 165.

132. Cal. Pat. R. 1247–51, 497; Treharne, *Baronial Plan of Reform*, 40; *Tout, Chapters*, VI 40.

133. Cal. Pat. R. 1247–58, 432–35.

134. Close R. 1254–56, 89–90, 135.

135. ibid., 425; Cal. Pat. R. 1247–58, 488, 524, 550.

136. *Ann. Monast.* (Rolls Ser.) II 310–11.

137. ibid., I *Theok.* 102–104: III Dunst. 189.

138. Close R. 1237–42, 22.

139. *Ann. Monast.* III Dunst. 150, 189.

140. ibid., I *Burt.* 318–20.

141. Matthew Paris, *Chron. Maj* V 451, 536; Treharne, *Baronial Plan of Reform*, 55–56.

142. arts. 7, 8, 9 (Stubbs, *Sel. Charters*, 374.)

143. Cal. Pat. R. 1258–66, 43, 58, 71.

144. *Ann. Monast.* (Rolls Ser.) I Burt. 478.

145. Cal. Pat. R. 1258–66, 60, 69, 85–86.

146. ibid., 1247–58, 550.

147. ibid., 1258–66, 273, 324; and see above, pp. 105–106.
148. Cal. Pat. R. 1258–66, 675.
149. E32/11, 29, 35, 72, 137, 140, 147.
150. E32/11/1, 1d; 140/4d; 158/3d; 194/1d; Hutchin, *Hist. of Dorset*, IV 79; Turner, *Sel. Forest Pleas*, 53, 61.
151. Cal. Pat. R. 1258–66, 435; 1272–81, 443; Treharne, *Baronial Plan of Reform*, 236, 301, 323, 328.
152. D.N.B., sub nom.
153. Cal. Pat. R. 1292–1301, 306; Cal. Fine R. 1307–19, 306.
154. E32/8; 12/21; 31; 43; 74/5; 161/1d, 8; *Coll. Hist. Staffs.* V i 166.
155. E32/161/1d; *New Forest Documents*, ed. Stagg, 33, 94.
156. DL39/1/8 (1298); C47/6A/4 (1300), printed 5th. Report of Commrs. of Inquiry into Woods and Forests 1789, App. 3; Stagg, op. cit., 33, 36.
157. See below, pp. 192–93.
158. E32/30/8, 28d; Bazeley, *Extent*, 155.
159. E32/188/8, 8d; Cal. Chart. R. 1257–1300, 348–49; *Coll. Hist. Staffs.* V i 166–68.
160. E32/76, ff. 14r.–15r., printed *Sherwood Forest Book*, 47–48; Cal. Close R. 1279–88, 404.
161. Cal. Pat. R. 1272–81, 237; C99/101; Turner, *Sel. Forest Pleas*, ci–cii.
162. E32/12/21; Fisher, *Forest of Essex*, 27–28. For the 'Stanestreet', see above, p. 6 n. 13.
163. E32/154/1; Greswell, *Forests of Somerset*, 88–89, 171–75.
164. C99,101; Turner, op. cit., cii n. 1.
165. C47/12/2/2, 4–6; Bazeley, *Extent*, 156, 171; *V.C.H. Wilts.* IV 399, 402, 408, 445.
166. Cal. Close R. 1272–79, 560.
167. Cal. Chart. R. 1257–1300, 247; Cal. Pat. 1272–81, 471; Cal. I.P.M. IV no. 348.
168. Bazeley, op. cit., 156–57.
169. Statutes of the Realm (Rec. Com.) I 120; Cal. Close R. 1296–1302, 134, 137.
170. E146/1/8; Cart. Eynsham Abbey (Rolls Ser.) II 92 sqq; V.C.H. Bucks. II 132.
171. Perambulations printed Collinson, *History of Somerset* III 56, from a register in Wells Cathedral: Greswell, *Forests of Somerset*, 89–90, 176–79, 265–74.
172. *Flores Historiarum* III 297; Petit-Dutaillis, *Studies* II 220.
173. Cal. Close R. 1296–1302, 298.
174. see H. Rothwell, 'Edward I and the struggle for the Charters 1297–1305,' in 'Studies . . . presented to F.M. Powicke' (O.U.P., 1948) 324.
175. Cal. Pat. R. 1292–1301, 424.
176. *Ann. Monast. IV Wigorn.*, 541.
177. Cal. Pat. R. 1292–1301, 454; Turner, *Sel. Forest Pleas*, civ.
178. C99/102/15.

179. C99/106.
180. Cal. Close R. 1296–1302, 387–88; Petit-Dutaillis, *Studies*, II 221–23.
181. Cal. Pat. R. 1292–1301, 506.
182. C99/102/15; Turner, op. cit., 119–121.
183. C47/11/38; *Coll. Hist. Staffs.* V i 178.
184. *Dom. Bk.* I 166b., 167, 182a; E32/255/2, 4, 7; Bazeley, *Extent*, 147, 159.
185. printed Appendix 4, Third Rept., Commrs. of Inquiry into Woods & Forests 1788, pp. 137–38.
186. See below, pp. 192–93.
187. Cantor, *Mediaeval Forests of Staffordshire*, 45, 46.
188. C47/113/18; *Coll. Hist. Staffs.* V i 178–80.
189. E146/3/33; C47/12/10/16; *V.C.H. Staffs.* II 348; IV 21, 54; *V.C.H. Worcs.* I 286, 295.
190. C99/102/15; Turner, *Sel. Forest Pleas* 116–17.
191. See above, p. 4.
192. Bazeley, *Extent*, 158; *V.C.H. Wilts.*, IV 402, 432, 444–57.
193. Bazeley, loc. cit.
194. Cal. Close R. 1296–1302, 408–409.
195. Rishanger, *Chronica*, 198; Petit-Dutaillis, *Studies*, II 223–25.
196. Cal. Pat. R. 1292–1301, 607.
197. Cal. Close R. 1302–1307, 323.
198. Rymer, *Foedera* I 978.
199. Statutes of the Realm I 147–49.
200. C47/12/10; E36/76 ff. 6v.–8r.; *Sherwood Forest Book*, 39–42.
201. Cal. Fine R. 1307–19, 1, 18.
202. ibid., 73; Cal. Pat. R. 1307–13, 295, 450–451.
203. Statutes of the Realm I 160–161; *Rot. Parl.* I 282–83.
204. Cal. Fine R. 1307–19, 116; Cal. Pat. R. 1307–13, 450–451, 464.
205. Cal. Fine R. 1307–19, 144.
206. Cal. Pat. R. 1307–13, 464.
207. Cal. Fine R. 1307–13, 230.
208. Cal. Close R. 1313–18, 224.
209. ibid., 225–26.
210. Cal. Pat. R. 1313–17, 296.
211. ibid., 324.
212. ibid., 296; Parl. Writs, II Div. 2, 158–9.
213. Cal. Close R. 1313–17, 272–74.
214. C47/11/6/23; Dermot, *Exmoor Forest*, 155–58.
215. Cal. Close R. 1313–17, 427; Cal. Pat. R. 1313–17, 529, 531–32.
216. ibid., 539; 1317–21, 240.
217. Cal. Close R. 1313–18, 550.
218. Cal. Pat. R. 1340–43, 190 ff.; Cal. Fine R. 1337–47, 230.
219. Cal. Close R. 1318–23, 523.
220. Cal. Fine R. 1319–27, 287; Stubbs, *Const. Hist.* II 368–370.

221. Cal. Close R. 1318–23, 634; 1323–27, 22.
222. Cal. Fine R. 1319–27, 238.
223. *Rot. Parl.* II 388.
224. Pickering Forest had been granted by Henry III in 1267 to his second son, Edmund, Earl of Lancaster and his heirs: see above, p. 144.
225. Cal. Fine R. 1319–27, 244; Cal. Close R. 1323–27, 15–16, 22; N. Riding Records, N.S., II 217–219, 257.
226. Cal. Close R. 1323–27, 539, 557.
227. *Rot. Parl.* II 10; Young, *Royal Forest*, 146.
228. Cal. Pat. R. 1327–30, 39; Statutes of the Realm I 255; Petit-Dutaillis, Studies, II 230–31.
229. Cal. Pat. R. 1327–30, 141; Cal. Close R. 1327–30, 212.
230. ibid., 124.
231. Stowe MS. 414, ff. 253 sqq. (*Collectanea de Forestis*); C47/11/8/16 sqq. (cited Neilson, 'The Forests' in *The English Government at Work 1327–36* 397–99; *V.C.H. Surrey* II 566.
232. *V.C.H. Staffs.* II 338–43, 348.
233. Cal. Fine R. 1327–37, 128.
234. Cal. Close R. 1330–33, 147.
235. Cal. I.P.M. VII p. 262; *V.C.H. Wilts.* IV 400–432, 444–457.
236. Cal. Pat. R. 1340–43, 190–191.
237. Cal. Close R. 1333–37, 72–73.
238. ibid., 1346–49, 522; Cal. Pat. R. 1345–48, 264.
239. ibid., 1330–34, 200.
240. E32/52, 132, 163–65, 304; E146/2/26–29.
241. Cal. Close R. 1333–37, 708; 1337–39, 110.
242. DL42/1/258ff.; E32/161; 163–65; 207 mm. 1–2, 11; N. Riding Records, N.S., III 67ff.; IV xiii.
243. E32/112, 113; 267/14; 268; Cal. Close R. 1346–49, 489, 592, 602–603.
244. ibid., 1341–43, 350, 519, 524.
245. E32/9, 15, 17, 18, 23, 26, 30, 43, 118 (for the southern forests 1361–77).
246. E32/217/3d; 271/5, 6, 6d; 300; 305/11; 310/7, 14; 315; 318/22; 319/3; 347.
247. Cal. Close R. 1339–41, 258.
248. Cal. Pat. R. 1354–58, 399, 449.
249. Rot. Parl. III 164.
250. ibid., II 311b., 367b; III 62a., 116a.
251. ibid., II 169b., 203b.
252. 'Poraillée' or 'Purale' originally meant the perambulation by which the Forest bounds were declared (ibid. II 169b.)
253. ibid., II 313a; III 18a.
254. ibid., II 169b., 313a, 367b.; III 18a., 62a., 116a., 164b.
255. ibid., II 367b.
256. ibid., 313a.; III 18a.

179

257. Cal. Pat. R. 1388–92, 406.
258. ibid., 1396–99, 415.
259. Cal. Fine R. 1405–13, 21–22.
260. Cal. Pat. R. 1413–16, 338; 1416–22, 129.
261. Cal. Close R. 1447–54, 392. On the death of the Duke of Warwick in 1446 Feckenham Forest reverted to the Crown.
262. Cal. Fine R 1327–37, 276; 1377–83, 257; Cal. Pat. R. 1388–92, 39; 1441–46, 191.
263. ibid., 1413–16, 389; 1446–52, 83; 1452–61, 88 etc.
264. ibid., 538; 1467–77, 258.
265. ibid., 1461–67, 46, 77; 1467–77, 107, 338.
266. Stubbs, *Const. Hist.* III 278.
267. Cal. Close R. 1422–29, 69, 260, 343, 471; 1429–35, 192, 257, 364; 1447–54, III, 256 etc.
268. DL39/2/5; DL39/2/11/1; Cardigan, *Wardens of Savernake*, 115–118.
269. See e.g. Cal. Pat. R. 1399–1401, 516; 1413–16, 413; 1461–67, 32.
270. DL39/2/2; Cox, *Royal Forest*, 118.
271. ibid., 94.
272. DL39/2/4; Cox, op. cit., 271.
273. See above, p. 126.
274. Cal. Close R. 1461–68, 43–44.
275. ibid., 1413–19, 75–76; Cal. Pat. R. 1452–61, 658.
276. *Rot. Parl.* III 273; 13 Richard II, cap. 13.
277. Petit-Dutaillis, *Studies*, II 242, 246–47.

CHAPTER 13

Tudor and Stuart Attempts to Revive the Forest System

1
The Forests Under the Tudors

On his accession Henry VII was faced with the task of restoring the reign of law in the forests as elsewhere. An Act of Parliament passed in the first year of his reign recited that great numbers of persons:

> som with paynted faces, som with Visors and otherwise disguised . . . have hunted . . . in divers places of this Realme . . . by color whereof have ensued in tymes past grete and heynous Rebellions, insurreccons, Rioutts, Robberies, murdres and other inconveniencies.

It was enacted that offenders were to be brought before a member of the King's Council or a Justice of the Peace for examination; hunting in disguise or by night, and wilful concealment of such offences were to be punished as felonies[1] – that is, by death and forfeiture of property.

The Forest courts were accordingly revived or infused with a new spirit of severity. 'Swainmotes' or 'swanimotes' were held in a number of southern forests – in Melchet, Melksham and Pewsham, Gillingham, Bernwood and Waltham, and in Windsor Forest in Berkshire and in Surrey.[2] In Chute Forest swanimotes were held at

Conholt three times a year, namely at the beginning of February, in June, July or August, and about Martinmas (11 November).[3] The local gentry and others were presented for taking the deer, which they had probably been accustomed to do for generations with little interference. Other presentments concerned the unwarranted felling of trees and cutting of branches in the forest coppices, and the overburdening of the forest pastures with unauthorized numbers of cattle, sheep and pigs.

To give judgment upon these presentments, the ancient machinery of the Forest Eyre was once more set in motion after a long period of general disuse. Between 1488 and 1490 eyres were held in the Berkshire and Surrey divisions of Windsor Forest, in Hampshire, Wiltshire, Northamptonshire, Essex, Buckinghamshire and Huntingdonshire.[4] The court rolls show that the Forest law had been generally disregarded, and that the king's deer had been hunted and the forest timber felled on a large scale.[5] At Andover in 1489 Sir Nicholas Lisle, hereditary warden of Chute Forest, was removed from office for unlawfully killing a score of deer, and for numerous offences relating to the forest covert and pastures;[6] he was, however, able to recover his office in 1500 on payment of a fine.[7] Claims by the forest landowners and inhabitants to various rights and privileges within the forest were also investigated at the Forest Eyre.[8]

Extensive districts had secured their freedom from the Forest law since the time of Edward III. At the Essex Forest Eyre held at Waltham Holy Cross in 1489, juries attended only from the hundreds of Becontree and Waltham Holy Cross and the half hundred of Waltham, plus four men and the reeve from only seventeen forest townships,[9] all in the south-western corner of Essex: that is to say, the forest of Essex had been reduced, roughly speaking, to the bounds laid down by the hotly contested peram-bulations of 1300. The Forest law still applied in some measure, however, to the purlieus, the outlying districts which had been put out of the forest during the fourteenth century – although in some parts of the country the authority of the Forest officers was disputed there. In 1591 it was stated in the Duchy of Lancaster Chancery Court that the manor of Hackness was 'within the precynct and liberties' of the forest of Pickering, and that

tyme out of mynde, when any deere of the said forrest . . . have commen
into the said manor of Hackness . . . the Rangers, and other officers of the
said forrest . . . have always used to fetch out the same with their houndes
and to rechase them into the said Forrest.

Thomas Constable and John Gilpin justified their 'unlawfull resys-
tance' to the Forest officers on the ground that the right of hunting
the deer in Hackness manor belonged exclusively to Sir John
Constable of Burton.[10]

The machinery of the ancient Forest courts was found at this time
to be cumbrous and ineffective. The comprehensive Forest Eyre of
1488–90 was not repeated until nearly 150 years later, as a desperate
expedient of the last decade of Charles I's personal rule. Henry VII
himself supplemented the eyre with judicial proceedings of other
kinds, such as the judicial inquiry in 1494 into offences in Pickering
Forest, which revealed extensive destruction of vert and venison.[11]
The Tudors also turned to the common law courts to enforce their
Forest rights. An Act of 1485 had already made hunting in disguise
or by night a felony; it was re-enacted several times[12] so that Forest
offenders could be prosecuted at Quarter Sessions or at Assizes.[13]

Even so, by the end of his reign Henry VII had decided that some
at least of his remoter forests were unprofitable assets. On
20 November 1508 he leased Exmoor and Neroche Forests to Sir
Edmund Carew for life, at an annual rent of £46. 13s. 4d.,

with . . . all courts and profits of courts and swainmotes, fines, herbage,
pannage and agistment, . . . with licence to hunt the deer, stags and bucks
and does, with dogs, greyhounds, bows and arrows and other instruments of
the chase, provided that at his death there be 100 deer left in the forest of
Exmoor, and 200 in that of Neroche.

This lease was renewed for 300 years, until the final disafforestment
and enclosure of those forests.[14]

Henry VIII hunted the deer with as much enthusiasm as his
Norman and Angevin predecessors.[15] He was the last king of
England to attempt to create a new royal forest – the forest of the
honour of Hampton Court, established in 1539 near his new palace
of Nonsuch near Epsom. However, it did not long survive him.

Hatfield Forest in Essex was a private chase which had escheated to the King in 1521; it too was granted away by Edward VI.[16] In 1537 he had made Thomas Cromwell Justice of the Forest north of Trent.[17] Cromwell obviously planned to bring the northern forests more closely under his control, and to ferret out encroachments upon the Forest rights of the Crown. Between June and September 1539 Cromwell's deputies held Forest Eyres in Sherwood, Galtres, Inglewood and other royal forests.[18] Their coming caused consternation among the local people: Sir Thomas Wharton, who sat in Cumberland in 1539 to hear pleas of Inglewood Forest, reported to Cromwell that 'no justice Court [i.e., Forest Eyre] had been held in that county within the memory of man'.[19] The proceedings were reported to the king himself; they included accusations of waste against forest landowners, one of whom was Sir William Parr, brother of Catherine Parr.[20]

But by this time the Crown was assessing the royal forests, not so much as hunting preserves but as sources of timber, especially for ship-building. As early as 1483 an Act had been passed, legalizing the enclosure of coppices in the forests where felling had taken place, until seedling beech and oak had grown again.[21] New officers had to be appointed for the new objective of woodland management for timber production. So in 1547 Henry VIII decreed the appointment of two Masters and two Surveyors of the Woods, one each for either side of the Trent, as officers of the Court of Augmentations. After the Court was absorbed in the Exchequer in 1554, that part of the Crown revenues was managed by 'Surveyors-General of Woods, Forests, Parks and Chases', responsible to the Exchequer.[22] The authority of the Justices of the Forest thereafter declined. Crown woods were sold by Exchequer warrant, and Forest offenders were prosecuted in the Court of Exchequer Chamber, instead of at the Forest Eyre.[23]

After Henry VIII's death and the accession of the nine-year-old Edward VI his subjects hoped for some relaxation of the Forest law. To dispel such hopes the Council of Regency issued, on 17 June 1548, a 'Proclamation (issued upon a false rumour that the King means to disafforest his ancient forest of Waltham, Essex, whereby ill- disposed persons have been stirred to destroy the vert and . . . kill . . . the deer).'

184

It was ordained that anyone hunting the deer in that forest without royal licence was to pay a fine and suffer three years' imprisonment. If after that he could not find sureties for his future good behaviour, he was to be banished. The deer were not to be fenced out of enclosures in the forest with 'unreasonable hedges and ditches', unless 'the greater part of the enclosure be sown with corn'.[24]

During the next two reigns the decline of the Forest administration continued, despite the fact that Elizabeth I was herself an ardent follower of the chase. In 1628 the Attorney-General said in the Court of Exchequer,

> The Inhabitants (of the forest of Waltham) were restrained from commoning with sheep as contrary to the forest laws during the reign of the late King Henry VIII . . . and of all other preceding Kings who took delight and pleasure in hunting. But afterward that Royall and princelie pleasure being not so much esteemed by the late King Edward the Sixt (by reason of his minoritie) and by the two succeeding Queenes (by reason of their sexe), the lesse care of the due execucon of the forest lawes consequentlie ensued, and the keeping of the Courts of Swainmote and Justice Seate [i.e., the Forest Eyre] became almost totallie neglected and disused; whereof the inhabitants of the said fforest . . . taking advantage, did by degrees, especiallie towards the end of the raigne of the late Queene Elizabethe, encroach upon the said fforest lawes by commoning with sheepe.[25]

Other counties present a similar picture. In Staffordshire the forest of Cannock had virtually ceased to exist by the end of Elizabeth's reign, and in Kinver Forest only Iverley Hay remained in the hands of the Crown, and even there the deer had disappeared, and the woods for the most part had been cut down.[26] In the Forest of Dean the verderers sat with the deputy Constable of St Briavels to hold attachment courts at Kensley every six weeks; fines were imposed for hunting with long bows, and for offences against the vert such as cutting great branches, rooting up hollies, hawthorns and hazels, and collecting 'Oke-cornes'.[27] But there was widespread despoliation of the woods by local landowners and by the charcoal-burners who produced the fuel necessary for the manufacture of iron – this despite Acts of 1559 and 1570 prohibiting them from using timber-trees needed to build ships.

Elizabeth followed precedents set by her ancestors in selling

Crown rights in some forests for ready money. In 1563 a number of landowners purchased the disafforestment of their estates in the forest of Essex in return for the substantial fine of £500.[28] In 1592 a grandiose proposal received consideration: an unnamed individual offered to farm all the queen's woods for £20,000 a year. The Lord Admiral, Lord Howard of Effingham, who later became Chief Justice of the Forest south of Trent,[29] was consulted, and stated his objections to the scheme. There were, he said, 180 parks, forests and chases belonging to the queen, and the rights proposed to be leased in them were worth far more than £40,000 a year. Leasing the herbage and pannage would disturb the deer in their lairs and deprive them of their pasture. The lease would be used as a pretext for the wholesale felling of timber, which even then was in short supply for building and repairing 'your Majesty's shyps, wych are the Jewells of your kingdom'. The suggestion that disputes should be referred to the Lord Treasurer, the Chancellor and the Court of Exchequer was an unwarrantable encroachment upon the jurisdiction of the Forest Justices in Eyre,

> who have always punished faults belonging to forests and parks. If so, there
> will be no cause to keep a justice court [Forest Eyre], nor to have verderers or
> regarders, for their offices, which had continued since the law of the forest,
> will be needless.[30]

Lord Howard's objections prevailed, but the mere fact that the project was entertained by the queen seems to show how low in importance the Forest had sunk.

2

The Forests Under the First Two Stuarts: the Last Attempt to Re-establish the Full Forest Administration

At the accession of James I the amount of land under Forest law was still considerable. Much of it had been enclosed, and pasture-farming was the predominant mode of agriculture. By this time it was generally considered that the forests were anachronistic and unprofitable. They were valued mainly as sources of timber for the Royal Navy but, in the absence of an effective forestry policy of conservation and production, the yields were small.[31]

James I was determined to restore the Forest system as an important part of his royal prerogative, and as a source of revenue as well as of pleasure in his favourite sport of hunting. In a proclamation made soon after his accession he declared his intention to enforce the Forest laws 'which are as ancient and authentic as the Great Charter'.[32] On occasion he took a personal interest in the apprehension and punishment of poachers who took his deer,[33] and his Attorney-General took proceedings in the Star Chamber against offenders in the Wiltshire forests.[34] The local Forest courts had fallen into disuse; in 1601 the regarders of Chippenham Forest had complained that there was great disorder 'for want of a swanmote court'.[35] James therefore ordained that these courts should be revived.[36] But in Braydon Forest, for example, the free tenants and village representatives showed reluctance to attend,[37] and in the Forest of Dean the attachment court, by now called the 'speech court', was ineffective in the face of large-scale destruction of the vert by the ironmasters.[38]

James's increasing financial difficulties impelled him to desperate measures. Timber was still required in large quantities for the Royal Navy: a warrant was issued in November 1611, for example, for felling 1,800 oaks in the New Forest and in Shotover, Stowood and Bernwood Forests for this purpose.[39] Crown woods in the Forest of Dean acquired new importance as a profitable source of wood and timber, especially for sale to the ironworks. But an effective policy of conservation and timber production required enclosure of the open forest wastes after felling, to protect the young shoots from grazing deer and cattle, which aroused violent opposition from commoners and 'free miners'.[40]

From 1604 onwards, Otho Nicholson and other commissioners inquired into 'assart lands' which had been brought into cultivation within the ancient Forest bounds laid down in 1300. These lands the king now claimed as his 'proper soil', and tenants were forced to compound with the commissioners by paying fines to the Crown and an annual rent thereafter. The Attorney-General took proceedings in the Court of Exchequer against those landowners who refused to compound: where necessary he obtained a writ of injunction sequestrating the assarted lands, which were then leased to other tenants. By 1616 the commissioners had raised over £25,000 by the enforcement of obsolescent Crown rights within the forest.[41]

But by 1613 even more desperate measures were in contemplation. The Spanish ambassador was reporting to his sovereign that James was 'five millions in debt', and intended to 'raise three millions by the sale of the Royal woods and of deer'.[42] The inquiries of Crown agents had revealed that some of the royal forests, such as Morfe, had become valueless as hunting-grounds through long neglect.[43] A jury declared that there was little timber left in Pickering Forest, and that 'for every redd deare in the fforest, there are 5,000 sheepe'.[44] The king therefore sought to raise money by leasing the soil of the forests to 'improvers'. Melchet Forest in Wiltshire finally passed out of the hands of the Crown in 1614, when it was leased to Sir Lawrence Hyde,[45] and in the same year John Waller and Thomas Purcell received a grant of Pamber Forest in Hampshire, 'consisting of the soil only, the woods being sold away and the deer gone'.[46] This was followed in 1622 by a special commission to Lord Cranfield and others 'to disforest and lease Bernwood Forest, Berkshire, Feckenham Forest, Worcestershire, and other forests and moors'.[47] Enclosure of the forest wastes by these 'improvers' deprived the forest inhabitants of their rights of common there. In 1620 the Lord President and the Council of the North reported to the Privy Council that the enclosure of the 'best part' of Galtres Forest had inflicted great hardship upon the poor of Easingwold and Kirkby. The wood required for fencing the enclosures had further reduced the forest cover, 'and the tumults arising there from searching for cattle etc.' had 'frightened away most of the deer'.[48] By 1623 the disafforestment and sale of the woods and wastes of Chippenham and Melksham Forests had been accomplished: Bowood Park alone was reserved to the Crown in that part of Wiltshire.[49]

Charles I's quarrels with his Parliaments and his inept foreign policy compelled him to continue the expedient of disafforesting and leasing the soil of various other forests. On 13 June 1627 Sir Miles

Fleetwood reported to Secretary Conway that in pursuance of the 'great service' he had undertaken for the king 'in the disafforestation of several forests, which have been very chargeable and without profit or pleasure', he had completed the disafforestment of the forest of Leicestershire. He begged the Secretary to remind the Duke of Buckingham, who was Chief Justice of the Forests south of Trent,[50] 'of his suit for a warrant to dispose of the bucks and deer in that forest to the gentlemen and inhabitants'.[51] On 27 June the Attorney-General sent to Buckingham warrants for the sale of Neroche, Selwood and Feckenham Forests,[52] and the disafforestment of Braydon was begun at about the same time.[53] It was hoped to raise £20,000 by the sale of the first two forests 'to supply a necessary service on the return of the fleet'[54] from the expedition against the island of Rhé. 'The several wastes and commonable lands' within Selwood Forest were to be divided: one-third to the Crown, one-third to the forest landowners, and one-third to those who had rights of common of pasture.[55]

In July 1627 Buckingham embarked upon his ill-fated expedition, which still further increased Charles I's financial embarrassments. To escape them the king, at the suit of Sir Allen Apsley, Victualler of the Navy, in 1629 granted the Forest of Galtres to his creditors in fee-farm, in consideration of a fine of £20,000.[56] As usual, the forest wastes were to be divided and enclosed. A proportion was to be allotted to the fifteen forest townships in lieu of their rights of common, and the remainder, as Crown lands, were to be leased to the king's creditors.[57] But the tenants of three of the forest townships, namely Alne, Tollerton and Newton, refused to agree to the disafforestment of Galtres Forest on the terms proposed by the royal commissioners, whereupon in March 1631 the king ordered that the lands of those townships should continue to be 'within the jurisdiction of a forest and the forest laws'.[58] The dispute was still continuing in 1637: the lessees of the disafforested lands complained that 'the people of the country adjacent will not pay any considerable rent for what they say have been their commons', although they had been allotted a considerable share of the forest wastes in lieu of common rights. The land itself was poor – 'wild and unmanured' – and the lessees were compelled to bring

Huguenot refugees 'from Hatfield chase', who would undertake to do what was necessary to bring it into cultivation and pay a reasonable rent.[59]

Similar arrangements were made in 1639 for the disafforestment of the Forest of the Peak. The wastes were to be divided into two 'moieties' – one for the king, and the other to be partitioned between the tenants, commoners and freeholders: all parties were to enclose and 'improve' their portions. The survey was completed in 1640 and the deer destroyed, but the planned disafforestment and partition was not then carried out because of the outbreak of the Civil War.[60] Schemes of the same kind were drawn up for the forests of Chute,[61] Pickering and Knaresborough,[62] and in the soke of Somersham within the forest of Huntingdon, which the Attorney-General reported 'had not been in use for a long time past'.[63] In the previous year the Crown had sold to Sir John Winter in the Forest of Dean 'all His Majesty's Coppices, Wood Ground and Waste Soil of the said Forest (except the Lea Bailey), with the Wood and Timber, and all his Mines of Iron and Coal, and Quarries', for £1,950. 12s. 8d. Winter, who employed 500 wood-cutters, felled timber trees on a large scale, and enclosed about 4,000 acres in coppices to promote growth: by 1641 the deer were 'almost destroyed'. A further 4,000 acres were allotted to commoners and the poor to compensate them for their loss of common rights, but since this was the poorest – indeed it was worthless – land, violent opposition was aroused among the commoners. In 1642 Winter's grant was rescinded by a vote of the House of Commons, because of his misappropriation of timber in the forest.[64]

Henry Rich, Earl of Holland, who was appointed Chief Justice of the southern forests on 25 May 1631,[65] was a pliable and ambitious servant of his royal master. He vigorously applied Charles's policy of raising money by reviving the ancient Forest administration. As Chief Forest Justice he put pressure upon landowners to purchase from the Crown freedom from the restrictions of long dormant Forest laws. On 14 February 1637, for example, he granted licence to Lady Mary Crane to cut down underwood in Stoke Park in Salcey Forest 'until she had made an agreement with His Majesty for the disafforestment thereof'.[66] Numerous other licences were issued – to hawk, fell and sell woods, plough up pastures, enclose small parcels of land on the forest wastes and build houses thereon, cut turf and peat, and to operate a brick kiln.[67] He ordered surveys to be made of royal parks such as Windsor and Grafton, and the enclosures to be repaired.[68] The earl also issued warrants for collecting the fines imposed at Forest Eyres: in 1638 a 'Messenger of His Majesty's Chamber in Ordinary or his deputy' was ordered to take into custody those who refused to pay.[69]

Under Holland's direction the Forest courts were again revived, and once again an attempt was made to fill an empty Treasury with Forest fines and amercements. In 1630 a jury declared that swanimotes in Essex 'hath bin discontinued for many yeares'.[70] But during the next decade they were once again held in Waltham Forest: offences were presented by juries from each ward of the forest, and proved by the Forest officers. At Chigwell in September 1632 a fine of 30s. was imposed for keeping an unexpeditated dog, £5 for killing a fawn, £20 for placing nets to take the game, and 50 marks for making a coney burrow, which was ordered to be stopped. The offenders had to enter into recognizances and find sureties to appear at the next 'Court of Justice Seat', as the Forest Eyre was now called: final judgment was pronounced there.[71]

The swanimotes were revived in the Northamptonshire forests also. In Rockingham, Whittlewood and Salcey Forests they met regularly three times a year. Large numbers of offenders, mainly poor people, were presented for Forest offences. The regard was held again after long discontinuance: presentments were enrolled, as in medieval times, for production at the Forest Eyre.[72] In the Forest of Dean a special swanimote was held on 10 June 1634: 800 presentments of offences against vert and venison, some referring to events forty years old, were drawn up for submission at the Forest Eyre in the following month.[73] Swanimote courts were also held during this period in a number of other southern forests, including Chute, the New Forest, Shotover and Stowood, Wychwood and Windsor.[74]

After a lapse of more than a century, the Forest justices were once again sent out on eyre in the southern forests, armed with articles of inquiry for local juries to answer. The first session was opened at

Stratford Langthorne, in Waltham Forest, on 21 September 1630.[75] After his appointment in 1631 as Chief Justice of the southern forests, the Earl of Holland took over the direction of the Forest Eyre, and presided at subsequent Justice Seats. During the next six years he held pleas of the Forests in six counties.[76] Since the Earl of Holland was 'a man of greater dignity than knowledge in the Lawes of the Forest',[77] he was assisted at various times by judges of the common law courts[78] who advised him on points of law.

At the Forest Eyre which opened before him at Windsor in September 1632, counsel for the Crown was Sir William Noy, the Attorney-General, a learned lawyer determined to re-establish Forest rights which had long been forgotten. But he became gravely ill, and in April 1634 was replaced by Sir John Finch, a much more intemperate champion of the king's Forest rights. Proceedings at these Forest Eyres followed the traditional pattern. Landowners and others who claimed rights and privileges within the forest were summoned to attend, and to produce warrant therefor. At the Essex Forest Eyre in October 1634, for example, the judges, after consulting with the Chief Justice of the King's Bench and the Barons of the Exchequer, decided that there was no right of common of pasture for sheep on the forest wastes. Fines were imposed for grazing sheep there, both upon those who held land within the forest bounds, and on 'purleymen' who did not.[79]

Juries were sworn to declare the bounds of the forests; they based their returns in the main on the perambulations of 1298 and 1300, which had put large areas out of the forest, and had many times been confirmed. But Finch produced earlier perambulations which he had discovered in the Exchequer. At the Gloucester Forest Eyre in July 1634 he produced perambulations of 1228 and 1282, 'both agreeing that the Bounds of the Forrest [of Dean] began at Gloucester Bridge, and so went to Monmouth Bridge and Chepstow Bridge, and came round again by the Severne to Gloucester.' Counsel for the 'Seventeen Towns', claimed by Finch to be within the forest bounds,[80] produced in rebuttal the perambulations of 1298 and 1300, and their confirmation by Act of Parliament in 1336, urging also that these towns had been out of the forest by 'the long and constant Usage ever since'. Finch, however, denounced the 1300 perambulation as 'false and erroneous', and coerced the Grand Jury and Forest officers into returning a verdict 'that the Meetes and Boundes of the Forrest of Deane ought to be according to the Perambulations made' in 1228 and 1282.[81]

At the adjourned session of the Essex 'Justice Seat' on 4 October 1634, Sir John Finch produced the Forest Eyre roll of 1277, according to which the bounds of the Forest of Essex were sworn to be 'from Bow Bridge to Catway Bridge in length,.and in breadth from the river of Thames to Stanstreet' – that is, the whole of the country south of 'Stanstreet' (or Stanestreet) was declared to be Forest.[82] Finch asserted that 'he would know how his master had lost every inch of it'. The Earl of Warwick, one of the judges, protested and asked for time to produce charters and other evidence so that 'we might still enjoy with quietness the possessions of our ancestors which had bin oute of the Forrest for three hundred and thirty yeares'. But Sir John:

> threatened and awed the jurors to give a verdict for the King, and by unlawful means did surprize the county, that they might not make defence, and did use several menacing wicked speeches and actions to the jury and others, for obtaining his unjust purpose aforesaid.[83]

On the following day the jury signed a verdict that the 1277 perambulation still set forth the true bounds. At an adjourned sitting at Stratford on 8 April the following year, Finch, now Chief Justice of the Common Pleas, himself delivered judgment that these bounds should be enforced.[84]

In other counties also 'an Attempt was made by Charles I again to enlarge the Forest'. On 21 June 1639, in the forest of Salcey, 'a new Perambulation was made, by which a considerable Extent of Country was added to it, and subjected to the Burthen of the Forest Laws'; this was described by the Report of 1790 as a 'violent and oppressive Measure'.[85] Even before this the six villages which had by long established custom sent representatives to the Salcey swani-motes were increased to forty-two, by an arbitrary re-imposition of the medieval bounds. The villagers naturally resisted: in December 1638 thirteen of them were each fined 40s. for failing to send representatives to the swanimotes, and men appointed by thirteen others were amerced for non-attendance.[86]

Penalties imposed for breaches of the Forest law were of course designed to fill an empty Treasury. At Gloucester in July 1634 the judges' proceedings were based partly upon the 800 presentments made at the swanimote held in the Forest of Dean in the previous month: 420 of these for unlawfully cutting and selling woods, 260 for illegal inclosures and other encroachments, 80 for taking the king's game and 10 for unauthorized operation of ironworks. Fines for these offences ranged from 2s. for taking a few branches, and between £2 and £10 for the unauthorized building of a cottage or house, to £100 for unwarranted taking of timber on a large scale. But Finch proceeded against the principal offenders, from whom it was hoped that substantial sums could be extracted, 'by way of a Speciall Indictment'. John Gibbons, a courtier, was fined £8,600 for exceeding the terms of his grant of land in the forest: between 1629 and 1634 he had, without warrant, cut down 4,000 oaks worth £1 apiece, spoiled certain coppices, and enclosed 94 acres.[87] Sir Basil Brooke of Madeley, an ironmaster, and George Mynne, a London merchant, who held the monopoly of the sale of wood to make iron, were sentenced to pay £59,039. 16s. 8d. for encroachments and unlawful destruction of the covert; Sir John Winter, another forest landowner and ironmaster, was fined £20,000 for taking wood without warrant.[88]

At subsequent Forest Eyres in other counties the judges were clearly determined to raise large sums by fining the forest landowners. At the Northampton Eyre for Rockingham Forest, which opened in September 1635, the late Earl of Salisbury was convicted of having assarted 2,300 acres of Brigstock Parks in 1604, destroying the vert and a thousand deer, and enclosing the parks. His heir was fined £20,000, even though his father had obtained a pardon from James I.[89] The Earl of Westmorland was fined £19,000, and Sir Christopher Hatton £12,000; Sir Giles Mompesson was adjudged to pay a total of £3,300 for felling timber even though he produced an Exchequer warrant.[90] The estimated totals of fines imposed on offenders in the Northamptonshire forests – Rockingham, Whittlewood and Salcey – was over £80,000.[91]

But the landed gentry were already heavily in debt, and collection of these huge fines was impracticable; only a small proportion was actually paid. Of the amercements for offences in the Forest of Dean, for example, Brooke's and Wynne's penalty was reduced in 1636 to £12,000, and Sir John Winter's to £4,000.[92] The Earl of Salisbury in 1638 paid £3,000 for remission of his £20,000 fine, and for recovery of his parks at Brigstock.[93]

These punitive Forest Eyres put pressure upon landowners to buy exemption from the Forest law. In November 1637 commissioners were appointed to compound with all offenders in the Forests of Dean, Essex, Rockingham, Whittlewood and Salcey – to buy their pardon and the disafforestment of their land.[94] In the Forest of Dean Sir John Winter paid £1,000 for the disafforestment of his extensive estates, and lesser men paid smaller sums.[95] Wadham College paid £240 in March 1640 in respect of its lands in Essex.[96] Altogether the Crown received £38,667 from landowners who compounded for their estates within the forests of Dean, Essex and Northamptonshire.[97] But many of the Forest fines were never paid, and others were reduced or evaded by claims to exemption, pardons or royal warrants.

Humbler folk also felt the weight of the Forest law. In December 1638 the Earl of Holland, as Chief Justice of the southern forests, was informed of persons who unlawfully took the game in Rockingham Forest with 'dogs, nets, crossbows, guns and other engines'. He therefore gave authority to one Edward Sawyer to make inquiries, and to search for evidence in all houses and places in Kettering and five miles around. 'All mayors and other officers' were ordered to assist him.[98] Similar commissions were issued to the Forest officers of Shotover and Stowood in January 1640, and of Windsor Forest in June 1642.[99] A number of offenders were arrested and committed to prison. In November 1638 John Elliott was in prison, having been fined for carrying venison stolen in Windsor Forest to London, 'contrary to the laws of the forest'. He petitioned the Chief Justice of the Forest to 'remit his fine and order his enlargement' on the ground that he was 'a very poor man with many children . . . and is altogether unable to pay the said fine.' Elliott was ordered to be released on payment of a reduced fine of 40s., and on giving a bond for his future good behaviour. [100]

By this time the law relating to the protection of the king's deer within the 'purlieus' or forest outskirts had become more clearly defined. The rangers of Waltham Forest exercised their office in the purlieus as well as within the forest itself. It was their duty to drive back with their hounds all deer which wandered out of the forest into their purlieus, and to present all offences against the venison, whether committed in the forest or in the purlieus, at the next attachment court or swanimote. [101] Only those who held land in freehold within the purlieus might hunt the deer there, and even they might not hunt by night, or on Sunday. Presentments for breaches of these purlieu laws were from time to time made at the Essex swanimotes in the sixteenth and early seventeenth centuries. [102]

Charles I's Forest policy caused indignation and alarm throughout England. Sir Thomas Wentworth was informed in 1635 that 'The Justice seat has been kept this Easter week and all Essex has become forest and so they say will all the counties of England but three – Kent, Surrey and Sussex'. [103] Gardiner's judgment was that

> as a means of improving revenue the revival of forest law proved largely abortive . . . Charles . . . allowed himself for the sake of a few thousand pounds to be regarded as a greedy and litigious landlord rather than as a just ruler or as a national king. [104]

The all-important class of landowners especially was inflamed against the king's personal regime. John Pym, speaking in the Short Parliament on 17 April 1640, enumerated the grievances of the king's subjects. He referred jestingly to 'that which somewhat sticks by me: it is the forest, and I might easily lose myself in it'. [105] A committee of the Commons a week later complained, among many other 'grievances in the civil government', of 'Forest fines, which of late have been too far enlarged'. [106] Agitation continued after the dissolution of the Short Parliament. In July the Grand Jury at the Berkshire Assizes petitioned the king, complaining that:

in the eastern parts of this county Your Majesty's forests of Windsor are particularly burdened with the innumerable increase of deer, which if they shall go on so fast, in ten years more will neither leave food nor room for any other creature in the forests.

It prayed for relief in respect of 'the rigid execution of forest laws in the extremity' and 'the exaction of inordinate fees by some officers under the Lord Chief Justice [of the Forest] in Eyre'.[107] In the next year there was a riot at Windsor. The rioters killed many deer, and threatened to pull down the palings of the park, so that the Earl of Holland, as Chief Justice of the Forest, obtained authority for the sheriff of Berkshire to raise the power of the county to apprehend the rioters.[108]

In December 1640 Sir John Finch, now Lord Keeper, was impeached by the Long Parliament. The principal charges against him related to ship money and his conduct concerning the forests; he saved himself by flight to the Continent.[109] Charles realized that he must abandon the attempt to re-assert the Forest rights enjoyed by his medieval predecessors. On 16 March 1641 the Earl of Holland told the House of Lords:

That His Majesty, understanding that the Forest Laws are grievous to the Subjects of this Kingdom . . . out of his Grace and Goodness to his people, is willing to lay down all the new Bounds of his Forests . . . reduced to the same Condition as they were before the late Justices Seat held.[110]

On 5 July Charles himself declared, 'I have bounded the Forests, not according to my right, but according to late customs'.[111]

In the same year an Act was passed declaring that from henceforth the boundaries of all the royal forests should be taken to extend no further than those 'commonly reputed, used or taken in the twentieth year of the reign of James I [1622–23]'. No places were to be taken to be within the forest if no Forest courts had been held, verderers elected or regards made in them since 1565. Commissioners nominated by the Lords and Commons were to ascertain the proper bounds of the forests by means of local inquiries, the perambulations returned into the Court of Chancery, and all places beyond the certified bounds were to be absolutely free from the

197

Forest law, with the proviso that the owners and occupiers of land left out of the forest were to retain 'such rights of common as anciently or accustomably they had enjoyed'.[112]

Accordingly, a perambulation of the forest of Essex was made on 16 August 1641, by a jury of twenty-four knights and an esquire, in the presence of fourteen royal commissioners and the officers of the Forest. The boundaries laid down followed fairly closely those of the perambulation of 1300. Some districts which had been forest in 1300 were however excluded in 1641. These were the liberty of Havering, including Hornchurch, Romford and Havering, with Havering Park, and part of the townships of Barking and Dagenham.[113] The Forest was restricted to the south-western corner of the county, and these limits remained until the final disappearance of the Forest in the nineteenth century. Similar perambulations were made in August and September 1641 for the Forests of Windsor, Wychwood, Shotover, and Stowood, Rockingham, Brigstock and King's Cliffe.[114] So ended a dispute between the Crown and its subjects which had gone on intermittently for more than four hundred years.

NOTES

1. I Hen. VII c. 7.
2. DL39/2/19; 3/1/15; 3/2; 3/18, 20; E146/1/10/6; C154/1–4; 5/20; 8–15.
3. DL39/2/9/26–32; 3/1/15; 3/32/10; E146/2/39.
4. DL39/2/7, 9, 11–13, 16–24; 3/1, 5, 6, 8, 32, 34; E146/1/10.
5. DL39/2/9, 19–22; 3/5, 6, 8, 34/1.
6. DL39/2/9/1.
7. Cal. Pat. R. 1494–1509, 219.
8. DL39/3/34/2d.
9. DL39/2/21–22; Fisher, *Forest of Essex*, 177.
10. DL1/78/11(A4); DLI/81/22(A15); N. Riding Records, N.S. I 240–42.
11. DL12/1/19; DL39/3/16; N. Riding Records, N.S. I 125–26, 140–45, 164.
12. 31 Hen. VIII c. 12; 32 Hen. VIII c. II; 3–4 Edw. VI c. 17.
13. P.A.J. Pettit, *Royal Forests of Northamptonshire*, 43–44.
14. Cal. Pat. R. 1494–1509, 621–22; Macdermot, *Exmoor Forest*, 219–76, 316–407.
15. See e.g. Lett. & Pap. Hen. VIII, IV pt. 2, 2031.
16. Coke, *Fourth Institute*, chap. 73, p. 301, citing 31 Hen. VIII c. 5; Cox, *Royal Forests*, 296–97; Oliver Rackham, *The Last Forest: the Story of Hatfield Forest* (London, 1989) p.95.
17. Lett. & Pap. Hen. VIII, XII pt. 2, 473.
18. ibid., XIV pt. 2, 35–36.
19. ibid., 38.
20. ibid., XV 502.
21. 22 Edw. IV c. 7.
22. *Guide to the P.R.O.* I 80–81; II 99.
23. Pettit, op. cit., 20.
24. Cal. Pat. R. 1547–48, 370.
25. E112/177/31; Fisher, *Forest of Essex*, 294–95.
26. *V.C.H. Staffs.* II 348.
27. E146/1/30–32; Hart, *Verderers of Dean*, 19–20.
28. Fisher, *Forest of Essex*, 48.
29. Cal. S.P. Dom. 1595–97, 438.
30. ibid., 1591–94, 288–89.
31. *New Historical Geography of England*, ed. Darby (C.U.P., 1973) 267, 272, 293; Pettit, op. cit., 124–28.
32. Cal. S.P. Add. 1580–1625, 451–52.
33. ibid., 552.
34. Sta. Cha. 8/7/9; 8/28/12, 15; 8/47/19; *V.C.H. Wilts.* IV 401.
35. E101/139/8/1; *V.C.H. Wilts.* IV 397.
36. Cal. S.P. Add. 1580–1625, 552.

37. E146/2/40/3, 4; DL39/4/23/1; 25/1; 27, 29–32; *V.C.H. Wilts.* IV 405.
38. E137/13/4/1–3; Hart, *Royal Forest*, 86, 94.
39. Cal. S.P. Dom. 1611–18, 85.
40. Hart, op. cit., 86–89, 101–107; Hammersley, 'Revival of Forest Laws' ('History' XLV, No. 154, 89–90)).
41. Cal. S.P. Dom. 1619–23, 566–73; 1623–25, 573–89; Pettit, op. cit., 71–82; Hart, *Royal Forest*, 100–101.
42. Cal. S.P. Dom. 1611–18, 199.
43. ibid., 1619–23, 288.
44. Norden's 'Survey' (DL42/124/1, printed N. Riding Records, N.S., I 28–29, 34.)
45. *V.C.H. Wilts.* IV 431.
46. Cal. S.P. Dom. 1611–18, 247.
47. ibid., 1619–23, 374.
48. ibid., 181.
49. *V.C.H. Wilts.* IV 412–14.
50. appointed in Nov. 1619 (Cal. S.P. Dom. 1619–23, 97.)
51. ibid., 1627–28, 214.
52. ibid., 232, 290.
53. *V.C.H. Wilts.*, IV 406–407.
54. Cal. S.P. Dom. 1627–28, 242; 1629–31, 141.
55. *V.C.H. Wilts.*, IV 417.
56. Cal. S.P. Dom. 1639–40, 39.
57. ibid., 1629–31, 425.
58. ibid., 529.
59. ibid., 1637, 195.
60. ibid., 1639–40, 502; DL/5/18; *V.C.H. Derby* I 412–13.
61. Cal. S.P. Dom. 1638–39, 592.
62. ibid., 1639–40, 198; 1640–41, 337.
63. ibid., 1638–39, 414.
64. Third Report of Commissioners of Inquiry into condition of Woods and Forests (1788), pp. 13–14; Hart, *Royal Forest*, 119–129.
65. Pat. R. 2567 m. 11.
66. SP 16/384, pp. 1–2.
67. ibid., pp. 33–38, 47–48, 51–52, 57–58, 99–103, 114–115; Cal. S.P. Dom. 1640, 180; 1640–41, 504.
68. SP 16/384, pp. 4–5, 14–15.
69. ibid., pp. 11–12, 24–25, 88–89.
70. C99/153; Fisher, *Forest of Essex*, 80–81.
71. C99/137, 140, 142, 143; Fisher, op. cit., 81–83, 99–100.
72. C99/60; 72; 74; 80/2, 3; 97; 104/5; Pettit, op. cit., 25–26, 85–86.
73. Hart, op. cit., 112–13.
74. C99/8, 49, 52, 60, 72, 74, 80, 82, 83, etc.
75. C99/129/1, 8, 21.

76. C99, 1, 3, 6, 10, 41, 56, 78, 94, 107, 132, 151.
77. Coke, 4 Inst., chap. 73, p. 315.
78. Cal. S.P. Dom. 1634–35, 143, 216.
79. C99/130, 153; Fisher, op. cit., 285, 297–98.
80. See above, p. 154.
81. 'Note of the Proceedings . . . delivered to the King by Sir John Finch', printed in 'Third Report of the Commissioners of Inquiry into Woods and Forests' 1788, App. No. 5, pp. 139–40.
82. E32/12; and see above, p. 155.
83. Statement by the Earl of Warwick (Cal. S.P. Dom. 1634–35, xxxiii–xxxvi): art. 3 of Finch's impeachment in 1640 (Cobbett, *State Trials*, IV, 11–12; *Journal of Sir Simonds d'Ewes* (ed. W. Notestein) 150–151.
84. Cal. S.P. Dom. 1634–35, 227–28; Fisher, *Forest of Essex*, 40–45.
85. Seventh Report, Commissioners of Inquiry into Woods & Forests (1790), p. 422, and App. 2, p. 440.
86. Pettit, op. cit., 88–89.
87. Cal. S.P. Dom. 1634–35, 143–44: Hart, 'Verderers and Speech-Court of Dean', 23.
88. C99/10–20; Hart, *Royal Forest*, 109–115; Hammersley, op. cit., 95–100.
89. C99/60/16; Strafford, *Letters*, II 117: Pettit, op. cit., 87.
90. C99/60; 83/15; 105/10; Pettit, loc. cit.
91. ibid., 88.
92. C99/10–20; Cal. S.P. Dom. 1634–35, 143, 182; Hart, *Royal Forest*, 109–115.
93. Cal. S.P. Dom. 1638–39, 171.
94. Pat. R. 13 Chas. I, pt. 14, 6d.; Pettit, op. cit., 89.
95. E401/1924, 1925; Hammersley, op. cit., 89–95.
96. Cal. S.P. Dom. 1639–40, 530.
97. Pettit, op. cit., 89.
98. Cal. S.P. Dom., 1638–39, 162.
99. ibid., 1639–40, 298; 1641–43, 346.
100. ibid., 1638–39, 109, 162.
101. Book of Oaths, 1649, fo. 296; Fisher, *Forest of Essex*, 166.
102. C99/140; John Manwood, *Treatise and Discourse of the Lawes of the Forrest* (London, 1598) ch. 20.
103. *Letters of the Earl of Strafford*, ed. W. Knowler (1739), Vol. I p. 413; R.C. Shaw, *Forest of Lancaster*, 204–205.
104. S.R. Gardiner, *History of England 1603–42* (1884) VIII 86; Pettit, op. cit., 92.
105. Cal. S.P. Dom. 1640, 47.
106. ibid., 76–79.
107. ibid., 1640, 466–67.
108. Cox, *Royal Forests*, 299.
109. Rushworth, *Hist. Collections*, IV 123–129; Cobbett, *State Trials*, IV 1–21.

110.   Rushworth IV 206; Fisher, op. cit., 48–49.
111.   Cal. S.P. Dom. 1641–43, 44.
112.   16 Car. I c. 16; Lords' Journals IV 349.
113.   C205/17/2; Fisher, op. cit., 177, 395, 400–403, and maps opp. pp. 29, 51.
114.   C205/17/1–5.

CHAPTER 14

The Forests Since the Restoration

1
The Commissioners of Woods and Forests. Statutory Disafforestment, Partition and 'Improvement'

Stuart schemes for felling timber and enclosing the forest wastes were interrupted by the outbreak of the Civil War. The Forest law fell into abeyance. Under the Commonwealth, money was desperately needed to pay the soldiers, and recourse was had once again to the forests. In 1651 Parliament appointed commissioners to sell Exmoor Forest, which was reported to be 'mountainous and cold ground, much beclouded with thick fogges and mists and . . . overgrown with heath and yielding but a poor kind of turf of little value there.'[1] But this measure, like a subsequent Act passed in October 1653 'for the Disafforestation, Sale and Improvement of Royal Forests',[2] proved ineffective.

After the Restoration, Charles II followed the example of his predecessors by granting away some of the remaining royal forests. In 1664 he disparked Clarendon Park, the last remnant of the royal forests in Wiltshire,[3] and granted it to the Duke of Albermarle. In the north the disafforestment of the Forest of the Peak, and schemes for inclosure of those portions of it which were suitable for arable or pasture, were completed by royal commissioners appointed in 1674.[4]

The expansion of the Royal Navy and the growth of the mercantile marine, however, intensified the alarm of the Navy

Board over the shortage of timber. The Crown made one last attempt to revive the Forest law and the Forest courts, not for the preservation of the king's hunting rights, but to promote the production of timber. In 1667 the Marquess of Worcester, as Constable of St Briavels and Warden of the Forest of Dean, was ordered to revive the Forest courts there and to see that the Forest laws were obeyed: their discontinuance had brought about 'great destruction of timber and retardment of its future growth'.[5]

But the reign of Charles II saw the end of the great Forest courts. On 15 September 1670 the Earl of Oxford, as Chief Justice of the southern forests, held the last Forest Eyre in the New Forest, at Lyndhurst.[6] The last 'Court of Justice Seat' in Waltham Forest sat at Stratford Langthorne on 30 September 1670: fines were imposed for killing deer and cutting oaks, assarts were arrented and enclosures ordered to be thrown down.[7] A like court for the Hampshire forests, held at Winchester on 11 September 1672 by Sir Thomas Fanshawe, deputy Justice of the Forest, brought the long history of the Forest Eyre in the southern forests to an end. North of Trent the last remaining royal forest was Sherwood: here the Marquess of Newcastle held a Forest Eyre in 1663, which was continued by his deputy by way of adjournment as late as 1676.[8]

The ancient Forest system was in fact cumbrous and inefficient: the attempt to revive it as an instrument of Crown policy was doomed to failure. The offices of 'Chief Justice and Justice in Eyre of His Majesty's Forests, Chases and Warrens' north and south of the Trent were held by noblemen such as the Dukes of Monmouth, Newcastle and Devonshire.[9] Their emoluments were increased in accordance with their rank and dignity,[10] but their offices were of course sinecures: the execution of Crown policy had long passed into the hands of the Surveyors-General of Woods and Forests. There were two of these, north and south of the Trent, until Thomas Hewett was appointed in 1715 to both Surveyorships, with an annual fee of £50 for each office.[11] They were, in the seventeenth and eighteenth centuries, responsible for the general management of this category of Crown properties – for the felling of timber in the forests for the Royal Navy, for repairs to Crown property, for royal gifts to subjects, or for sale; for dealing with claims to customary rights in the Forest, for paying the keepers' wages and for providing hay for the deer in times of scarcity.[12] The Surveyors-General frequently complained of depredations by local people upon the forest woods,[13] and on one occasion at least appealed for aid to the titular head of the Forest administration. In 1714 Edward Wilcox, as Surveyor-General of His Majesty's Woods south of Trent, complained to the Lord Treasurer that:

> the neighbouring people of Salcey Forest have appeared in such great strength in the forest that the keepers are unable to oppose their cutting down many trees there, and forty of the best trees in Whittlewood have likewise been cut down.

He added a hopeful postscript:

> If a messenger be sent by the Lord Chief Justice in Eyre to take into custody some of the most substantial, as was done on the return of King Charles the Second, it may prevent further destruction.[14]

By the end of the eighteenth century the Forest was regarded as an unprofitable anachronism. Arthur Young wrote in 1807:

> The adjacent Forests of Epping and Hainault are viewed as an intolerable nuisance . . . the farmers uniformly declare that the privilege of commonage is by no means equal to the one-tenth part of the losses they constantly sustain from the deer in breaking down their fences, trespassing upon their fields, and destroying their crops either ripe or green.

He maintained that the forest wastes wanted 'only inclosure to be highly productive' of corn: a general Enclosure Act would make them 'profitable to the Community'.[15]

A royal Commission was appointed to inquire into the condition of Crown woods and forests, and published a series of seventeen Reports between 1787 and 1793.[16] The Commissioners reported that north of the Trent there survived only Sherwood Forest, while south of that river there were the New Forest, Aliceholt and Woolmer, and Bere Forests in Hampshire, Windsor Forest in Berkshire, the Forest of Dean in Gloucestershire, Waltham or

Epping Forest in Essex, Whittlewood, Salcey and Rockingham Forests in Northamptonshire, and Wychwood Forest in Oxfordshire.[17] The general picture was one of neglect and decline. In 1736 the Conservator and Supervisor of the Forest of Dean had reported to the Treasury, 'Within the last thirty years those Elections [of Forest officers] had been neglected, the Courts discontinued, and offenders left unpunished.' The ancient Forest offices of verderer, regarder and agister had 'become merely nominal and . . . bestowed rather as Marks of Favour and Distinction upon Gentlemen of Consideration in the Neighbourhood, than as Appointments of real Use or Responsibility.'[18] By the end of the century a similar report was made concerning the verderers of Rockingham Forest,[19] and in 1789 the Rt. Hon. Frederick Montague gave evidence to the Commissioners that regarders and agisters were not appointed in Bere Porchester Forest, and that there was no supervision of rights of common there.[20]

In some forests the local Forest courts also had fallen into abeyance. In Rockingham and Whittlewood they appear to have been discontinued after the time of Charles I,[21] and in 1789 the Rt. Hon. Frederick Montague gave evidence to the Commissioners that no Court of Attachment or Swanimote had been held in Salcey Forest since he became Ranger, 'and I doubt whether such Courts have been held ever since the Rangership has been in my Family, which is about 120 years'.[22] No swanimote was held after 1769 in Bere Porchester Forest: in that year the court could not be opened because no verderers attended.[23]

There had been an attempt, through Acts of Parliament, to revive the election of local Forest officers and the holding of local Forest courts in some forests; these measures were intended to preserve the forest woods and to increase timber production by enclosure of the forest wastes. Such was the Dean Forest (Reafforestation) Act of 1667.[24] But though the forest officers, together with four men and the reeve from each forest vill, and a jury of twelve held their 'Speech Court' once a year at Kensley in the presence of the deputy constable of St Briavels, the proceedings were largely ineffective: the violent opposition of the commoners frustrated the attempt to enclose the forest wastes.[25] Similarly in the New Forest an Act of 1697[26] gave statutory powers to the local 'Verderers' Court' to impose fines for such offences as stealing timber, burning the heath and destroying the covert. A later Act of 1819[27] gave it jurisdiction over the exercise of common rights in the New Forest. Two thousand acres of coppices were to be enclosed and planted with oak and beech, and a 'rolling programme' of further enclosures was projected as the trees matured. But here too the 'rolling programme' aroused intense opposition from the commoners, whose rights it threatened. In any case the statutory policy of enclosure and planting was too late. As the Commissioners said in 1788, 'An Oak must grow a Hundred Years, or more, before it comes to Maturity.'[28] Indeed, 1862 was the last year in which a considerable quantity of New Forest timber was supplied to the Royal Navy.[29]

In Waltham Forest Attachment Courts, attended by the verderers, foresters and woodwards, continued to be held until the middle of the nineteenth century. These courts supervised common rights on the forest wastes. They oversaw the reeves of the forest parishes, who branded the commoners' cattle, the number depending on the size of the commoners' holdings. Twice a year the reeves 'drove' the Forest, and removed and impounded all unbranded cattle. These Attachment Courts were also responsible for preventing illegal enclosures, and for giving landowners leave to cut timber in their own woods: thousands of acres of woodland in Essex were cleared during the eighteenth century by their leave, and with the licence of the Chief Justice of the Forest.[30] This process continued during the nineteenth century. The unenclosed wastes in Epping Forest were consequently reduced from 12,000 acres in 1777 to 3,500 acres in 1871, by illegal enclosures by the lords of the forest manors, and by sale of Crown rights by the Commissioners of Woods and Forests which amounted to disafforestment.[31]

The Commissioners therefore reported on the forests as potential sources of profit to the Crown and to the local landowners. They said of Sherwood Forest, 'No Deer being now kept for the King in any Part of the Forest, except Thorney Woods, the Forestrial Rights are productive of no Profit or Advantage'.[32] Salcey Forest, although 'a valuable Property, . . . the greatest part of it Wood Land, fully planted, and the Soil the most excellent for the Growth of Oak' was nevertheless 'unproductive to the Proprietor'.[33] In the Forest of Dean, as in the other forests, there was widespread destruction of the woods, by the 'free miners', by wood-stealers who lived by shipping stolen timber to Bristol, by the cottagers and other forest inhabitants, and by the Forest officers themselves. There was no effective management of the woods for profitable timber production, and regeneration was prevented because the young shoots were eaten by the deer and by commoners' cattle, which roamed the forests at will. Yet the Crown derived little profit from the herds of deer which still remained in some forests: the Forest of Dean, for example, had in 1788 'supplied only Four Bucks and Four Does Annually for the last Seven Years'.[34]

The Reports gave close attention to the vexed question of enclosures and commoners' rights in the forest. The legal entitlement to common of pasture was defined by the 'couchant and levant rule' – that is to say, commoners were allowed common for no more cattle than they could keep on their own land during the winter months when they were excluded from the forest. But, as a result of the decay of the Forest organization, there was widespread disregard of these regulations.[35] The assistant Deputy Surveyor in the Forest of Dean reported in 1788 that:

> the Number of the Cottages and Encroachments in the Forest . . . is nearly doubled since he had known it. The Persons who inhabit the Cottages are chiefly poor Labouring People, who are induced to seek Habitations in the Forest for the Advantages of living Rent free, and having the Benefit of Pasturage for a Cow or a few Sheep, and of keeping Pigs in the Woods; but many Encroachments have been made by People of Substance. The Cattle of the Cottagers are impounded when the Forest is driven by the Keepers, as all other Cattle are; and when the Owners take them from the Pound (paying the usual Fees to the Keepers) they turn them again into the Forest, having no other Means of maintaining them . . . The Cottagers . . . are detrimental to the Forest, by cutting Wood for Fuel, and for building Huts, and making Fences to the Patches which they inclose from the Forest; by keeping Pigs, Sheep etc. in the Forest all the Year; and by stealing Timber.[36]

In the New Forest evidence was given that:

> Swine and Cattle of all Kinds, commonable or not commonable, are suffered to go in the Forest at all Times, without Regard to the Fence Month and

Winter Haining and without any Restriction as to Number, or Proof that
they belong to those who have Right of Common.[37]

The Commissioners therefore divided the forests into two
classes. In the Forests of Dean, New Forest and Aliceholt and
Woolmer, the Crown was the principal landowner. Their 'Vicinity
to the Dockyards' made them a vital source of timber for the Royal
Navy; therefore it was 'a National Object to keep and to improve'
them.[38] The deer were to be removed, because they ate young trees
and crops. These forests were to be freed from the Forest law, the
commoners compensated for loss of their common rights, and lands
allocated to the Crown were to be enclosed for timber production.[39]

The second class of forests were those like Whittlewood, Salcey,
Rockingham, Wychwood and Sherwood, where the soil was for the
most part owned by local landowners. The great obstacle to the
efficient economic exploitation of forests such as Salcey, said the
Commissioners, was that 'the Interest in this Forest, exclusive of the
Right of the Commoners, is divided between Three different
Proprietors' – i.e., the Crown, to which belonged 'the great Timber
and Saplings', the principal owner of the woodlands, in this case the
Duke of Grafton, and the hereditary Warden of the Forest, who had
the 'Care of the Deer': by exercising his right of cutting 'Browse-
wood' for them, he prevented the proper growth of 'Timber
Trees'.[40] 'In Rockingham Forest,' they said, 'where the Crown has
little property left, where a considerable part of the Land is already
in Tillage or Pasture, and the Country pretty fully inhabited, it
cannot be desirable that those (Forest) Laws should be continued':
their 'Restraints and Burthens . . . by impeding its Improvement,
must be a loss to the Public as well as to the Proprietors'.[41] The
Commissioners recommended therefore that these Forests also
should be disafforested. The Forest rights of the Crown should be
sold to the landowners who owned the soil, or exchanged for an
apportionment of land for enclosure and economic development.
Commoners would receive an allotment of land. The Thirteenth
Report concluded:

Those who have Rights of Common would receive an Equivalent for those Rights; and even the Cottagers living on the Borders of the Forest, who, by our Information, at present waste their Time in pilfering in the Woods, would find useful Employment, from the Demand for Labour which the Inclosure and Improvement of the Wastes would create, and might perhaps be led to Habits of Industry.[42]

In 1810 the management of the whole of the Crown's landed estates were placed by statute[43] under three Commissioners of Woods, Forests and Land Revenues, to whom all the powers of the two Surveyors-General of Woods and Forests were transferred. And when the offices of the Chief Justices of the Forest were finally abolished by statute in 1817,[44] their powers and duties also were taken over by the First Commissioner.

From the end of the eighteenth century onward, the agents of the Crown acted upon the recommendations of the Commissioners of Inquiry, and actively promoted the disafforestment, enclosure and 'improvement' of the forest wastes. In 1795 and 1796 Acts enabled the Crown to sell to local landowners the various Walks of Rockingham Forest, 'freed . . . from . . . the Duties and Burthens . . . of . . . the Laws and Customs of the Forest'. The purpose of these Acts was stated to be to enable the purchasers to exclude the deer and 'commonable cattle', after compensation paid to the commoners, and to enclose the forest wastes and 'use (them) as Farms'.[45] In 1812 the deer were removed from the forests of Aliceholt and Woolmer, and two-thirds of the area were enclosed as a 'Nursery for Timber'.[46] Between 1810 and 1855 Acts were passed for the disafforestment of the forests of 'South, otherwise East Bere' (Bere Porchester),[47] Delamare,[48] Windsor,[49] Exmoor,[50] Sherwood,[51] Salcey,[52] Hainault,[53] Wychwood,[54] Whittlewood[55] and Woolmer.[56] Commissioners were appointed to 'divide, allot and inclose' the open forest wastes. A proportion was allotted to the Crown 'in severalty', varying according to the area of the forest wastes in which the property in the soil belonged to the Crown. In Windsor Forest, for example, the Crown's share was nine thirty-seconds, and in Exmoor twelve twenty-seconds. These Crown lands were freed from the common rights hitherto exercised over them, in compensation for the extinguishment of royal forest rights: in

Windsor Forest the Commissioners of Woods and Forests were given powers to purchase compulsorily the cottages built on them.[57]

The Commissioners of Woods and Forests reported in 1812 that about 100,000 acres of suitable land would need to be enclosed and planted to meet the Royal Navy's requirements of oak timber, but that neglect of the royal forests 'had produced . . . an almost total despair with regard to the prospect of Naval Timber from those Plantations.'[58] It was hoped to use the Crown allotment in Exmoor Forest for this purpose, but after partition the Commissioners decided that it would not in fact be suitable, and in 1818 it was sold for £50,000 to a Mr Knight, who enclosed it.[59]

The remainder of the forest wastes was in most cases divided between the lords of the manors and the commoners, in proportion to the value of their interests: the allotments were then to be fenced at the expense of the proprietors.[60] The loss of their common rights of course caused great hardship among the poor of the forest districts. So in 1831 the commoners rioted in the Forest of Dean, threw down the enclosures, and drove their cattle and sheep into the coppices: they had to be suppressed by soldiers.[61] Some later Acts endeavoured to meet this problem by making an allotment to the 'Rectors, Churchwardens and Overseers of the Poor' of the forest parishes, who were as trustees to apply the income for the benefit of the poor.[62] Poor widows in Barking and Dagenham parishes in the Forest of Hainault had formerly been allowed one load of wood yearly from the 'King's woods': the disafforesting Act of 1851 provided that an equivalent sum should be invested in Consols, and the income applied to a distribution of coal at Christmas to the widows.[63] Some later Acts, such as that of 1853 disafforesting Wychwood Forest, did not extinguish common rights: common fields were to be set and cleared in each parish in compensation for the common rights which the forest inhabitants had previously enjoyed over the whole forest waste.[64]

The offices of Lord Warden, Ranger, and other Forest offices were in most cases abolished, and compensation allowed by the Acts to the holders.[65] The deer remaining at large were removed, and on completion of the work of the Commissioners the forests were declared to be disafforested, and no one henceforth liable to pay any penalty for hunting therein, except in enclosed parks.[66]

In the Forest of Dean poaching was rife, and there were frequent violent clashes between keepers and poachers. In 1850 therefore the deer were officially banished, and in five years they had all been killed off.[67] The deer had become very numerous by this time in the New Forest, and there were numerous complaints about their depredations. Consequently the Deer Removal Act of 1851[68] ordered them to be destroyed in the New Forest also. But the attempt to remove the deer failed in both forests, because fresh stock kept coming in from adjoining woods. It was realized furthermore that grazing by the deer was essential to the survival of the open 'lawns' in the New Forest, and so the 1851 Act was abandoned.[69]

This Act was unsuccessful also in its attempt to develop the New Forest as a source of timber by a 'rolling programme' of inclosure.[70] Determined protests were made against it, not only by the commoners, but also by the environmentalists. The agents of the Crown consequently became disillusioned about the New Forest as a Crown asset: it barely escaped the fate of the other royal forests. A Bill was actually introduced into the Commons in 1871 to disafforest it,[71] but was withdrawn because of the strength of the opposition. Another Select Committee reported in 1875 that 'the continued operation of the Deer Removal Act 1851' would 'render the rights of common existing over the New Forest worthless, and by so doing . . . extinguish a large class of small freeholders and tenants of whom the highest character has been given'; furthermore it would 'destroy almost the only specimen left in England of a primeval forest, a priceless source of enjoyment to all classes of the nation'. The Select Committee considered that a balance should be struck between the two conflicting interests:

> while the portion of the Forest at present planted under the Acts may properly be managed with a view to producing the most profitable crop of trees, the remainder of the Forest should henceforth, in the interest of the nation at large, be managed with a view to the preservation of its natural aspect and condition as a Forest of surpassing beauty and unique character.[72]

The New Forest Act of 1877[73] accordingly represented a change of policy. The Crown's powers of inclosure were greatly limited, and statutory definition was given to the commoners' rights, which they could freely exercise under the supervision of the verderers: the Court of Verderers was reconstituted for this purpose. Grievances arising from restrictions on commoners' rights during the fence month and the period of winter heyning were overcome. The verderers were enabled, in return for an annual payment of £1, to secure for the commoners the right to turn out their animals during these periods from year to year. Provision was also made for the preservation of the picturesque character and ornamental value of the New Forest.[74] Nevertheless controversies continued between the verderers, as protectors of the commoners' rights, and the officers of the Crown, who wished to enclose and encoppice to promote the growth and sale of timber.

Epping Forest was the last remaining portion of the forest of Essex: environmentalist objectives were achieved there by different means. The rights of the commoners were finally championed by the Corporation of the City of London, which wished to see Epping Forest preserved as an open space. By a suit in the Court of Chancery[75] the Corporation vindicated commoners' rights over the whole of the waste land within the forest 'according to the assize and custom of the Forest'. It obtained an injunction ordering enclosures made during the previous twenty years, amounting to nearly 3,000 acres, to be thrown down, and restraining further enclosures. In 1875 and 1876 the Corporation purchased 3,000 acres of the open waste lands of the forest manors. Finally, by the Epping Forest Act of 1878[76] what remained of the forest of Essex was disafforested. Crown rights over vert and venison, the Forest courts and offices, and the burdens and restrictions of the Forest laws and customs were abolished. The Corporation of London was appointed Conservators of the Forest, with the duty of protecting and managing the forest as an open space for the recreation and enjoyment of the public: a duty it discharged through an Epping Forest Committee. The rights of registered commoners were to continue unchanged. They were to elect, as members of the Committee, four verderers, who were required to be resident in one of the forest parishes. These verderers were no longer to be officers of the Crown administering the forest law on its behalf. They were instead to be guardians of the interests of the commoners and of local interests generally, but they were to have no greater powers than any other members of the Committee. The Conservators were empowered to regulate the rights exercised by registered commoners – e.g., to depasture horses, cattle and sheep, and to agist swine, and to exclude animals for which no common rights existed. The twelve forest parishes were to continue to nominate reeves for appointment by the Conservators, and the reeves to mark commoners' cattle, receive the fees therefor, and impound uncommonable cattle. They were to use a scale of marking laid down by the Forest Court of Attachment in 1790 – that is, one horse or two cows for each £4 per annum rent paid by the commoner, and one horse or two cows 'for every poor cottager having a family and right of commoning'.[77]

2
Epilogue: the Forests Today

Of all the forests established in England by the Norman kings, some remnants of the ancient Forest system still survive in three. In the Forest of Dean alone the four verderers are still elected as they were in medieval times – by the freeholders of the county called together in County Court by the sheriff.[78] In the New Forest their appointment is now regulated by the New Forest Act of 1949,[79] which provides that there shall be ten verderers in that Forest: the Official Verderer appointed by the Queen, and four others by the Forestry Commissioners, the Minister of Agriculture and others, together with five elected by the Commoners. The New Forest verderers appoint three agisters to supervise the commonable animals. In Epping Forest also verderers are still appointed: their appointment and functions have been reconstituted by the Epping Forest Act of 1878.[80]

The purposes and administration of these ancient forests have of course changed fundamentally. The Forestry (Transfer of Woods) Act of 1923[81] transferred the property in them to the Forestry

Commissioners, who were made responsible for their care and management. Since 1923 they have been, not royal forests, but state forests. The office of Surveyor-General of Woods and Forests, created in the eighteenth century, has been discontinued, but 'Deputy Surveyors' manage the New Forest and the Forest of Dean for the Forestry Commissioners. The foresters today, unlike their medieval counterparts, are primarily responsible for felling, thinning, preparation and sale of timber, and the establishment of new plantations. They are also concerned with recreational facilities and amenities, and the conservation of the forest flora and fauna.[82]

Despite attempts in the middle of the nineteenth century to kill them off, the deer have returned. In the Forest of Dean there is a small herd of fallow deer around the Speech House in the centre of the Forest, and a large one in Highmeadow.[83] In the New Forest there are four species – a few red deer, fallow and roe deer, and the Japanese Sika deer, introduced probably in 1904.[84] In each of the two Ranges of the New Forest there is a Head Keeper, with six beat keepers under him, who take censuses of the deer, cull them in due season, guard against poachers and check pests. They also patrol camp sites and parking and picnic places.[85]

Rights of common are still exercised in both forests. In the New Forest the most important is common of pasture, which enables about 350 commoners to depasture some 3,000 ponies, 2,000 cattle and a few sheep on about 4,500 acres of open forest throughout the year. Common of mast carries the right to turn pigs on to the forest. The 'pannage season' was fixed by medieval custom, but since the New Forest Act of 1964[86] the Forestry Commissioners, after consultation with the verderers, may fix any suitable term of no less than sixty days. Common of firewood, or estovers, is enjoyed by about eighty commoners. Common of Turbary – the right to cut turf for fuel – and Common of Marl – to dig marl for fertilizer – are now virtually obsolete.[87]

Verderers continue to hold their courts in the New Forest and in the Forest of Dean. In the New Forest the duties of the Verderers' Court are now mainly administrative, and are concerned with the supervision and administration of rights of common on the open forest. They have statutory powers to make by-laws concerning the number, health and welfare of commoners' animals, and payments for marking such animals, and for pigs turned out in pannage time. They can take measures for the burning of the heaths, the clearing of drains, and the repair and maintenance of the Forest pounds: these measures they carry out through the agency or with the permission of the Forestry Commissioners. The verderers appoint three agisters whose duty it is to supervise the animals on the forest commons, brand and mark them, collect the grazing fees for the verderers, and attend the Verderers' Court. The verderers also have powers for the preservation of the natural beauty and the flora and fauna of the forest. Since they are primarily concerned with the rights of commoners, and the Forestry Commission with timber production, there has naturally in the past been a divergence of interest and policy in the New Forest between these two authorities.[88]

The Official Verderer and four other verderers nominated by the Lord Chancellor retain judicial powers in the New Forest. They sit every two months in the Verderers' Hall in the Queen's House at Lyndhurst, and deal with cases concerning common rights, unlawful enclosures, purprestures and encroachments. Any member of the public can make a 'presentment' there, so continuing the medieval accusatorial procedure.[89]

The 'Speech Court' in the Forest of Dean is still scheduled to be held every forty days, but the verderers' sittings are formal, and their court is usually adjourned until there is sufficient business. Such matters as are dealt with are administrative questions, such as those concerning common rights. It has been found more convenient to leave jurisdiction in cases concerning offences against the vert and venison to the ordinary petty sessions.[90]

These two forests have therefore survived into the twentieth century by a remarkable process of transformation. In the twelfth and thirteenth centuries the Forest law, courts and officers constituted a mighty system which paralleled the common law itself, and operated over a third of England. Created for their pleasure by arbitrary decrees of tyrannical Norman kings, the Forests were exploited by their Stuart successors to support their personal government. Then in the eighteenth century there was conflict between Crown programmes of economic development and the interests of the commoners. The epitaph upon the old Forest system was finally written in the Wild Creatures and Forest Laws Act of 1971, which abolished the sovereign's prerogative right to wild creatures (except royal fish and swans), and abrogated the Forest law, except in so far as it relates to the appointment and functions of verderers.[91] The modern concept was summed up by the Earl of Radnor, Chairman of the Forestry Commission, when he wrote in 1961:

> The New Forest is at once a great national reserve of timber, a grazing ground for several thousand cattle and ponies owned by the Commoners, and a region for recreation and the enjoyment of scenery and wild life which, being open to the public, at large, has much of the character of a National Park.[92]

It nevertheless 'remains a unique memorial of Norman England'.[93]

NOTES

1. E317/18; Land Revenue Miscellaneous Book, 294, fo. 58; Greswell, *Forests of Somerset*, 195; McDermot, *Exmoor Forest*, 299–306.
2. Firth and Rait, II 783–812.
3. Cal. S.P. Dom. 1660–61, 285–86; 1663–64, 275, 502; *V.C.H. Wilts.* IV 401, 431.
4. *V.C.H. Derby*, I 412–13.
5. Cal. S.P. Dom. 1677, 368; Hart, *Verderers and Speech-Court of Dean*, 27.
6. Cal. S.P. Dom. 1670, 175–77, 182.
7. E32/5, 6, 8; Fisher, *Forest of Essex*, 94, 100, 159.
8. 14th. Report of Commrs. of Woods & Forests, 1793, App. 8, p. 1121; Apps. 15 and 16, pp. 1128–32.
9. Cal. S.P. Dom. 1672–73, 201–202; 1676–77, 574; G.E.C. IV 344.
10. by £1,033. 6s. 8d. a year south of Trent in 1713, and by £1,000 a year north of Trent in 1732 (Cal. Treas. Bks. XXVII, part II (1713), 447; 1731–34, 470.
11. ibid., XXIX part II (1714–15), 323–24.
12. Cal. S.P. Dom. 1663–64, 585: 1667, 83; Cal. Treas. Pap. 1702–1707, 363, 374, 381, 400, 411, 430, 594, 595; 1708–14, 599; 1720–28, 89; Cal. Treas. Bks. & Papers, 1729–30, 26; 1731–34, 302.
13. Cal. Treas. Pap. 1720–28, 49; Cal. Treas. Bks. & Pap. 1729–30, 26.
14. Cal. Treas. Pap. 1714–19, 7.
15. *General View of the Agriculture of the County of Essex* (London, 1807) I 32; II 151–53; Addison, *Epping Forest*, 16.
16. 'House of Commons Sessional Papers of the 18th Century' (facsimile edn., ed. Sheila Lambert) Vols. 76, 77, 78 (pub. Scholarly Resources Inc., Delaware, 1975).
17. Third Rept., 1788, App. No. 1, p. 55.
18. ibid., pp. 22, 25.
19. Eighth Rept., 1792, p. 474; Ninth Rept. 1792, p. 538.
20. Thirteenth Rept., 1792, p. 1052.
21. Eighth Rept., 1792, p. 474; Ninth Rept. 1792, p. 538.
22. Seventh Rept., 1790, App. 10, p. 452.
23. Thirteenth Rept., 1792, p. 1052.
24. 19 & 20 Car. II c. 8.
25. G.R.O. D36/Q2 (09); Return of 1691 Commission (Cal. Treas. Bks. IX Part IV, 1495–96); Hart, *Verderers and Speech-Court of Dean*, 35–43, and *Verderers and Forest Laws of Dean*, 109–114; D.W. Young, 'History of the Forest Woodlands', in *New Forest* (H.M.S.O., 1961) 29–30.
26. 9 Will. 3, c. 33.
27. 59 Geo. III c. 86 s, 1.

28. Third Report 1788, p. 5.
29. *New Forest* (H.M.S.O., 1961), 29–31; *Explore the New Forest* (H.M.S.O., 1981) 14, 23–24, 40.
30. Commissioners of Sewers v. Glasse (1874) L.R. 19 EQ. 142; Fisher, *Forest of Essex*, 180–83, 241–42, 299–304.
31. Addison, *Epping Forest*, 26, 45–46.
32. Fourteenth Rept., 1793, p. 1103.
33. Seventh Rept., 1790, p. 428.
34. Third Rept., 1788, pp. 4, 24–25, 41–42; App. No. 37, pp. 185–86; App. No. 39 p. 189; Fifth Rept., 1789, pp. 222–23; Sixth Rept., 1790, p. 354.
35. Pettit, *Royal Forests of Northamptonshire*, 153–163, 184.
36. Third Rept., 1788, App. No. 39, p. 189.
37. Fifth Rept., 1789, pp. 222–23.
38. Seventh Rept., 1790, pp. 421, 426.
39. Third Rept., 1788, pp. 41–42; Fifth Rept. 1789, pp. 231, 235; Sixth Rept., 1790, p. 354.
40. 7th Rept., 1790, pp. 423, 424, 426, 428–29.
41. Ninth Rept., 1792, 558–559.
42. Seventh Rept., 432; Eighth Rept., 480; Ninth Rept., 551; Tenth Rept., 620; Thirteenth Rept., 1054–55; Fourteenth Rept., 1106.
43. 50 Geo. III c. 65.
44. 57 Geo. III c. 61; 10 Geo. IV c. 95.
45. 35 Geo. III c. 40; 36 Geo. III. cc. 62–64.
46. 52 Geo. III cc. 71, 72.
47. 50 Geo. III c. ccxviii.
48. 52 Geo. III c. 136.
49. 53 Geo. III c. 158; 55 Geo. III c. 122.
50. 55 Geo. III c. 138.
51. 58 Geo. III c. 100.
52. 6 Geo. IV c. 132.
53. 14 & 15 Vict. c. 43; 21 & 22 Vict. c. 37.
54. 16 & 17 Vict. c. 36.
55. 16 & 17 Vict. c. 42.
56. 18 & 19 Vict. c. 46.
57. 53 Geo. III c. 158 s. 16.
58. First Report 1812, Part 2, pp. 22–26, 161.
59. ibid., p. 28; Second Rept., 1816, 33–34; App. No. 31, 155–59: Third Rept., 1819, 34–35.
60. 5 Geo. IV c. 99 s. 85.
61. Hart, *Verderers and Forest Laws of Dean*, 136.
62. 5 Geo. IV c. 99 s. 31; 6 Geo. IV c. 132 s. 18.
63. 14 & 15 Vict. c. 43.
64. 16 & 17 Vict. c. 36 s. 7.
65. 53 Geo. III c. 158. s. 47; 14 & 15 Vict. c. 43; 16 & 17 Vict. c. 36 s. 19.

66. 53 Geo. III c. 158 s. 64.

67. Hart, *Royal Forest*, 216–18.

68. 14 & 15 Vict. c. 76.

69. Rept. of Sel. Committee of the House of Commons on the New Forest Removal Act, 1868 (P.P. 1867–68, VIII, p. 663.)

70. *The New Forest* (H.M.S.O., 1961), 31, 57; Explore the New Forest (H.M.S.O., 1981), 43.

71. P.P. 1871, IV pp. 317–49.

72. ibid., 1875, XIII, p. 13 (ss. 57, 60).

73. 40 & 41 Vict., c. cxxi.

74. *The New Forest*, 33–34, 59; *Explore the New Forest* (H.M.S.O., 1981), 21, 37; *Report of the New Forest Committee 1947* (Cmd. 7245) pp. 10–12.

75. Commissioners of Sewers of the City of London v. Glasse (1874) 19 L.R. Eq. 134.

76. 41 & 42 Vict. c. ccxiii.

77. ss. 29, 33 (I) (viii).

78. Hart, *Verderers and Speech-Court of Dean*, 66–67; *Verderers and Forest Laws of Dean*, 17, 157–58.

79. 12 & 13 Geo. 6, c. 69.

80. 41 & 42 Vict., c. ccxiii, s. 30.

81. 13 & 14 Geo. 5, c. 21, s. 1.

82. *Explore the New Forest*, 41.

83. Hart, *Royal Forest*, 243.

84. ex inf. Mr F.A. Courtier, Head Forester Conservation, Forestry Commission, Minstead.

85. *Explore the New Forest*, 42–43; *Report of the New Forest Committee 1947* (Cmd. 7245) p. 17.

86. c. 83, s. 7.

87. Hart, op. cit., 241–43; H.C. Pasmore, 'The Commoner', in *Explore the New Forest*, 33–35.

88. *Report of the New Forest Committee 1947* (Cmd. 7245) pp. 17, 56.

89. *The New Forest*, 2, 34–35, 55–59: *Explore the New Forest*, 36–39.

90. Hart, *Verderers and Speech-Court of Dean*, 62; *Verderers and Forest Laws of Dean*, 167–68, 194.

91. c. 47, ss. I (a), 2.

92. Foreword, *The New Forest*, (H.M.S.O., 1961), v.

93. H.C. Darby, *New Historical Geography of England* (C.U.P., 1973) 57.

Appendix

List of the Royal Forests of England, with Dates of Disafforestment, or Alienation.

FOREST	COUNTY	DISAFFORESTED OR ALIENATED	AUTHORITIES
ACORNBURY	Hereford		
ALICEHOLT	Hampshire	1812	52 Geo. III c. 72
ALLERDALE (award of INGLEWOOD FOREST— q.v.)	Cumberland		E32/29, 30: Cal. I.P.M. IV pp. 183–84: Cal. Pat. R. 1292–1301, 486
ALNWICK	Northumberland	1280	Cal. Chart. R. 1257–1300, 247
ALVESTON	Gloucester		
AMOUNDERNESS (incl. BLEASDALE, FULWOOD, and MYERSCOUGH)	Lancashire		
ARCHENFIELD	Hereford	1251	Cal. Chart. R. 1226–57, 369
ASHURST	Sussex		Pipe R. 1166, 89
BAGSHOT (part of WINDSOR FOREST)	Surrey		
BECONTREE	Essex		
BEDFORDSHIRE	Bedfordshire	Part Disafforested in 1191	Pipe R. 1191, 134
BERE	Dorset	1269	Granted to Edmund Earl of Lancaster (Cal. Chart. R. 1257–1300, 227–28)
BERE ASHLEY (otherwise BERE-NEXT-WINCHESTER or LITTLE BERE)	Hampshire		E32/310/22: DL39/2/11/17, 24

FOREST	COUNTY	DISAFFORESTED OR ALIENATED	AUTHORITIES
BERE PORCHESTER	Hampshire	1810	50 Geo. III c. ccxviii. (wherein called 'the Forest of South, otherwise East Bere.')
BERKSHIRE		1227	The greater part of the county disafforested, except the eastern part, which remained in Windsor Forest. (Cal. Chart. R. 1226–57, 39)
BERNWOOD	Buckinghamshire (part, incl. BRILL & PANSHILL) Oxford (part)	1622	Cal. S.P. Dom. 1619–23, 374
BLACKMOOR	Dorset		
BLACKMORE (Otherwise MELKSHAM)	Wiltshire	1277	Cal. Close R. 1272–79, 560 V.C.H. Wilts. IV 407
BOLSOVER	Derby		
BRAYDON	Wiltshire	1630	Close R. 36 Hen. III m. 14d; Bazeley, *Extent*, 160
BREWOOD	Shropshire	1204	V.C.H. Wilts. IV 405–407 Rot. Chart. 122
BRIGSTOCK (part of ROCKINGHAM FOREST q.v.) BRIGSTOCK PARK	Northampton		
BRILL (part of BERNWOOD q.v.)	Buckingham		
BUCKHOLT (part of CLARENDON FOREST)	Hampshire	1638	Cal. S.P. Dom. 1637–38, 171
CARLISLE (otherwise INGLEWOOD FOREST q.v.)	Cumberland		
CANNOCK	Stafford		
CHEDDAR (otherwise MENDIP FOREST q.v.)	Somerset		
CHELMSFORD	Essex		

FOREST	COUNTY	DISAFFORESTED OR ALIENATED	AUTHORITIES
CHIPPENHAM	Wiltshire	1618–23 (except 'Bowood or Pewsham New Park)	V.C.H. Wilts. IV 413–14
CHUTE	Hampshire (part, incl. FINKLEY & DOILEY FORESTS) Wiltshire (part)	1639–61	V.C.H. Wilts. IV 426–27
CIRENCESTER (? Braydon Forest)	Gloucester		
CLARENDON (incl. PENCHET & BUCKHOLT)	Wiltshire	1577–1610	Pipe R. 1185, 77 V.C.H. Wilts. IV 431
Clarendon Park disparked	Hampshire		
CLAVERLEY and WORFIELD	Shropshire	1664	Pipe R. 1209, 146 Dom. Bk. I 154b
CORNBURY (otherwise WYCHWOOD)	Oxford		
CORNWALL (except two woods and two moors disafforested in 1215)		1204	Rot. Chart. R. 122b., 206: Rot. Litt. Claus. 1204–24, 197
DARTMOOR. All Devon disaff. outside Dartmoor & Exmoor. Dartmoor granted to Earls of Cornwall. Dartmoor annexed to Duchy of Cornwall	Devon	1204	Rot. Chart. R., 132: Cal. Chart. R. 1257–1300, 247
DEAN	Gloucester (part). Hereford (part)	After 1337	
DELAMARE (Otherwise 'the forests of Mara & Moudrem'). Escheated to the Crown after the death of the Earl of Chester 1237: subsequently under jurisdiction of the Justice of Chester. Never part	Cheshire	1812	52 Geo. III c. 136. Hewitt, 'Mediaeval Cheshire', and Stewar-Brown, 'Serjeants of the Peace', and 'Armories of Cheshire' (E.H.R. xxix (1941), 12, 14, 48, 51–55)

223

FOREST	COUNTY	DISAFFORESTED OR ALIENATED	AUTHORITIES
HAY OF HEREFORD	Hereford		
HORWOOD	Gloucester		
HUNTINGDON (in 13th century, embraced the whole county, incl. forests or 'hays' of WEYBRIDGE, SAPLEY & HARTHAY)			
INGLEWOOD (Sometimes also incl. forest of ALLERDALE)	Cumberland		
ISLE OF WIGHT, FOREST OF	Hampshire		Cal. Pat. R. 1330–34, 355
KEYNSHAM (otherwise KINGSWOOD)	Gloucester (part) Somerset (part)		Rot. Litt. Claus. I 344, 352, 360: II 54: Cal. Pat. R. 1281–92, 153, 519: Cal. Close R. 1396–99, 165: 1409–13, 251
KESTEVEN (the 'forest of the march')	Lincoln	1230	Pipe R. 1209, 76. Cal. Chart. R. 1226–57, 122
KILPECK	Hereford		
KING'S CLIFFE (part of ROCKINGHAM FOREST)	Northampton		
KINVER	Stafford (part) Worcester (part)		
KNARESBOROUGH	Yorkshire		
LEE or LEIGHFIELD. (otherwise the forest of Rutland)	Rutland		
LONG FOREST (incl. LONGMYND or STRATTONDALE, and STAPELWOOD, BURSWOOD, LYTHWOOD and STAPLETON.)	Shropshire		Cal. Pat. R. 1467–77, 451, 528, 555

FOREST	COUNTY	DISAFFORESTED OR ALIENATED	AUTHORITIES
LONSDALE (incl. WYRESDALE q.v. and QUERNMORE.) Alienated with AMOUNDERNESS (q.v.)	Lancashire	1267	
LINWOOD (part of the NEW FOREST q.v.)	Hampshire		Pipe R. 1209, 163
LYTHWOOD (part of LONG FOREST q.v.)	Shropshire		
MACCLESFIELD. Escheated to the Crown in 1237 (see DELAMARE)	Cheshire		
MALVERN. Granted by Edward I to Gilbert de Clare, Earl of Gloucester, on his marriage to the King's daughter	Worcester	1290	Cox, Royal Forests, 227
MARLBOROUGH (otherwise SAVERNAKE q.v.)	Wiltshire		Pipe R. 1130, 17
MELCHET	Wiltshire	1577–1614	V.C.H. Wilts. IV 431
MELKSHAM. What remained of the forest granted to the Earl of Anglesey	Wiltshire	1623	ibid., 414
MENDIP (otherwise CHEDDAR)	Somerset		
MORFE	Shropshire		
NEROCHE. Sold by the Crown	Somerset	1627–29	Cal. S.P. Dom. 1625–29, 336, 344: 1627–28, 214: 1629–31, 141
NEW FOREST	Hampshire		
NEW FOREST	Stafford	1204	Rot. Chart., 122
NORTH PETHERTON			
NORTHUMBERLAND	Somerset	1280	Cal. Charr. R. 1257–1300, 247

FOREST	COUNTY	DISAFFORESTED OR ALIENATED	AUTHORITIES
OMBERSLEY & HOREWELL	Worcester	1229	ibid., 1226–57, 102
ONGAR	Essex		
OUSE & DERWENT, FOREST BETWEEN	Yorkshire	1234	Close R. 1231–34, 477
OXFORD & STAMFORD BRIDGES, Forest between (incl. forests of Rockingham, King's Cliffe & Salcey, Whittlewood, Bernwood, Shotover & Huntingdon)	Northampton (part) Buckingham (part) Oxford (part) Huntingdon (part)		
PAMBER. Granted away to John Waller & Thos. Pursell	Hampshire	1614	Cal. S.P. Dom. 1611–18, 247
PENCHET (otherwise CLARENDON)	Wiltshire		V.C.H. Wilts. IV 427 n. I
PANSHILL (part of BERNWOOD q.v.)	Buckingham		
PEAK	Derby	1639–1674	Cal. S.P. Dom. 1639–40, 502: Rot. Parl. II 49: V.C.H. Derby I 397 seqq
PEWSHAM (otherwise CHIPPENHAM)	Wiltshire		
PICKERING	Yorkshire	1639	Cal. S.P. Dom. 1639–40, 198: 1640–41, 337
POWERSTOCK	Dorset		
PURBECK. Granted to the Duke of Somerset	Dorset	1550	Cal. Pat. R. 1549–51, 430–32
RYEDALE	Yorkshire	1204	Rot. Chart., 121

FOREST	COUNTY	DISAFFORESTED OR ALIENATED	AUTHORITIES
ROCKINGHAM (incl. BRIGSTOCK, KING'S CLIFFE, & NORTHAMPTON PARK)	Northampton		
Disaff. 1638, except bailiwicks of Rockingham, Brigstock & King's Cliffe, disaff. 1795–1796		1638	Cal. S.P. Dom. 1637–38, 424–25 35 Geo. III c. 40: 36 Geo. III cc. 62, 63, 64
RUTLAND. Granted to Edward Duke of Albemarle		1398	Cal. Pat. R. 1396–99, 415
SALCEY	Buckingham (part) Northampton (part)	1825	6 Geo. IV c. 132
SAPLEY	Huntingdon		
SAUVEY Disaff. 1236, except royal demesne vill & wood of Withcote	Leicester	1236	Cal. Chart. R. 1226–57; 193: Close R. 1234–37, 51 Cal. S.P. Dom. 1627–28, 214
Remainder disaff. 1627			
SAVERNAKE. Granted 1550 to the Duke of Somerset	Wiltshire. Berkshire (part)	1550	
SCALBY (part of PICKERING)	Yorkshire		
SELWOOD	Wiltshire (part) Somerset (part)	1627–29	Cal. Pat. R. 1549–51, 430–32 Cal. S.P. Dom. 1627–28, 214: 1629–31, 141
SHERWOOD	Nottingham		
SHIRLET	Shropshire		
SHOTOVER (incl. STOWOOD)	Oxford	1818	58 Geo. III c. 100
SPAUNTON	Yorkshire		
STOWOOD (see SHOTOVER)	Oxford		
SURREY – 'south of the Guildford road'		1191	Pipe R. 1190, 155: 1191, 134

FOREST	COUNTY	DISAFFORESTED OR ALIENATED	AUTHORITIES
TREVILLE. Granted to John of Monmouth	Hereford	1230	Close R. 1227–31, 296
WALTHAM	Essex		
WEYBRIDGE	Huntingdon		
WHITTLEWOOD	Northampton (part) Oxford (part) Buckingham (part)	1824–53	5 Geo. IV c. 99: 16 & 17 Vict. c. 42
WINDSOR	Hampshire (bailiwicks of BAGSHOT & EVERSLEY) Berkshire (part) Surrey (part)	1813	53. Geo. III c. 158
WIRRAL	Cheshire	1376	Cal. Chart. R. 1341–1417, 230–31
WOODSTOCK	Oxford		
WOOLMER	Hampshire	1855	18 & 19 Vict. c. 46
WREKIN (otherwise forest of MOUNT GILBERT – incl. WELLINGTON & WOMBRIDGE)	Shropshire		
WYCHWOOD	Oxford	1853	16 & 17 Vict. c. 36
WYRESDALE	Lancashire	1204	Rot. Chart., 123a

INDEX

Abbots, responsible for production of monks who committed Forest offences, 81; imprisoned for Forest offences, 84

Abingdon (Berks.), abbey of, 12; abbot of, acts as Justice for Forest pleas, 66

Agisters, 35, 55, 57, 65, 125, 129, 159, 214; office honorary by eighteenth century, 206

Agistment, 19, 35, 36, 57, 149

Alconbury, king's demesne woods in Huntingdonshire Forest, 139

Alexander III, Pope, concessions obtained from Henry II regarding clerical privilege do not include forest trespasses, 81

Alfred, king of England, excelled in hunting, 7

Allexton, Peter of, (otherwise Peter de Neville, q.v.) forester of fee of Rutland Forest, 18; gaol at, 106–7

Alice Holt (Hants), Forest of, 5, 147, 205, 209; dissafforestment of, (1812), 210

Almain, Henry of, nephew to Henry III, appointed Warden of forests between Oxford and Stamford bridges (1269), 94

Alrewas (Staffs.), hay of, in Cannock Forest, 104

Alvric the huntsman, lands held by, of Edward the Confessor, 8

Amesbury (Wilts.), royal manor of, in Chute Forest, 10

Amounderness (Lancs.), Forest of, granted to Earl of Lancaster (1267), 144; Forest Eyre held in (1334), 166

Anglo-Saxon Chronicle, describes the Conqueror's establishment of the Forest, 3

Anstey (Yorks.), wapentake of, disafforestment of (1190), 136

Archenfield (Hereford), Forest of, 11; disafforestment of, 144

Arrow (Warks.), wood of, in Feckenham Forest, re-afforested by Edward II, 163

Ashwood (Staffs.), in Kinver Forest, declared in Domesday to be 'waste on account of the Forest', 12

Assarts in the Forest, 15, 16, 19, 20, 43, 45, 57, 65, 101, 138, 194; leasing of, 90, 187–8; cultivation of, 105

Assize, Justices of, 76

Assizes, General, Forest offenders tried at, 183

Assize of the Forest (1198), 20, 127

Attachment Courts, 37–40, 127, 170–1, 185, 196, 207, 214, 216; ineffective temp. James I, 187; discontinued in Salcey and Bere Porchester Forests in eighteenth century, 206

Attorneys at the Forest Eyre, 56

Badgers, right to hunt, 104

Barking (Essex), nuns of, lands and

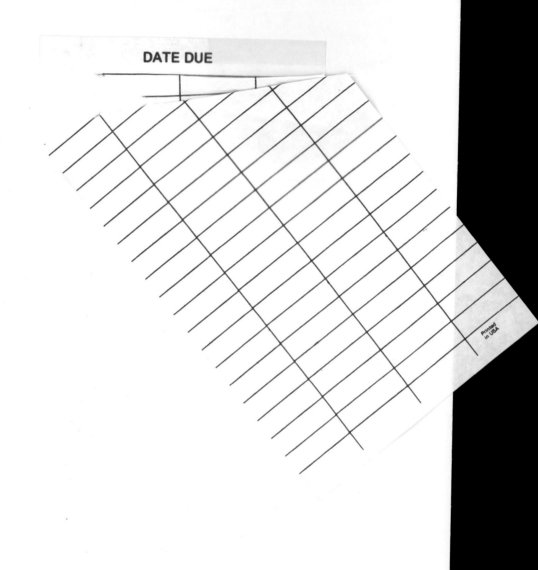

DATE DUE

Printed in USA